CORPORATE PLANNING

JOHN ARGENTI

CORPORATE PLANNING

A Practical Guide

1969
DOW JONES-IRWIN, INC.
Homewood, Illinois

To my Wife

THIS book was originally written as a guide to managers in Britain who wished to introduce corporate planning into their companies. Consequently, all the examples and calculations refer to conditions in Britain: the Stock Exchange is mentioned rather than Wall Street; "shareholders" are referred to, not "stockholders"; the calculations are made using the tax structure of Britain; the rates of growth that are used to set targets are more appropriate to Britain than America. The author believes, however, that none of these differences will in any way stand between the American reader and this British book, for what is being offered here is a description of a system of corporate planning. It is the system and the philosophy that lies behind it that are important, not the tables of figures, or the calculations, or the case studies.

For the convenience of the American reader, all monetary figures are expressed in terms of the dollar.

The philosophy of corporate planning will be well known to senior managers in America; the author believes, however, that the system developed in Britain and described here may be of considerable interest to the American reader.

CONTENTS

I Introduction   *page* 11

II Introduction to the Corporate Planning System   13

III The Need for Corporate Planning   20

IV Step 1 Determine the Objective   27

V Step 1 . . . Who Decides How Much   36

VI Step 1 . . . and Decide on a Profit Target   44

VII Step 2 Prepare a Forecast   70

VIII Step 2 . . . and Declare the Probable Error   110

IX Step 3 Calculate the Gap and Decide the Task   119

X Step 4 Determine the Constraints   127

XI Step 4 . . . and Determine the Means   136

XII Step 4 . . . Draw Up the Policy Statements   166

XIII Step 5 Draw Up the Plan   183

XIV Monitoring, Revising, Timing   189

XV How Far Ahead Should One Forecast?   202

XVI Organizing for Planning   214

XVII The Essence of Corporate Planning   231

APPENDIX

1 Outline of the Five Step Process   238

2 List of Management Techniques   239

3 A Practical Application of Decision Theory   256

4 A Glossary of Terms   266

INDEX   270

9

CHAPTER I

INTRODUCTION

CORPORATE Planning is concerned with problems of the kind that can only be tackled by the top levels of company management: it is true that its influence is felt at every level of a company and it extends to every part and activity, but its prime function is to examine and illuminate decisions on overall company strategy at the top. A book on corporate planning must therefore be written with Directors and senior executives mainly in mind but this is not to forget those who aspire to that level, or all those who wish to increase their understanding of company policy. Since such men seldom seem to have the time to wade through voluminous textbooks, it seemed appropriate to prepare as short a book as possible.

Although this book is short, it is intended as something rather more than a mere introduction to the subject. It is hoped that on completing it the reader will be able to introduce corporate planning into his own company with a very clear idea of why he is introducing it, what to expect from it, how to start, what to avoid on the way. In other words this is essentially a *practical* guide to the subject designed for people who are actually going to employ it. Although essentially practical in aim the book must also deal with theoretical aspects since in corporate planning as in many other disciplines the theory inspires and informs the practice and the practice confirms and modifies the theory.

A considerable effort has been made to write this book in plain English. Some English books on management subjects do sometimes contain woolly generalizations and meaningless abstractions; a very serious effort has been made in this book to keep one's feet firmly on the ground by the liberal use of specific practical examples – by doing so it is difficult for an author to pass off his ill-considered thoughts as though they were general principles of management. Nor, it is hoped, will the reader find

any of that racy jargon sometimes found in American management literature, of which a typical example would be: 'one of
management's main tasks is to control the marketing dynamic'.
At first sight this phrase is pregnant with new thought; a
second glance is enough to see the meaning fade away to nothing
leaving only a lingering admiration for the audacity of its
author. Nor does this book contain any mathematical equations. It is hoped that plain words alone will be enough to
transmit the idea of corporate planning with sufficient clarity
to allow the reader to apply it successfully in practice in his
own company.

One more word of introduction: a company is a very complex organization acting in and reacting to its very complex
environment. When one is concerned with the analysis of very
complex systems such as these it really is essential to tackle the
job in a thoroughly disciplined, rigorous, logical, systematic,
methodical way – otherwise the mind is confused by the sheer
variety and number of factors involved. Although corporate
planning has achieved remarkable results for the firms into
which it has been introduced, these results might have been
greater and achieved more quickly had a really systematic
version of corporate planning existed. Until recently it did not,
but a highly disciplined version of corporate planning has now
been developed as a result of several years study and practical
experience and is introduced in this book. As the reader will
notice the corporate planning process has here been broken
down into a logical sequence of precise well-defined steps each
of which is clearly signposted and fully described.

It is this development that leads the author to suggest that,
using this disciplined system, corporate planning can now
lifted out of the hands of its few high priests and placed into
those of the average senior executive.

Pettistree Lodge
Near Woodbridge
Suffolk

CHAPTER II

INTRODUCTION TO THE
CORPORATE PLANNING SYSTEM

Corporate Planning's pedigree – a definition – lack of discipline in early forms – the need for professional standards – introduction to the Five Step process.

CORPORATE Planning was first started in the United States in the late 1950s and it is now being used, in one form or another, in several hundred companies there. In Britain only a few dozen are yet using it and only a very few have been doing so for more than three or four years. It seems to have sprung from four basic premises:

1 Before drawing up a plan which is designed to do something, decide what it is you want it to do.

2 In these days of rapid change it is necessary to look ahead as far as possible to anticipate these changes.

3 Instead of treating a company as a collection of departments, treat it as a corporate whole.

4 Take full account of the company's environment before drawing up any plans.

Although they may appear somewhat naive, each of these sentences does contain a kernel of truth and when joined into one concept a new and powerful management approach emerged.

A Definition
By borrowing the nub from each of these four sentences, the idea of corporate planning can be defined as follows: it is to determine the long term goals of a company as a whole and then to generate plans designed to achieve these goals bearing in mind probable changes in its environment. Three points must be made about this definition straight away. Firstly, it is a

rather informal one and does not measure up to the high standard of logic that was mentioned in Chapter I. It will do for the present, but it must be tightened up later on. Secondly, this definition will probably be acceptable to most of those who practise corporate planning, for it is sufficiently imprecise to embrace most of the current shades of opinion among the experts: very soon we will part company with some of them.

Thirdly, and very important, many people will object that if this is all there is to corporate planning, well, most companies are doing it already. This may be true: many companies do know where they are going and how to get there without any prompting for corporate planners. And yet, do they really know? It will be seen later on how the corporate planning approach uncovers unjustified assumptions, explodes long-held convictions, uproots old wives' tales, exposes many accepted management generalizations as just cocktail-party half-truths. Some companies who now pursue their clear-cut goals with such enviable concentration may find that in fact they are moving vigorously in the wrong direction. Nevertheless it is most certainly true that a few companies do undoubtedly achieve success year after year, time after time; they neither use corporate planning nor do they need to for they are doing by intuition and entrepreneurial flair what most companies can do only through corporate planning. For most companies it is only through the corporate planning approach that they can sensibly and realistically decide exactly what they want to do, what sort of company they want to become and how they are going to achieve it.

Lack of discipline in early forms
With what has been said so far few experts would disagree. Corporate planning has achieved considerable success. Through it company policies and plans do become more sensible, more purposeful, more appropriate, more successful. There have been few failures. And yet there has been something lacking— the disciplined methodology, the logical system, the precise definition of terms, that was briefly mentioned in Chapter 1. One can search almost in vain to discover *exactly* what corporate planning is and how it should be done. One seldom finds a clear set of instructions to guide the would-be corporate planner – perhaps this is due to the desire of the high priests of the art to

preserve their mystique – but if corporate planning is a discrete and distinct branch of management science then, surely, there is a right and a wrong way of going about it. If so, then a book on corporate planning ought to have at least one chapter which starts . . . . 'When you start work on your first day as a company's corporate planner, take off your hat and coat, sit at your desk and . . . .' and then it should tell him what to do next! In fact almost the whole of this book is devoted to describing exactly what he should do. This book is essentially a detailed description of how to do corporate planning. It is not an attempt to forecast the future or to prepare a suitable plan for any particular company: it is an attempt to show *how* to forecast and *how* to plan.

The need for professional standards
Does it really matter if corporate planning is done systematically or not? It matters as much as in any other process. A doctor can treat a patient first and diagnose afterwards: if he does so it may not matter. If the patient is given cough mixture when he has a broken leg no harm may be done so long as this is eventually discovered. It may not matter if his appendix is removed when he only had a headache. But although there must be occasions when no harm is done by such eccentricity there must also be occasions when treating a patient before diagnosing his ailment has disastrous results. So it is with corporate planning.

Again, there may be occasions when an architect can meaningfully design an apartment complex without knowing where it is to be built; and occasions when, on the contrary, such a procedure would not only represent a total failure of professional standards but would also be disastrous. So it is with corporate planning – it will sometimes do no harm to take step 3 before step 2 but on some occasions it would not only waste time, not merely represent a failure of professional standards, but would be a very costly blunder. It is a feature of the professions that in each there is a right and a wrong way of doing a job, there is a disciplined approach, a systematic sequence of steps that is recognized to yield better results more efficiently than any other possible sequence of steps. In such a sequence the omission or transposition of any step can prejudice either the result itself or the efficiency with which the result is obtained.

The more complex the task the more essential does it become to tackle it systematically. Corporate planning deals with the long term future of a company within its environment – a combination of two highly complex systems. A disciplined approach is surely essential. Furthermore, corporate planning must exhibit a discipline fully up to the standards acceptable to the professions, for it is an activity that can only be carried out at Board level, and increasingly these days, company directors are drawn from the professions; accountants, scientists, engineers, lawyers, and the like. They will surely expect from the corporate planner a standard of intellectual discipline similar to their own.

It is not necessary to dwell further on the need for a disciplined methodology in corporate planning. Indeed it has only been necessary to discuss it at such length because of the evident lack of it in some of the literature so far. One more word might not be out of place, however: a really successful system can only be evolved from a blend of careful theoretical consideration together with much practical experience. In such a process of evolution the practice modifies the theory, the theory points to new more powerful practical applications until a system emerges that is both intellectually satisfying and pragmatically useful. The system of corporate planning that is about to be described emerged in this way.

Introduction to the Five Step process
Corporate Planning is a process, that is to say it is an activity carried out in a sequence of steps taken in a certain order. A manufacturing process consists essentially of taking materials through a sequence of steps each one modifying the material until it emerges as a finished product at the end. In any complex process it may be possible to identify hundreds of steps, some of which may be so small as to advance the process only imperceptibly, others so important that to omit them in describing the process would make the description unintelligible. The corporate planner must take hundreds of steps to complete his work but it is possible to describe the process meaningfully by saying that it is essentially a five step process. Every one of the hundreds of detailed steps he takes comes into one or other of these five main ones. These are as follows:

(1) Determine the company's objective and decide on a target.
(2) Prepare a forecast and declare the probable error.
(3) Calculate the planning gap and decide the task.
(4) Decide constraints and means.
(5) Draw up the plan.

This partially describes the process. Many other features must be discussed before it can be claimed that a complete description has been given but this must wait until the five steps themselves have been explained. One important point must be mentioned, however. The process of corporate planning is an unending one, it is a repetitive cycle – in fact it contains two cycles. Step 1 has to be reviewed independently of and for different reasons from the review of the other steps which are repeated much more frequently, probably many times a year. Suggestions as to how and when these reviews are carried out will be given in detail in a later chapter, but it is important to realize now that the process of corporate planning is continuous and not, as suggested by the partial description above, a once-through linear one.

As has been said before, the sequence of steps outlined above is only one out of many possible steps and many possible sequences; this particular one has been chosen partly because it can be seen to be more logical than any other, but chiefly because it gives the best practical results. Fewer errors will be made if it is used and less time wasted by the corporate planner who, without prior knowledge of this sequence can work for weeks on step 2 only to find that much of it is rendered useless by some fact that he would have discovered if he had taken step 1 first. He can waste even more time trying to decide what to do having just completed a step or even trying to decide whether he has completed a step or not. There is little excuse for a corporate planner to lose his way today for the route and the staging posts are now clearly marked by those who have gone before.

Referring back to the list of the 5 steps it will have been noticed that most of the steps consist of two substeps and it may be asked why the process is not better described as a 9-step process as follows:

(1) Determine the company's objective.
(2) Decide on a target.

(3) Prepare a forecast.
(4) Declare its probable errors.
(5) Calculate the planning gap.
(6) Decide the task.
(7) Decide constraints.
(8) Decide means.
(9) Draw up the plan.

This would be fairly satisfactory. However, as will be seen later, to decide on a target is a task so intimately connected with determining the objective that to separate these detracts from the description of the process rather than clarifies it. On the other hand the task of preparing a forecast is so totally distinct from deciding a target that it must be treated as a distinct and separate step. Similar explanations can be offered for choosing the classification of the other steps into a 5 step rather than a 9 step process.

But if the process is described more adequately in 5 steps rather than in 9 or some higher number, it might be asked whether it could be still better described in fewer steps. Probably not. It would detract from the description to try to force any further contraction in the number of steps; these five are the minimum by which the process can meaningfully be described. There is just one contraction that can be made that means something, namely the amalgamation of steps 1, 2 and 3 together and steps 4 and 5 together, but this would yield a definition of corporate planning rather than a description of the process used by corporate planners. The definition it would yield has already been quoted: 'to determine the goals of a company' (steps 1, 2 and 3) 'and to generate plans designed to achieve these' (steps 4 and 5). These, it will be recalled, are the twin tasks that corporate planning is designed to tackle.

Summary of Chapter II

The function of corporate planning is to decide what a company's long term objectives are and how to achieve them. Some companies do know the answers to both these questions but a great many do not – and if they do not know exactly what they want to do how are they to decide how to do it? Corporate planning takes full account of the company's environment before drawing up plans and lays much emphasis on taking a long look ahead. A particular 5 step process recently developed offers a practical way of doing corporate planning, since it forces the corporate planner to tackle his complicated task in a thoroughly rigorous, systematic way.

CHAPTER III

THE NEED FOR
CORPORATE PLANNING

When companies need corporate planning – how companies plan – the budget does not give the company a target – departmental planning – why this is not adequate as a long range planning system.

BEFORE studying the Five Step Process of corporate planning in detail a little more thought must be given to the reasons for introducing corporate planning into a company. Sooner or later most companies run out of steam, reach a plateau, lose their way. There are at first sight dozens of reasons why this may happen; the product on which their prosperity is based becomes outdated, or they have grown so fast that the management cannot cope with the administrative problems, or the man who built up the firm retires leaving a managerial vacuum, and so on. It is almost certainly true, however, that there are not dozens of reasons for a company starting to slip, but only three: the company no longer has a clear objective, or it does not know how to achieve it, or it lacks energetic leadership. Since it is the first two of these managerial problems that corporate planning is designed to solve, companies in this position could profitably adopt this approach, although since prevention is better than cure, it would be sensible to introduce corporate planning *before* a company starts to stagnate. Companies of all types and sizes can lose their way: the least that corporate planning should achieve for a company is to prevent stagnation and at best it will yield much more.

How Companies Plan
All companies plan. In some the planning is very informal, amounting to no more than the managing director playing a hunch about some future event – he may think that the economy

is entering a decline and order a reduction of stocks or he feels in his bones that demand for the company's products will rise next year and order the building of a new plant. There is nothing wrong with this way of running a business (except that not all companies are blest with managing directors who have the right hunches and the courage to play them), but it is physically impossible for a managing director to take all the necessary decisions in a company over a certain size – probably a few hundred employees is the maximum.

Most companies over this size have a formal planning system which consists of two elements. There is the annual budget which indicates what profit the company will make based on what each department expects to do during the following year and there are the departmental planning activities.

Unfortunately neither the budget nor the departmental planning are really suitable alternatives to corporate planning.

The budget does not give the company a target

It has been said in previous chapters that companies need an objective, a target, something to aim at. It may be suggested that most companies already have a target in the form of the annual budget.

Unfortunately this target is a delusion. It is not a target but a forecast: a target is what the company *wants* to happen, a forecast is what it *expects* will happen. Consider how the budget is prepared. Every year the accountants ask each department what they expect to happen next year. The Sales department forecasts what they expect to sell, the Production department says what it thinks this will cost to produce in terms of overtime, electricity, etc. The Purchasing department says what it will have to buy and at what price, the Research department says what it expects to spend and so on. If any department cannot forecast what some activity will cost next year they instruct the accounts department to put in the same figure as last year. All these costs and revenues are collected and collated by the accounts department and, shortly before the start of the financial year the budget is presented to the Board. From it they can see what profit the company is expecting to make.

Now what has really been happening here? In effect, the accounts department has been passing the hat round on behalf of the Board. Each department, each executive, has been asked what effort they will make on behalf of the company and they have said to the accounts department 'I think I will be able to buy these components for $21 per thousand next year' or 'I hope to sell 3 per cent more next year' or 'I'm afraid I won't improve productivity at all next year'. When all these individual offerings, effective and useless, ambitious and insipid, powerful and feeble are added up, the result is next year's profits. This may be excellent or execrable, it all depends on how much effort each executive thinks he will make. Surely this is an upside-down tail-wagging-dog charade! It represents an abdication of management by the directors to the employees. Surely the directors should tell the employees what profit the company will make next year and hence what effort each man has to make to achieve this?[1]

The budget was prepared as a *forecast* – it is the sum of what everyone expected he was going to be able to do. But it is used as if it was a *target* for if the Sales department do actually achieve the level of sales they said they would everyone is delighted, hats are thrown in the air, telegrams are sent by the Chairman. Everyone behaves as though they *wanted* this level of sales quite forgetting that it was not what they wanted but what they *expected* – quite possibly poles apart.

So, in many cases, companies who think they have a profit target have only got a profit forecast. To achieve a forecast is excellent if, and only if, that forecast is also the level of achievement that the company really wanted to aim at, i.e. if it was also the target. The trouble is that few companies know what level of profits they should aim at. They do not know how to calculate a profit target. Some have to find something else to aim at that they can calculate, and so they aim to improve sales or share of the market or some other factor that can more easily be measured and which they believe to be related to profit.

The budget procedure does not give the company a profit target or any other sort of target. It can never therefore be the instrument for reinvigorating a company by giving it an objective or setting it on the right path. All it can do is to draw attention to the company's expectations, good or bad.

[1] The jargon words to distinguish between these two approaches are respectively 'bottom-up' and 'top-down' management.

Departmental Planning

The second limb of the planning system used by most companies is planning at the departmental level. This is often of two types. One is operational planning, for example planning an advertising campaign, building a factory, scheduling production, routing delivery vehicles or the itinerary of salesmen. This short term planning is vital to the company's day-to-day efficiency. The introduction of corporate planning does not affect it in any way – except that a skilled corporate planner may be able to advise on planning techniques.

The second type of departmental planning is long range, for example preparing a proposal to build a new factory, replace a major machine, sell retail in addition to wholesale, raise a loan and so on. In most companies these far-reaching projects are proposed and prepared by the relevant operating departments. This type of planning would be affected by the introduction of corporate planning. How it would be affected will be discussed much later on when the question of how a company's organisation needs to be changed when corporate planning is introduced.

Why this is not an adequate long range planning system

Long range planning done solely or mainly at departmental level has a number of disadvantages:

(1) When the budget is being prepared each department tells the accountants what they hope to do next year – this, it was suggested, is upside-down – the company should tell *them* what to do. It is similarly upside-down for the operating departments to initiate long range plans because (*a*) their plans may be inadequate (*b*) they may be too ambitious, thus straining the company's resources and (*c*) they may not be in line with the direction in which the company should be going. To illustrate this last point: the production department might be preparing plans to improve the efficiency of a plant producing product A when what should be happening is the elimination of product A in favour of product B.

(2) Until a department submits their plan to the managing director no one capable of taking an overall company view would have studied it. The managing director is probably the only man in the company who can take the company view. Unfortunately he is also the only senior executive without a

staff of his own so even when he does get a departmental plan
to study he has no one who also takes the company view
to discuss it with. This is a particularly serious disadvantage
when two different departmental plans are competing for
limited resources and the managing director has to chose between
them.

(3) One way of arbitrating between two mutually exclusive
plans is to refer them to an *overall* company plan. To prepare
one, even in outline, is a major task but one which the managing director is best suited to do – unfortunately he seldom has
the time. Since it is to be a *company* plan he cannot ask any
specialist department to do it for him.

(4) Departmental plans very often aim to achieve departmental objectives. The sales department may prepare a plan to
increase sales volume but from the overall company's view-
point what matters is profit, not sales volume. In most cases an
increase of sales volume does mean an increase in profit, but not
always. Departmental objectives may even be positively inimical
to company objectives.

(5) Plans are based on forecasts. Salesmen are not always
the most appropriate people to forecast sales levels nor are
buyers always the best forecasters of price movements. It is only
human for a salesman to forecast low if he has any reason to
think that his forecast will become a target against which his
performance is to be judged. For the same reason a buyer
may forecast high. Also, current success or failure may colour,
perhaps quite irrelevantly, a long range forecast.

(6) In many departments the people who draw up the long
range departmental plans are also the people responsible for
its day-to-day running. Inevitably they attend to immediate
problems first and give less attention to long range planning
than may be desirable. It is possibly true that most of a company's profits for this year were made last year – that is to
say, the long range plans have a greater effect on profits than
do day-to-day operating efficiencies. If this is so then there is a
case for spending *more* time and giving *greater* priority to long
range planning than to day-to-day crises.

(7) Some executives thoroughly enjoy the practical side of
their work but shun abstract thought: long range planning and
forecasting, which call for a certain amount of this, may therefore be skimped by such men.

(8) The rate of change in a company's environment is now so rapid, the complexities so great, that it has become impossible for a busy executive to think out all the implications of each change that might affect his department. A company that fails to anticipate a relevant change is at a disadvantage to one that does. Predicting what these changes will be requires painstaking analysis. Drawing up a plan to meet them needs time. So great is the penalty for backing the wrong horse that before placing one's bet much more careful analysis is needed today than previously.

Summary of Chapter III
Until a few decades ago nearly all companies were run by one man – the owner. These men were fully alive to the purpose for which the company came into being and why it continued to exist. Nowadays, while there are many small companies run by the owner, there are also an enormous number of medium sized and large companies run by professional managers and directors. Many of them have failed to decide what the objective of the company really is – they do not know, the company does not know, the budget does not tell them, although they may think that it does. If they do not know what the company is really trying to do they will never know how to do it. 'If you don't know where you're going, any road will do.'

But matters are worse than this. Not only have many companies no clear idea of what they want, they are also unable to plan efficiently. In the small company one man – again the owner – does all the long range planning himself and he no doubt makes very sure that the plans are tailored to achieve the company's objective. In larger companies the planning effort has become diffuse because it has been distributed to half a dozen departments and dozens of officials. Many are too busy to do it properly, some do not know how to do it and others do not want to; even if they did they can only take a departmental view of any plan.

Thus all modern companies, except those small enough to be run by the owner, may be without a clear objective *and* without the planning mechanism needed to achieve it if they had one! These companies run the risk of stagnation, of running out of steam, reaching a plateau for long periods at a time. Corporate planning offers an approach to these twin problems.

Only one man is needed to do this in most companies although in the very large organizations as many as half a dozen may be required to man a corporate planning department. His task is not to usurp the job of the Managing Director in setting objectives, but to help him to do it; nor is it his task to usurp the departmental planning activities but to supplement and redirect them.

CHAPTER IV

STEP 1.
DETERMINE THE OBJECTIVE

A philosophical step – the corporate planner starts work –
some objectives are proposed and tested – three different
types – 'survival'.

THE reader will recall that Step 1 of the Five Step process was
described in Chapter II as follows:

'Determine the company's objective and decide on a target.'
It was also stated in Chapter I that although this book is
intended as a practical guide, the more theoretical aspects of
corporate planning must not be ignored. In fact, and this is the
best moment to say this, unless the theory holds water the practice will not hold water either. Corporate planners who put an
ill-conceived theory into practice run the risk of finding flaws
in the system *after* they have recommended a company to take
some action that is later discovered to be ill-founded. Certain
parts of the corporate planning process result almost entirely
from logical considerations while other parts are largely of a
practical, empirical nature.

The parts most dependent on logic are the first stage of Step 1
and the first stage of Step 4 – i.e. 'determine the objective' and
'decide constraints'; this latter will be discussed in Chapter X.
There is, perhaps, more need for the philosophical discussion of
management principles and practice than is often realized by
managers, some of whom seem to think that as men of action
they are called upon only to take prompt and vigorous action
to do their job. Some deep reflection on basic premises might
not be out of place, however, and at this first stage in the
corporate planning process it is particularly appropriate.

The purpose of the next few chapters is to describe the corporate planning process. The best way of doing this is possibly
to follow the route that would be taken by a corporate planner

from the start of his task to its completion – by so doing the difficulties that he may meet can be discussed in the order and in the context in which he will meet them in real life.

The corporate planner starts work

He will be able to start work on 'determining the objective' the very day he starts his job as a company's corporate planner. This is because at this stage he need know almost nothing about the company he is working for since the objective of every company is the same. In spite of this universality of objective few companies have thought out what it is and the corporate planner's first job is to act as a catalyst in the company's efforts to define it.

Before trying to decide what a company's objective is it is sensible to ask what the word means. The objective for which the corporate planner is looking is something fundamental to the nature of a company and which distinguishes it from other types of organization; it is therefore something permanent and unalterable. It is the reason for the very existence of the company, that for which it came into being and what it is for now. It is that which, if the company fails to achieve it, the company itself fails. It is its permanent unalterable purpose or raison d'être.

Some objectives are proposed and tested

The corporate planner can now start asking the company's directors to suggest what they think their company's objective is, but it is so important to identify the objective correctly – everything else that the company does depends on this – that he will submit each of their suggestions to three test questions designed to establish whether they are indeed the *permanent unalterable raison d'être* of the company. The directors will probably make several suggestions as to what the objective may be; for example:

To increase our share of the market,
To increase the volume of sales,
To lead our industry in technology,
To increase production,
To be good employers,
To make a profit.

Now let us test the first of these – 'to increase our share of the market'. Since a company's objective is something permanent and unalterable, we would expect the company never to abandon it. So if we asked 'under what circumstances would the company *not* try to increase its share of the market?' we would expect the answer 'none'. But we do not get that answer to this question. There are many occasions when a company might *not* aim to increase its share of the market. If it had 2 or 3 per cent of the market it might, by increasing its share to, say, 5 per cent, attract the unwelcome attention of a large competitor. Or if it had 31 per cent of the market it might, by increasing it to over $33\frac{1}{3}$ per cent, attract the attention of the Monopolies Commission. If the market was subject to violent fluctuations or if it was contracting, the company might prefer to diversify into some other market rather than increase its share of the present one.

'To increase our share of the market' has failed the first test question, but even so, the other two questions should be tried. If this suggestion really was a genuine objective we would expect the reply to the question, 'why does the company want to increase its share of the market'? to be, 'in order to survive', since we also defined the company's objective as its raison d'être – i.e. reason for continuing in existence. But we do not get this reply. We have noted that the company does not always wish to try to increase its share, but on the occasions when it does, it does so in order to improve its profits. Again, not a satisfactory answer, but we will try the third question, which is a contrary to the second: the second asked why the company wanted to do something, the third asks what would happen if the company failed to do it; it is a cross-check on the second question.

The third question, therefore, is, 'If the company failed to increase its share of the market, would it fail as a company and therefore cease to exist'? If increasing its share of the market was the genuine objective, we would expect to be able to answer 'yes', but we do not get this answer; a company whose share of the market is not increasing may not be in a healthy state, but there are few cases when this failing alone could cause its demise.

This suggestion has failed all three test questions. 'To increase our share of the market' is not this company's objective, nor is it any company's in spite of some assertions to the contrary in some of the literature. The second suggestion, 'to increase the volume of sales' is so similar to the first that an identical set of replies would be obtained from the three test questions. The third suggestion was, 'to lead our industry in technology', and this will be put through the triple test quite quickly:

Question 1:	Under what circumstances would the company *not* try to lead the industry in technology.
Answer required:	None.
Actual answer:	Many, e.g. if it was more profitable to buy know-how from another company.
Question 2:	Why does the company want to lead the industry in technology?
Answer required:	In order to survive.
Actual answer:	To improve profits by keeping its product ahead of competitors.
Question 3:	If the company failed to lead the industry in technology, would it fail as a company?
Answer required:	Yes.
Actual answer:	No.

The pattern of answers obtained with this suggested objective is similar to the last two. A genuine objective would have given the answers:

1. 'None.'
2. 'In order to survive.'
3. 'Yes.'

but we have been obtaining the pattern:

1. 'If it did not improve profits.'
2. 'To improve profits.'
3. 'No.'

A similar pattern would be obtained with 'to increase production' and many other similar suggestions. However, two other possibilities remain in the list proposed by the directors: 'to be a good employer' and 'to make a profit'. Test the first one:

Question 1:	Under what circumstances would the company *not* try to be a good employer?

Answer required:	None.
Actual answer:	None.
Question 2:	Why does the company want to be a good employer.
Answer required:	In order to survive.
Actual answer:	To improve profits; because it is the right thing to do, etc.
Question 3:	If the company failed to be a good employer, would it fail as a company?
Answer required:	Yes.
Actual answer:	No.

Now, although this suggestion has clearly failed to pass the test – it failed two out of three questions – it differs in kind from the previous 'objectives' tested in that under *no* circumstances would the company *not* try to be good employers (Question 1); for all the other 'objectives' in the list so far tested there *were* circumstances under which it might not try to achieve them. Even so, the 'good employer' suggestion has failed the test because it failed two of the questions.

Finally the last suggested objective must be tested: this was, 'to make a profit'.

Question 1:	Under what circumstances would the company *not* try to make a profit?
Answer required:	None.
Actual answer:	None.
Question 2:	Why does the company want to make a profit?
Answer required:	In order to survive.
Actual answer:	In order to survive.
Question 3:	If the company failed to make a profit, would it fail as a company and cease to exist?
Answer required:	Yes.
Actual answer:	Yes.

Quite evidently this has passed the test and the true objective of the company – indeed of all companies – is 'to make a profit'. What a discovery! The reader will have met this statement with astonishment – 'do you mean to tell me', he will be saying, 'that I have waded through the last few pages just to be told that – of course the objective of a company is to make a profit!' But that is not the conclusion we have reached. The conclusion is that the *only* objective of a company is to make a profit. There is no other 'objective' whatever, in spite of the fact that most companies apparently think there are. Companies do not have several objectives, they have one, and only one.

Three different types

What, then, is the nature of the other suggested objectives that were listed on page 28 and which appear so often as objectives in books on management and in the Board Minutes of companies? The three patterns of reply to the three questions were:

Pattern A	*Pattern B*	*Pattern C* The True Objective
1. If it did not improve profits	None	None
2. To improve profits, etc.	To improve profits etc.	To survive
3. No	No	Yes

Pattern A is obtained from suggestions that are really the *means by which* the company hopes to achieve its objective, that is to say, any action that the company believes will lead to an improvement in profits. If they do not think it will lead to an improvement then they will not do it.

Pattern B is obtained from suggestions that are *constraints* on the achievement of the objective, that is to say, any action that the company will *not* take – even if not taking it makes the objective harder to achieve, or any action the company feels it *must* take even though taking it makes the objective harder to achieve. Thus a company might wish to be good employers because by encouraging good human relations profits could be improved. But even if it could be proved that *bad* human relations actually caused an improvement in profits the company might decide that it would be morally wrong to foster bad human relations in order to improve profits. Means and Constraints are discussed at length later on,[1] meanwhile let us summarize the last few pages in three definitions.

OBJECTIVE. A company has one and only one permanent, unalterable raison d'être, namely to make a profit.

[1] See Chapters X and XI.

MEANS are those actions which a company may take if it believes that they will improve profits. It will not take them if it believes they will not improve profits.

CONSTRAINTS are those actions which a company will take *whether or not* they improve profits because the company believes them to be the right things to do on moral grounds.

'Survival'

There is one other suggested objective that has not been considered yet, because it is in a somewhat different logical category to the ones so far mentioned. It must be taken seriously since it appears in many management books and is frequently stated to be the most fundamental objective of all – namely survival. It certainly sounds deeply significant, undeniable, almost mystically self-evident. But let it be put to the test of the three questions:

Question 1:	Under what circumstances would the company *not* try to survive?
Answer required:	None.
Actual answer:	If it became apparent that it could not make a profit.
Question 2:	Why does the company wish to survive?
Answer required:	In order to survive.
Actual answer:	To make a profit.
Question 3:	If the company failed to survive would it fail as a company and cease to exist?
Answer required:	Yes.
Actual answer:	Yes.

This suggestion has failed the test. It did pass question 3 but it only did so by a trick! We asked in effect, 'If the company failed to survive, would it fail to survive?' and so of course the answer was 'yes'. Not only was question 3 a logical tangle but question 2 was as well when taken with the answer required to pass the test: 'The company wishes to survive in order to survive', would have been the correct answer! One can hardly imagine a more confusing verbal muddle – it rivals *Alice in Wonderland*. The way out of it all is shown in question 1 which reveals that if a company is incapable of making a profit no one would want it to survive. A company is not there to survive just for the sake of survival *but in order to do something else* – i.e.

make a profit. The idea that a company's objective is to survive for the sake of survival is merely a special case of a general misconception that all organizations wish to survive for survival's sake. No organization wishes to do this, all wish to survive in order to do something else – what that 'something else' is depends on the type of organization, but for companies it is, as we have seen, to make a profit. That survival has been accepted as an objective for organizations may be due to confusing the purpose of organizations with that of organisms. There are very good reasons for thinking that bacteria, or a frog or a cabbage react to their environment in a manner consistent with the desire to survive. We do not know *why* they want to survive, because we did not create them. We do create organizations knowing full well what their purpose is. In the one case the organism wishes to survive – perhaps just for the sake of survival, perhaps for some unknown purpose. In the other case companies wish to survive for a clear and distinct purpose allotted to them by we, their creators. Organizations are very like organisms in many ways but this is certainly not one of them.

The anomaly provided by the two statements 'A company wishes to survive in order to make a profit' and 'A company wishes to make a profit in order to survive' which is thrown up by Question 2 is thus capable of solution. Companies do not wish to survive, or to be more accurate, the people who benefit from the company do not wish it to survive. They do wish it to make a profit. If it does not make a profit they will not wish it to survive. We see therefore that 'A company wishes to make a profit in order to survive' is a false statement: it *is* correct to say 'A company wishes to survive in order to make a profit', i.e. profit is the unalterable permanent raison d'être, its objective.

Summary of Chapter IV
The corporate planner's first job is to help the directors to determine their company's objective. It has been a surprisingly difficult task requiring quite a deep logical analysis of their various suggestions. He warned them that he was looking for something that was permanent and unalterable, the company's reason for being in existence at all. By testing each suggestion with three questions he identified no less than three quite different logical groups: the real objective, the

Means, and the Constraints; i.e. what the company was really trying to do, the actions it would take to achieve it, and the actions it would not allow itself to take even if that made the job harder. 'Survival' was shown to be a red herring. 'To make a profit' was the one and only true objective.

This is not a surprising conclusion, the only surprise is that anyone should come to any other conclusion. Unfortunately they do, for the management literature, company policy statements and speeches at conferences all mention a bewildering variety of 'objectives' from which the Managing Directors are supposed to choose. As a result some companies have not clearly identified their objective, some have several, some have none.

Why need the corporate planner take such trouble to define the objective correctly? The answer contains the very essence of corporate planning: *if a company does not know what it wants, it cannot decide how to get it.* Many companies do not know and have to be content to drift through their environment reacting only to stimuli so painful that they just have to do something to stop it hurting. Other companies have several 'objectives' and, sooner or later, when a conflict between them develops, they find they have no single overall criterion by which to judge priority.

It is sometimes said that British companies still tend to be 'production-orientated' instead of 'sales-orientated'. This may be so; perhaps it is even more true to say that they are not sufficiently 'profit-orientated'. Determining the objective correctly really does matter. It is not just an academic discussion taking place in a philosophical vacuum, it really does have practical consequences of great importance to individual companies, to the economy of a country and to the standard of living of its citizens.

CHAPTER V

STEP 1
. . . WHO DECIDES HOW MUCH

The morality of profit – profits are due to the owners –
types of ownership – public companies.

IN the last chapter it was concluded that a company exists to
do one thing only; to make a profit. This conclusion is both
obvious and surprising: obvious because everyone knew all
along that companies exist to make a profit, surprising because
it turned out to be the *only* objective. Many people will com-
plain that this is a highly immoral conclusion, but to make this
objection is to misunderstand the full implications of the role
of the constraints. The existence of these preclude a company
from attempting to make a profit by all means fair or foul;
profit may be pursued only within certain moral and legal
bounds – the moral bounds being set by the company itself
from its own moral conscience or by public opinion and the
legal bounds set, of course, by the State. These matters will be
further considered in Chapter X on Constraints.

Although the existence of constraints in the system undoubtedly removes the objections of most people to the making
of profits, there remains a minority of people who believe that
profits are immoral no matter how they are made. The
corporate planner can only take note of these views; profit-
making organizations exist and that is the salient fact. One day,
perhaps, the number of people who believe that profit, however made, is wrong, may grow so large that profit as an aim
will become taboo in countries that are now capitalist. At
present only the trend is there to be borne in mind from time
to time; when companies may no longer seek to make a profit,
someone, perhaps the corporate planner, will have to help them
to discover what they are to do.

Profit, then, is still a legitimate objective in our society.
To whom this profit is due is a second, more urgent moral

problem. Two or three generations ago it was unquestionable that profits should go to those who had invested their capital in the company and to no one else. Nowadays it is suggested that it should go to shareholders, employees, customers and the government in proportions that are hotly disputed. Unfortunately the corporate planner cannot get on with his work until this dispute is settled, for it will be recalled that Step 1 of the Five Step process was described in Chapter III as 'Determine the objective and decide on a target'. He has determined the objective as 'to make a profit' and now wishes to decide on a target – a profit target – for the company to aim at. He cannot do so until he knows who is to receive this profit. It is not up to the corporate planner to decide the target, it is his job only to advise on an appropriate level – but who is he supposed to be advising?

Profits are due to the owners
The assumption is going to be made here that profit is still due to the owners of the company and to no one else. This is not as arbitrary as it may seem. Firstly 'the owners' are not always capitalists who buy shares in a company but who have no other relationship with it, for companies can be, and are, owned by the employees (as in partnerships), by the customers (as in co-operatives), by the suppliers (marketing co-operatives), and by the State (nationalized industries). Secondly, any payment made to any group of people other than the owners can be considered to be the cost of a constraint. Thus a profit-sharing bonus paid to an employee (who is not also an owner) is no different in kind to the money the company spends on providing him with a canteen to have his meals in. If the company feels it has a moral or legal obligation to provide him with a canteen that is a constraint upon making higher profits; in just the same way a company who feels it desirable or necessary to pay him part of their profits is also acting on a constraint. The taxes paid to the State out of profits is another constraint. These are things that a company does, voluntarily of its own conscience or of legal necessity, which make its objective the more difficult to attain.

There is a trend in the social climate of this country against owners of companies who have no other stake in it than their capital. The amount of profit left over for them is a decreasing proportion of Gross Trading Profits. Increasingly it is society, rather than the shareholder, who dictates how much of the profit he may have. This is a trend the corporate planner cannot ignore, for, if continued, it must make the rewards of capital less attractive and promote the rise of those other types of shareholding which involve some other, more active, relationship with a company.[1] This trend is also considered further in Chapter X.

Profit, then, is considered to be that which is due to the owners of the company, whoever they may be, as far as this discussion is concerned, and this means that the corporate planner can say to them 'this company exists to make a profit for you; how much should it be?' Let it be clearly understood that it is the owners who decide whether a company is achieving its objective and if it is not, have the power to end it. It is they who say whether it is to survive or not. If they are satisfied with their profits, they will allow it to survive, if not they will wind it up. To check this conclusion, put it to the test of the three questions used to identify the objective in the previous chapter. We know that 'to make a profit' passed this test: will 'to make that profit which satisfies the owners' pass it?

Question 1:	Under what circumstances would the company *not* want to make that profit which satisfies the owners?
Answer required:	None.
Actual answer:	None.
Question 2:	Why does the company want to make that profit which satisfies the owners?
Answer required:	In order to survive.
Actual answer:	In order to survive.
Question 3:	If the company failed to make that profit which satisfies the owners would it fail as a company and cease to exist?
Answer required:	Yes.
Actual answer:	Yes.

Types of Ownership

It appears that this refinement of the crude 'to make a profit' agreed in the last chapter is acceptable and all that remains is

[1] It could lead to the wider ownership of shares, of course. It depends on which way the political cat jumps!

for the corporate planner to ask the owners what profit would
satisfy them. He must find out, therefore, who the owners
are so that at this stage in Step 1 he must, for the first time,
ask a question about his particular company – previously he
needed to know nothing about it since 'to make a profit' is so
generalized a conclusion that it would apply to all companies.
Not all companies are owned by the same type of owner,
however. A company can be:

Privately owned by one man or his family or by several
families,
Partnerships (employees),
Co-operatives (customers or suppliers),
Publicly owned, i.e. shareholding members of the public.
State owned or nationalized,
Mixed.

It would be easy if the owner was one man. Suppose he was
aged eighty-five, single, and the company yielded him an
income of $250,000 per annum. What profit would satisfy him?
Probably he would ask no more than that his income should
rise at the same rate as inflation or at least that it did not fall
significantly over the next ten years or until his death. Or
again, if the sole owner was aged thirty, married with five
sons whose names were down for Eton. He could give a very
clear indication of what profits his company would have to
make; he would certainly abandon it if it failed to yield more
than he could earn elsewhere and might be satisfied if it
enabled him to pay his impending school fees.

Such examples may appear trivial. And yet it is questionable
whether the proprietors of businesses have really set down even
on the back of an envelope what they do want from their
companies and exactly what the implication of this would be.
Some need not do so – those whose income will exceed their
needs for years ahead and who are therefore more than satisfied.
Others would be well advised to set down what they want and
use that as the starting point for determining the scale of future
operations and the effort this might call for from them.

Perhaps the owners are several families: here the problem is
not so simple but it should be possible to set down what would
satisfy all or most of the members. In some cases it would be
necessary to determine their needs for only a year or two ahead,
in others it might be sensible to think ahead to the needs of the

generation who will inherit the business. If the owners know what they want from the business they will be some way towards seeing what they must do to get it.

Perhaps the owners are the employees, or customers, or suppliers. Here the difficulties are considerable, partly because there may be large numbers of them but mainly because their demands are different; the rewards that satisfy some would not satisfy others. And yet there will surely be some level of reward for membership below which the employees, customers or suppliers would withdraw their support leading to the collapse of the organization. The corporate planner would have to determine what this level was, a task in these types of organization that is even more difficult than in publicly owned companies, because the relationship between member and organization is a dual one. He is an employee and shareholder at the same time and while expecting the same or rather better treatment as an employee of any other similar company, he expects something also as an owner – but what? Not, perhaps the same return on his capital as if he was a shareholder only. He may expect some say in the management of the organization, indeed he may feel that this is a sufficient 'return' – he may need no share of the profit at all and therefore the company need pay no dividends. The corporate planner must help the organization to find out what exactly is expected of it; otherwise it cannot know how to tackle the job. There are signs today that co-operatives and partnerships are not achieving the success that might be expected of them; one cannot help wondering whether it is because they have not sufficiently defined the real goal to which they should be aiming.

It has been said many times that if those who are directing the affairs of an organization do not know precisely what it is for, they will find it impossible to determine precisely what actions to take. The absence of a clear purpose may account for the relative failure of many state-owned or nationalized industries. It is not hard to appreciate the arguments behind nationalization, the trouble is that there are several such arguments: (1) if a profit is to be made it should go, not to shareholders, employees, customers, suppliers, but to the nation. (2) If an essential social service is to be performed, it should be provided at cost, not at cost plus a profit margin. (3) If the economy is to be controlled for the benefit of all, then the state must have direct control over a significant proportion of industry. (4) If there are to be monopolies, they should be owned by the nation. (5) If employers cannot be trusted to treat employees with humanity the state must show them how. And so on. Each argument may be sufficient to justify an act of nationalization: the merits of the case are of no relevance to this discussion. What is relevant is that nationalized industries exist but those who control them are not always clear what purpose to ascribe to them. If the intention is to use them as an economic regulator then when the economy is in one state they should aim to make a profit, when in another, a loss. If the objective is to provide a social service at cost (i.e. in effect to give the profit to the customer), then they should aim at neither profit nor loss. If the aim is to ensure that the profit goes to the nation then the aim must be to sell their services at the market price and place the profits in the hands of the nation. Each of these aims can be pursued singly but not together: an organization cannot aim to make a profit or loss depending on the state of the economy *and* make neither profit nor loss *and* make a profit all at the same time. It may not matter very much which of these aims the nation, through the government, chooses but it must choose one or the other. Having done so those who direct these industries could clearly see how to go about it.

Public Companies

Finally, consider the company whose shares are held by the public. For this type of organization also there is a level of achievement that satisfies the owners and below which the organization would cease to exist. At first sight this may appear to be untrue in this case since if a shareholder is not satisfied he will sell his shares and buy some of another company: but someone buys the shares that he sells and the company survives in spite of the original shareholder's dissatisfaction. It survives only because the new shareholder believes he will be satisfied with the company's performance – either he is, in which case the company will continue to survive at this new lower requirement, or he is not, is which case eventually the company is wound up. The corporate planner has to help the company decide what profits the company must make in order to be able to give its shareholders a satisfactory return on their capital. How he can do this is described in the next chapter.

So great is the power of the board of directors of a publicly owned company and so diffuse and fragmented the voice of the shareholders that, although theirs is legally and ultimately the sole authority over the company, the directors have the effective power to determine the objective of the company and the profit target. Few boards in fact do either – it is the burden of this book that they should do so – but if they do, they may well consider that 'to make that profit which satisfies the share-holders' is too low an aim. They may feel that, in order to prove their competence as managers, they should aim to more than satisfy the shareholders or even to astound them! Certainly a managing director who is also the owner of the company may set whatever target he chooses depending upon his needs, ambitions, his vigour or his laziness. But may the directors of a company owned by others set the target at whatever level they wish? Clearly to set the target below that which would satisfy the shareholders would be totally irresponsible and would lead either to the Board's dismissal or the company's failure. May they set the target higher than the satisfaction level? The answer must be, yes, providing that in attempting to achieve this goal they do not significantly increase the risk of investing in the company. The shareholder will have placed his money in the firm knowing the risk attendant upon that investment and knowing the level of return that he expects from it. He may not mind if the company shifts its business interests into new fields (if this alters the balance of his portfolio he can quite easily redress it) but he may mind very much if the risk of losing some of his capital is significantly altered. He will, on the other hand, be delighted if the management of the company achieves a better than satisfactory return without incurring greater risks. This does not mean that a board is not entitled to move into a field of greater risk; it only means that they should alert the share-holder of this intention.

Summary of Chapter V
The objective of all companies is to make a profit and it must be sufficient, after meeting the cost of all the constraints, to allow a satisfactory return on the owner's capital. Only the owners can say what 'satisfactory' means to them and it is part of the corporate planner's job to advise the directors what this is. If he can consult the owners, whether one man, a family, several

families, the employees, the customers, the suppliers, the nation, he should do so; if not he may have to use indirect means of estimating their requirements.

There is no reason to think that all owners demand an ambitious and challenging target to be set, although most will require as good a return on their money as they can get elsewhere. A board of directors may not set the company a target below the level that would satisfy the shareholders: they may set a target higher than that which would satisfy them provided that in order to achieve it they did not appreciably increase the risk of the shareholder's investment.

In all this the corporate planner must bear in mind the increasing trend for society to dictate what proportion of a company's profit may be returned to the shareholders.

CHAPTER VI

STEP 1 . . . AND DECIDE ON A PROFIT TARGET

A target is an objective expressed in figures – maximizing profits – return on company's capital – return on shareholder's capital – D.C.F. – an ideal tool – choosing a target figure – an example – notes on policy and methodology – revising the targets.

THE conclusion of the last chapter was that a company should aim to make enough profit to allow the owners to receive a return that satisfies them. Now the corporate planner must attempt to put a figure on this intention; the word 'target' is used in only one sense in this book, namely as a numerical, quantitative, expression of an aim; it is an objective expressed in figures. We asked '*what* is a company for?' in Chapter IV; we asked '*who* gets the profit?' in Chapter V; now we must ask '*how much* profit should they get?'

Considerable care has been taken so far to ensure that no unwarrantable assumption, no overhasty conclusion, no arbitrary assertion has been made. The point has been made before that unless the theory is right, the practice may be impaired. A company aiming at some objective that sounds valid but which, if closely inspected would be seen to be meaningless, is bound to be trying to do the impossible or to achieve the useless; to aim at survival for its own sake is one such mirage-objective. Before demonstrating a valid method of setting a profit target, two more false ones must be discussed; both are often used today, but both, in their different ways, are useless.

Maximize Profits
The first is that a company should aim to maximize profits (sometimes the word optimize is used instead of maximize, sometimes Net Present Value is used instead of profit and although these alternatives do not mean quite the same things the

objections apply to all statements of this type). The problem is to know what 'maximize' means. The word 'maximum' has a clear meaning in ordinary life – the maximum speed of my car is 92 m.p.h. But what is the maximum profit for your company; $22 a year, or $209,000 or $29 million? Who is to say? Or perhaps 'maximize' means 'make as much profit as you can under the circumstances in which you find yourself'? Well, yes of course! This is little more than an exhortation and quite ignores the possibility that one could alter the circumstances to allow more profit to be made. Even if a definitive meaning could be attached to this word there are three good reasons for not accepting it as a valid profit target:

(a) Some companies do not want to aim at maximum possible profits: the owners would be perfectly happy with less. Why should they strain every fibre to screw the last penny out when, in their particular private circumstances, their income from this company is already perfectly sufficient for their needs.

(b) Suppose a company is so severely up against it that, despite every possible action to maximize profits, it ends the year with a loss. It has achieved its target – it did maximize profits!

(c) Take a company that everyone knows could have made a better profit than it did last year – i.e. by common consent it has failed to maximize profits. If that profit was far above the average performance for its industry and far better than any of its previous profits surely no one would claim that the company had somehow *failed* in any important sense of that word.

It is difficult to see how this concept could have gained such easy acceptance; the only explanation that comes to mind is that it sounds impressive but does not call for any precise action. The aim to 'optimize our Net Present Value', is one of those racy, tough, scientific, dynamic, pieces of meaningless jargon that unfortunately fools some of the people some of the time.

Return on Capital Employed
The second possible method of setting a profit target is as old as Accounting. It has meaning and a certain usefulness and may be treated with some respect. This is the Return on Capital, or

Return on Assets Employed that is quoted in every Chairman's Report – i.e. the ratio between trading profit and balance sheet capital employed. It is not meaningless but is gradually becoming so for purely practical reasons; there is also one objection on theoretical grounds.

The theoretical objection is simply that 'Return on Capital' is return on the *company's* capital not on *shareholder's* capital. There is a relationship between the two since the shareholder owns the company and therefore its capital, but this fact is small compensation to a shareholder who has to sell some of his shares when the Stock Exchange value stands below the asset value. If the company exists to yield a satisfactory return to the shareholder then it is return on *his* capital that is the right measure, it is this that should be the starting point in setting the target. Regardless of this theoretical consideration these are the following reasons why Return on Capital is a poor tool for setting the target and a poor yardstick for measuring success in achieving it:

(*a*) Balance sheet capital values can be altered by revaluing the assets thus altering the Return on Capital ratio.

(*b*) Stocks and work in progress can be valued high or low at will (within limits) thus altering the capital value and hence the ratio.

(*c*) The rate of depreciation can be altered; if this is reduced, the 'profits' may rise thus altering the ratio.

(*d*) It is nowadays possible to lease plant and equipment rather than buy it. Although these items may not appear as a capital asset in the books they may improve profits. This can alter the ratio.

(*e*) If a company spends no capital for a whole financial year the asset value shown in its annual accounts will decline due to the effect of depreciation; if profits do not fall that year – and they may not – its Return on Capital will rise indicating an apparent improvement in its efficiency.

(*f*) If, as seems probable, the Investment Grants on Capital Expenditure (Finance Act 1966) are to be treated in the balance sheets as reducing the value of new plant and machinery by 25 per cent (45 per cent in development areas, etc.) this will depress the Asset Value of the company – eventually by up to 25 per cent of the plant and machinery bought over the next decade or so. Thus a return on capital of 10 per cent today could rise to as high as 13 per cent thus indicating, quite spuriously, an improvement in efficiency.

Such elasticity in a yardstick is intolerable.

Return on Shareholder's Capital

If the company's objective is to satisfy the shareholder (or, if the directors are keen to show their prowess, to more than satisfy them) then the starting point in setting a target must be the return on *shareholder's* capital. The company must decide whether it wants to aim only at the lowest permissible target – just to satisfy them – or to be much more ambitious and astonish them, or something in between. It must decide what race it wants to enter for and where it wants to come in. Having done so it need merely ask what return would satisfy (more than satisfy, etc.) a shareholder and aim for that. But how is this to be measured?

A shareholder who buys shares for $100 expects an annual dividend of about $5, i.e. a gross dividend yield of about 5 per cent, this being very approximately the average dividend yield on equities over the past forty years or so. Of course it has fluctuated widely – from under 4 per cent to over 6 per cent at times of exceptional economic stress – but 5 per cent has been the most usual rate of interest. Of course it varies from company to company and industry to industry as well as from time to time, but this is a reasonable middle figure to quote. If personal tax on unearned income is around 40 per cent for the average shareholder, this gross dividend of 5 per cent becomes only 3 per cent in his hands. This may be an appropriate figure for any given company or it may not, it depends upon its history, its industry and many other factors – but the appropriate figure can be established for any given company.

Dividends are not the only rewards a shareholder receives, however. Chief among the others is capital gains and growth in the amount of the dividend. Thus a shareholder who buys shares for $100 would expect something more than a net dividend of $3 every year and then only to be able to sell for $100 some years later. On the contrary, he would expect the dividend to rise at a fairly steady rate over the years and the share valuation to rise with it. Over the past forty years or so dividends and Stock Exchange valuations have risen by 4½ per cent per annum – again a very approximate figure but one which would not have been unacceptable to the average shareholder with an average portfolio. In the past ten years the rise has been closer to 6 per cent per annum. This may or may not be the right figure for any given company to choose; certainly it is not an exciting rate of growth but for an average company it would be acceptable in the future if the future is to be the same as the past ten years.

Apparently we have therefore to consider two figures in setting a target return to shareholders: net dividend yield and capital gain – 3 per cent and 6 per cent respectively on an average over the past ten years. If a company decides that it will take these two figures as being appropriate for its own share-holders then it can easily calculate what returns it should aim to give its shareholders for as far ahead as it likes. Thus suppose the current Stock Exchange valuation of its ordinary shares is $2,400,000 and that it has just paid out a total dividend of $120,000 for the year its gross dividend yield is 5 per cent. Next year it will have to pay out 6 per cent more than this; i.e. $127,200 and its Stock Exchange valuation will become $2,544,000. The following year it must pay out 6 per cent more again, $134,832, and the Stock Exchange valuation will rise to $2,696,640. And so on; a shareholder who bought $100 worth of shares and received $5, $5.30, $5.618 in gross dividends would be satisfied with this return and, if he wished to sell out at the end of the third year for $112.36 he would be satisfied with this, too.

But, this is nonsense, it will be said. Surely it is not really being suggested that things will work out like this? Is it really being suggested that this company can so order its affairs as to raise its dividends by *precisely* $7,200 and by *precisely* $7,632 in these two years? And is it really being suggested that the Stock Exchange valuation will rise exactly in line with this so as to leave the gross dividend yield at precisely 5.0000 per cent? No, it is not! These figures were given an absurd accuracy intentionally, to show how absurd it would be to expect such accuracy. Of course a company has no such precise control over the dividends it can afford to pay each year and it certainly has no such control over the Stock Exchange valuation. What then *is* being suggested? Merely that a company can *aim* to achieve this sort of result rather than some other. Of course it will not succeed to five decimal places every year or any year. But it may achieve these orders of magnitude over a period of several years; it may not pay out exactly 6 per cent more each year, but perhaps by the second year its dividend will have risen, not to exactly $134,832, but perhaps to $132,000 or to $144,000 or some figure not too dissimilar from the target. This is the whole point: this company has decided to aim at a definite return on its owner's money; if it gets near this, slightly above some years, slightly below in others, it will satisfy its shareholders.

The Discounted Cash Flow Method
It is necessary to refine the method of target setting introduced above. So long as there are two figures to be set (dividend yield and rate of growth) there is a possibility of confusion and dilemma. This is less likely to occur in companies where shares are quoted on a Stock Exchange since 5 per cent yield and 6 per cent growth has become a fairly well established duet in the past ten years. But shareholders may prefer some other combination: 6 per cent yield and 5 per cent growth, or 10 per cent and 1 per cent, or 0 per cent and 11 per cent. And how does one decide which is better, 5 per cent and 6 per cent or 6 per cent and 5 per cent? It would be preferable to have to manipulate only one figure rather than two. The concept of discounted cash flow (d.c.f.) allows us to combine all types of return to shareholder – including such exceptional receipts as bonus issues – into one figure. This concept must now be described.

Suppose $100 was invested in a fund earning 10 per cent interest. It would be possible to receive this interest in many different ways – the returns could flow back in many different patterns:

(1) It could be paid out at the rate of $10 every year until the shareholder withdrew his $100.

(2) No annual interest at all, instead it could be left in the fund to earn 10 per cent on an increasing investment. Eventually it could all be paid back in one lump sum. For example:

Year 0: $100 put in fund, earns $10 which is reinvested –
Year 1: $110 in fund earns $11 which is reinvested –
Year 2: $121 in fund earns $12.10 which is reinvested –
Year 3: $133.10 in fund earns $13.30 and is paid out as a lump sum of $146.40.

(3) Only part of the interest might be paid out, the rest of the annual income being reinvested. For example:

Year 0: $100 yields $10 of which $3 is paid out and $7 reinvested –
Year 1: $107 yields $10.70 of which $3 is paid out and $7.70 reinvested –
Year 2: $114.70 yields $11.47 of which $3 is paid out and $8.47 reinvested:
Year 3: $123.17 yields $12.317 and is returned as a lump sum of $135.487.

(4) Or the annual payment could be made to rise in proportion to the capital value of the fund at the time. For example:

Year 0: $100 yields $10 of which $3 is paid out and $7 reinvested:
Year 1: $107 yields $10.70 of which $3.20 is paid out and $7.50 reinvested:
Year 2: $114.50 yields $11.40 of which $3.40 is paid out and $8.00 reinvested:
Year 3: $122.50 yields $12.30 which is paid out as a lump sum of $134.80.

(Notice that the annual payment rises at 7 per cent per annum – the same rate at which the capital left in the fund is rising).

So these four patterns can be obtained from £100 invested at 10 per cent:

(1)	or	(2)	or	(3)	or	(4)
$ 10		$ 0		$ 3		$ 3
10		0		3		3.20
10		0		3		3.40
110		146.40		135.50		134.80

The point is that these four patterns of payments are all of exactly equal value (correct to one place of decimals). Many other patterns of income and capital gains over any period can be devised while remaining within the rules of the game – that is that the capital remaining in the fund earns 10 per cent interest.

Now turn back to the task in hand: to devise a target return to shareholders using one figure only to include annual dividend payments, capital gains, bonus issues and so on. Clearly the d.c.f. method outlined above fits the bill admirably. Suppose a shareholder was content with an investment that yielded 10 per cent interest and invested $100 in a company that gave this overall return. He would be equally satisfied with any of the four patterns of receipts calculated above, since they are all of equal value. But suppose none of these were convenient for his particular private needs: suppose he wished to invest $100 and then receive three equal annual payments, what should these be? They should be:

Year 0: $100 yields $10 and $40.20 is paid out leaving:
Year 1: $69.80 yields $7.00 and $40.20 is paid out leaving:
Year 2: $36.60 yields $3.60 and $40.20 is paid out leaving:
Year 3: 0

Or he may require a high return followed by a much lower one; $75 followed by $40 the next year, for example. Or a declining income over three years: $60, $40 and $17. Or he may decide to sell some of his shares after a few years, or never to sell them, or to buy some more after a few years – whatever pattern is required the returns due can be calculated given the initial investment and the interest rate. Such flexibility is seen normally only in privately owned companies in which the owner can determine how he takes his returns; in publicly owned companies it is rare to find much intentional deviation from a dividend yield of 5 per cent before tax.

This method may be used to determine the return that a shareholder has received from a company. Suppose Mr A pays $100 for some shares in January 1960, receives a dividend of $5 in 1960, $8 in 1961, $20 in 1962 when he also sells 10 shares for $12. In 1963 he sells the rest for $104.20. What has been his d.c.f. return? The answer is 15 per cent.[1] This calculation can be checked like this:

Year 0: $100 invested at 15 per cent yields $15. He received $5 and the capital remaining was:
Year 1: $110 invested at 15 per cent yields $16.50. He received $8 and the capital remaining was:

[1] This calculation is made using specially prepared Tables of Interest Rates such as will be found in all books on Discounted Cash Flow.

Year 2: $118.50 invested at 15 per cent yields $17.70. He received
$32 and the capital remaining was:
Year 3: $104.20.

Compare this with the very different experience of Mr B. He
invested $1,000 in January 1962 but the company passed the
dividend that year. In 1963 he received $48 and then he sold
out for $1,271 in 1964. What was his d.c.f. return? In fact it was
also 15 per cent – *exactly* the same as Mr A's, not at all the 'very
different experience' suggested above! Check the calculation:

Year 0: $1,000 invested at 15 per cent yields $150. He received
$0 and the capital remaining was:
Year 1: $1,150 invested at 15 per cent yields $173. He received
$48 and the capital remaining was:
Year 2: $1,271

An Ideal Tool

It is difficult to imagine a more versatile tool than d.c.f. for the
purpose we have in mind. The corporate planner has merely to
list all the payments made to shareholders over the past few
years, taking in to the calculation the Stock Exchange valuation
of the company's ordinary shares, and he can calculate the d.c.f.
return that the company has given the shareholders in the past.
He then needs to know whether this was satisfactory which can
be determined by reference to a similar calculation made for
other companies in the same industry or in similar industries
or similar companies in other industries or the average for all
industries or the top few companies in England or
America; whatever criterion is felt to be appropriate. Thus if a
company considers itself about average he can compare its past
record with that of the average company. If it considers itself
one of the top few firms in the world it can compare its record
with theirs. He must of course take care not to choose exceptional starting and ending years for his calculations: thus if a
company's record is:

	Stock Exchange Valuation of Ordinary Shares $	Total Gross Dividends $	Yield %
1960	2,962,000	112,500	3.8
1961	2,429,000	123,800	5.1
1962	2,688,000	131,700	4.9
1963	2,856,000	142,800	5.0
etc.			

It might be wise to consider the high capital valuation and the yield of 3.8 per cent in 1960 as being exceptional and to check this result with the valuations and the yields for other similar companies in that year. By this type of calculation the corporate planner can arrive at the d.c.f. return enjoyed by shareholders of his company in the past and can gauge whether or not it has been satisfactory compared with other similar companies. Unfortunately this does not tell him what return the company should aim to give them in the future. He must now consider this.

Choosing a Target Figure
In fact, he must consider three questions. Have the shareholders been satisfied in the past; if not what would have satisfied them? Secondly, even if they have been satisfied in the past, do the company's executives think they should have done better? Using the replies to these questions, together with a considered opinion about the future, he thirdly needs to decide whether the company should aim at the same d.c.f. return in the future as achieved in the past or one that is higher or lower. Let us assume that a company has yielded 9 per cent d.c.f. return to shareholders over the past fifteen years, say, and that this was similar to industry in general.[1] The company believes it could have improved on this slightly, since some of its competitors did much better. Then, if the future is to be the same as the past, the target should be a little more than 9 per cent – say 10 per cent. The company might well settle for 10 per cent, to provide an extra challenge to their own abilities as managers, but now a new factor must be brought in: they believe that profits in all fields throughout business in Britain will be harder to earn in the next ten years than in the past fifteen years. So they decide that to achieve 9 per cent will be as much as they can hope for, but still rather better than a shareholder might expect from a similar investment elsewhere. So they settle for this and it is then up to the corporate planner to show what this means in terms of dividends, capital gains, profits and many other factors. Another company, perhaps less ambitious, might have chosen 8 per cent in similar circumstances, but no company would have chosen a figure lower than

[1] This was, in fact, approximately the d.c.f. return on an average portfolio for this period.

the lowest return that shareholders might be expected to be satisfied with. To do so would be grossly irresponsible. Nor should any company set the target so much higher than its past achievements as to subject the shareholders' capital to undue risk. In all cases the corporate planner must take account of the probable future trend of rewards to shareholders in general; if the economic future for the next five years is bleak this should be reflected in the target return. If governmental policy is anti-capitalist then this must be reflected. What he must not allow is the easy assumption that as his company is facing difficult times it can afford to lower its target. The only case for setting a target return that is lower than their past achievement is when shareholders *as a class* are thought to be facing harder times, if most or all companies seem likely to lower their rewards to shareholders.

Similarly if it is thought that shareholders can look forward to better times, then a company should raise its sights for its own shareholders. Naturally most companies, when asked to consider a target of this sort will incline to decide one that represents a rather better performance than it has achieved in the past – this part of the corporate planning process gives the company a chance to stand facing the future and deliberately throw down a gauntlet.

An Example
Take the case of a company whose stock market valuation and dividend payments have been as follows:

Year	Stock Exchange Valuation	Total Gross Dividend Paid Out	Total Net Dividend Paid Out
	$	$	$
1957	1,200,000	60,000	36,000
1958	1,274,400	60,000	36,000
1959	1,276,800	64,800	38,900
1960	1,428,000	72,000	43,200
1961	1,468,800	81,600	49,000
1962	1,612,800	72,000	43,200
1963	1,706,400	81,600	49,000
1964	1,684,800	84,000	50,400
1965	1,941,600	93,600	56,200
1966	2,066,400	100,800	60,500
1967	2,160,000	108,000	64,800

Although there is a considerable year to year variation in these figures, the upward trend is approximately 6 per cent per annum.

The corporate planner can calculate the d.c.f. return to shareholder that this flow of dividends represents on the Stock Exchange valuation of 1957 (i.e. the initial capital value) together with the valuation in 1967: it is 9 per cent. Or he can do the same calculation for a shareholder who bought in 1961 and sold in 1965 (9.2 per cent) – or for any other years. Had the dividend yield remained exactly constant each year and had the rate of growth in dividend and Stock Exchange valuation been constant each year, then no matter when a shareholder bought or sold, the d.c.f. return would have been the same – exactly 9 per cent. As it happens there were year to year variations and a slightly variable performance is the result.

This company now has to decide what target to aim at for the next ten years or so. They believe that profits from all businesses are going to be harder to earn in future, that few shareholders expect as good a return in future as in the past ten years (9 per cent) – indeed they will be lucky to get 8 per cent d.c.f. Even so the company feels that they should try to do at least as well in the future as in the past and decide to set themselves the ambitious target of 10 per cent d.c.f. return to shareholders: if they succeed the shareholders should be well pleased. The corporate planner now has to translate this return-to-shareholder target into a profit target for the company.

He knows that a return of 10 per cent d.c.f. can be given by any number of different patterns of income. In family businesses the proprietors can decide how they want their returns to be streamed. But assuming the hypothetical company whose record we are now discussing (let us call it Hypothetics Ltd.) is owned by members of the public, tradition has it that they expect an annual income before tax representing about 5 per cent of the capital value of the company. Now if the gross dividend is to be 5 per cent, (3 per cent net), and the d.c.f. return is to be 10 per cent at what rate must the dividend increase each year (and with it the Stock Exchange valuation)? The answer is 7 per cent per annum. A net income of $3 per annum on an investment of $100 is 3 per cent. But an income of $3, $3.21, $3.43, etc. (rising at 7 per cent per annum) is a *d.c.f.* return of 10 per cent. An income from $100 of $3, $3.18,

$3.38 etc. (i.e. rising at 6 per cent per annum) is a d.c.f. return of 9 per cent. An income of $8 rising at 5 per cent per annum is 13 per cent d.c.f. And so on; the after tax dividend yield plus the rate of growth equals the d.c.f. return.

However this is only true if the income goes on rising indefinitely – i.e. if a shareholder *never* sold the shares he holds. If he did sell them then the price he gets for them must reflect the same rate of growth as the dividend. Thus if he requires 12 per cent d.c.f. return then: *either* he must receive 5 per cent growing at 7 per cent per annum indefinitely *or* he must receive 5 per cent growing at 7 per cent per annum until he sells and when he sells he must make a capital gain of 7 per cent per annum over the years he has held the shares. Thus the corporate planner knows that if Hypothetics shareholders are to receive 10 per cent d.c.f. and if they expect the traditional net dividend yield of 3 per cent then the dividend payments *and* the Stock Exchange valuation must rise by 7 per cent per annum. The company intends, therefore, to aim to bring about the following results:

Share Price Index		Stock Exchange Valuation $	Gross Dividends $	Approximate Gross Dividend Yield per cent
100	1967 (actual result)	2,160,000	108,000	5
105	1968	2,304,000	115,200	5
110	1969	2,472,000	123,600	5
116	1970	2,640,000	132,000	5
122	1971	2,832,000	141,600	5
128	1972	3,024,000	151,200	5
134	1973	3,240,000	162,000	5
141	1974	3,456,000	172,800	5
148	1975	3,696,000	184,800	5
155	1976	3,960,000	198,000	5
163	1977	4,224,000	211,200	5

It will be noticed that the company expects the Share Price Index (e.g. The Times or Financial Times Index) to grow at only 5 per cent per annum. Assume the net dividend yield of the shares represented in this Index is 3 per cent. Now 3 per cent net dividend growing at 5 per cent per annum equals 8 per cent d.c.f. return to shareholders – this, it will be recalled, is the return that Hypothetics think the average shareholder will get in the next ten years – not as good as the 9 per cent they have enjoyed in the past ten years. This table also shows the dividends that Hypothetics would like to be able to pay over the next ten years together with the concomitant rise in share valuation giving a 10 per cent d.c.f. return (3 per cent growing at 7 per cent per annum). Now what profits will it have to make in order to be able to make these payments? Clearly, if dividend cover remains constant, if the rate of taxation in all its forms remains constant, if the company's gearing remains constant, then, to finance a *dividend* growing at 7 per cent per annum the *profits* must grow at 7 per cent per annum.

Hypothetics' dividend cover was 1.4 in 1967, it paid corporation tax at 40 per cent and its gross profits were $252,000. This must now grow at 7 per cent per annum if the company is to achieve its target. Their profits in 1968 must therefore be about $268,800, in 1969 $288,000, then $309,600 and so on, until, in ten years time its profits would have to be $496,800 – very nearly double the present figure.

The company's profit target is set.

Notes on Policy and Methodology
In order to preserve the thread of the argument in this chapter certain technical details have so far been avoided. More importantly, certain matters of principle, which do not stand in the main stream of the argument, have been so far ignored. In other words simplicity has been the keynote so that the discussion can proceed step by step without turning aside to consider certain technical details and certain ancillary matters of company policy. These miscellaneous factors – and some of them are of considerable importance – must now be considered.
Inflation
All records of money values include inflation. A record of share values such as:

| 1960 | $42,072 | 1962 | $48,043 |
| 1961 | $46,291 | 1963 | $53,366 |

shows an upward movement of about 10 per cent per annum. But this may include the effects of inflation; if the figures were taken from actual unedited historical records then inflation is certainly included. Only if the statistician who produced this list of figures has consciously and intentionally corrected them to present day values is the 10 per cent increase in value a real and genuine one. If they have not been corrected in this way (and if they have the author of the list should certainly have said so) then the real improvement in their value has only been about 7 per cent per annum – the other 3 per cent or so being due to the effect of inflation.

In this book we have already seen that rates of growth in dividends and capital values of around 6 per cent per annum are normal for the past ten years or so. (A few companies can show much better rates of growth – 20 per cent per annum is very exceptional. Many companies show rates of less than 4 per cent.) So we are normally dealing with fairly low numbers. All figures so far quoted or suggested include inflation. It will be realized that as inflation has been 3 per cent per annum over the past ten years or so this is a very large proportion of figures such as the 6 per cent that have been discussed. In other words a company whose share value has risen by 6 per cent has *really* only shown a growth of 3 per cent – the rest of its apparent growth, about half of it, is due to inflation.
sterling.

In this book, to avoid confusion, all past records will be quoted with inflation *included*. Thus 7 per cent per annum means a real growth of about 4 per cent and inflation of 3 per cent. If a figure of $100 is mentioned relating to 1961, it means $100 at 1961 values. Equally, all projections into the future will assume inflation continues at 3 per cent. Suppose one drew a graph of a company's asset values over the past ten years:

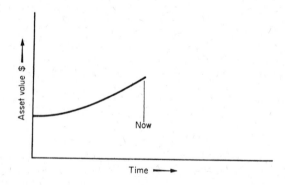

Suppose one now wishes to project this trend into the future:

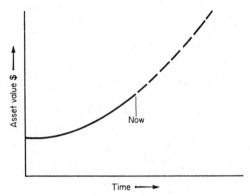

This projection assumes inflation will continue in the future as in the past. The mistake is often made of making a forecast in terms of present-day values and comparing it with past performance. This is fatal! Since we are usually dealing with rates of *real* growth of around 3 or 4 per cent per annum, an error of as much as 100 per cent can be made in comparing real growth with an inflated growth.

A consequence of these thoughts is that a company whose profits have risen by 3 per cent per annum over the past ten years *hasn't grown at all!*

Of all the traps that lie in wait for unskilled corporate planners the phenomenon of inflation is probably the best concealed. One can so easily forget that if someone claims that production of pig iron has increased by 6 per cent per annum he really means 6 per cent; if someone says that profits have increased by 6 per cent per annum he really means 3 per cent! It is so easy to forget that one cannot compare a forecast of future financial statistics with a record of past financial statistics unless both contain (or do not contain) inflation. All records do contain it – unless someone has *consciously* adjusted them to real values. On the other hand most forecasts are in real terms – unless someone has *consciously* added inflation in.

If a company chooses a target of 10 per cent d.c.f. to shareholders this figure includes inflation; without inflation it would be 7 per cent. If the company decides upon a 3 per cent after-tax dividend yield and 7 per cent growth in dividends and if it therefore aims to improve profits by 7 per cent per annum, this also includes inflation. In real terms profits need increase by only about half that figure; the other half will be provided automatically by the effects of inflation assuming it continues at its present rate. Thus if the target profit for 1976 is $500,000, this is the figure the company hopes *actually to see in the balance sheet* for that year. So often a company sets its target in present-day terms and is delighted when it achieves it – quite forgetting that it has not achieved it! In real terms they have missed it by 3 per cent per annum!

Taxation

Discounted Cash Flow deals with *cash* flows, i.e. income after all taxes. Taxation is one of the largest 'costs' facing a company today and it must certainly not be ignored as it has been so far in this book. Three types of tax must be considered.

Firstly, the shareholder's dividend is taxed at about 40 per cent for most people. So it is not true that a shareholder receives $5 per annum from an investment of $100, he only receives $3 or so. While gross dividend yields are, and have been, around 5 per cent, net dividend yield is nearer 3 per cent.

But it does not end here. Shareholders also suffer a capital gains tax of, frequently, 30 per cent. Thus if a company aims to increase its share value by 7 per cent per annum and if a shareholder sells his shares, realizing this gain, he will be taxed on it at 30 per cent. He will therefore only get 30 per cent of the 7 per cent gain as actual *cash*. Now take two shareholders who both have shares in companies earning 12 per cent d.c.f. but shareholder A takes it all as dividend with no capital gain and shareholder B takes no dividend, only a capital gain:

SHAREHOLDER A

1964 Invests $100 takes $12 dividend = $7.40 after tax.
1965 Invests $100 takes $12 dividend = $7.40 after tax.
1966 Sells at $100. No gains to tax = $100 cash.

SHAREHOLDER B

1964 Invests $100. Takes no dividend.
1965 Capital now $112. Takes no dividend.
1966 Capital now $126.40. Sells. Pays gains tax of $7.90 on $26.40, receives $118.50 cash.

To the extent that it is possible to do so it would be better to follow B's course than A's; however, the shareholders' own preferences for an annual income rather than a postponed lump sum, the tax laws and the willingness of a company to adopt B's pattern, all severely limit the extent to which this can be done. Nevertheless there must be an optimum mix of dividend and growth for any given company and any given shareholder at any given time. So far as is known little effort is made by most companies to find it.

Finally, company taxation must be considered. The corporate planner, in calculating the profit target from the return to shareholder's target has to take account of company taxation. He must attempt to forecast whether it will become more or less severe over the years. It is hard to believe that its severity will decline over industry in general over the next few years although the rate of increase may well be less for some companies than for others who may be in 'less socially desirable' industries.[1]

The Merits of the d.c.f. method

If a company has no intention of attempting to tailor its payments to shareholders to suit them, if it decides to adopt the traditional 3 per cent net yield, then it does not need to set its target return to shareholders in terms of d.c.f. It can simply set it as yield and growth – two figures. But many companies will wish to consider some alternatives either to minimize the effect of taxation on the shareholder or on the company, or, better still, on both. Also, by using d.c.f., it can determine whether a high income now followed by a period of lower income is worth the same to a shareholder as some other pattern. And it can test dividend against capital gains (making the calculation afresh after each change in the tax laws relating to companies or individuals); it can compare one company's record with another, it can see what extra dividend should be paid next year in order to get back on target if this year's dividend was below target. All these hitherto difficult questions become easy.

Using d.c.f. it can see that the endless discussion as to whether a company should seek to give priority to short term shareholders or long term ones is empty. For if the net dividend yield is a constant 3 per cent and if the dividends and share valuation increase regularly by 7 per cent, it does not matter when a shareholder buys or when he sells or even if he never sells,

---

[1] Company taxation has in fact *declined* over the past ten years or so.

he will still receive 10 per cent d.c.f. Only the fluctuations of the stock market will cause some to do better and others worse than 10 per cent.

Deciding the target level
The reader may have gained the impression that 10 per cent d.c.f. was a suitable target for *all* companies in the next ten years. This is not so. Some, in shipping for example, have achieved less than 8 per cent and would be bold to aim for 10 per cent over the next ten years – and yet, if they fail to get this (and many will fail on present showing) they will surely be wound up. Other companies, in oils for example, have achieved as much as 16 per cent d.c.f. Again, they would be bold to aim at as high a figure in the future. Nevertheless, while no company should aim as low as 8 per cent a few could reasonably expect to achieve twice that figure. It is up to each company to decide how ambitious it wishes to be.

Accuracy of the Calculations
It has been pointed out that no company can possibly guarantee to raise its dividends by precisely a given percentage each year. Still less can it ensure that the Stock Exchange will value its shares at precisely twenty times the total dividend paid out. This being so there is singularly little sense in setting a target that is accurate to several places of decimals. If this year's dividends totalled $464,225 and if the target calls for a growth of 7 per cent then, to be accurate, next year's dividend should be $496,720.75. One has only to suggest this figure to see its absurdity. A figure of $496,800 is the nearest one could possibly hope for; a figure of $489,600 or even $480,000 is quite near enough. However, it must be noted that a dividend of $489,600 represents a growth of 6 per cent over the previous year's $463,200; and a dividend of $480,000 is only about $3\frac{1}{2}$ per cent better than $463,200. So, clearly, if the aim was a 7 per cent increase and if the company felt able to declare a dividend of only $480,000 then, to get back on target, its dividend the following year must be above the target figure by an amount similar to this shortfall (or, to be more correct, by an amount similar to the net present value of the shortfall – i.e. about 10 per cent greater than the shortfall if the target return was 10 per cent).

Since a company cannot control its destiny with any great accuracy there is no point in setting the target with great accuracy. In fact, the corporate planner does not need to make extraordinary efforts to obtain accuracy in setting the target – he need only ensure that the targets are at an *appropriate* level. An error of 1 per cent in setting the growth target has comparatively little effect on the figures over even quite a number of years. Thus a target of 6 per cent growth on a profit of $240,000 requires a profit of $303,120 in the fifth year while a target of 7 per cent requires one of $314,400 in the fifth year. It is extremely unlikely that any company can control its profits to such a fine degree. Not too much time should be spent, therefore, in sophisticated refinement of such targets: it is necessary only to ensure that the right order of magnitude is being chosen. This is not to say that an error of 1 per cent should not be avoided if possible. Even 1 per cent over many years mounts up formidably even when the difference is between 6 per cent and 7 per cent; it is greater between 16 per cent and 17 per cent. Again: a growth of $7\frac{1}{2}$ per cent per annum means the profits double in ten years while a growth of 10 per cent per annum means doubling in only seven years or so. Differences of this magnitude are certainly too great to tolerate.

Loans

The reader will be aware that all the discussion above concerning dividend and growth refers to ordinary shares. Loan capital normally bears a fixed rate of interest and once this has been stated it remains constant regardless of the prosperity of the company; nor is there normally any question of capital appreciation. However, one class of loans are of interest here: convertible loans. The interest lies in the fact that when a company issues a convertible loan it has in mind a Stock Exchange price for the ordinary shares at which the loan can be converted to ordinary shares – furthermore it has a particular date in mind when this price should be reached. In other words companies do try to predict what value their ordinary shares will have many years ahead. This point is made here in order to show that setting a growth target based on Stock Exchange valuation, which is part of the target-setting process recommended in this book, is a perfectly practicable suggestion.

Dividend Cover

One easy way to ensure that dividends paid out each year meet the company's target is to pay them at the expense of dividend cover. This is not always a dangerous expedient but it must be deprecated in most cases especially when cover is already low or when the company's profits are liable to severe fluctuations. Obviously if dividend cover is too low or too high at the time the target is being set, the necessary adjustment to this must be borne in mind when setting the target.

Return on Capital

At first sight the fact that the profit target is expressed as one relating to volume of profit only, suggests that the concept of 'return on capital' has been dropped. One can well imagine someone objecting that a target that only called for a rise in the *amount* of profit must fail to take into consideration the *efficiency* of the capital employed. If this were so it would indeed be a serious failing. However, the concept of return on capital is included, not in the company's profit target but in the target for return on *shareholder's* capital. It is inserted one stage further back than usual. Traditionally, a company tends not to consider the return that a shareholder receives at all – except when the dividend is declared, of course, but dividends are only part of the shareholder's return; growth of the dividend and share valuation over the years must be considered as well. Too often, they are not. Instead the company's executives concentrate on the Return on Capital Employed figure – i.e. return on the *company's* capital – as an indicator of their efficiency. The concept of return on capital, or the efficiency with which capital is employed, most certainly is included in the d.c.f. method of setting targets – in the right place, though, at the starting point for all target setting, with the owner's capital; not with the rather meaningless hotch-potch of items that make up the Capital Employed figure. Furthermore, the highly appropriate discounted cash flow method is used to measure this efficiency rather than the oversimple Profit/Capital Employed ratio which can be such a flexible yardstick.

One other point is worth noting about the traditional Return on Capital Employed. While it purports to measure the efficiency with which the company is employing its capital (and it does not do this very well, as we have seen) it is completely silent on the matter of growth in the volume of profits. That is to say, a company aiming at a Return on Capital Employed of 10 per cent cannot tell from this whether it should aim to invest more or less capital next year compared with last year. Thus efficiency is measured (poorly) but growth is not.

Incidentally, there is no fixed relation between a given d.c.f. target and a Return on Capital Employed figure. Two companies who both return 10 per cent d.c.f. to their shareholders may have widely different Returns on Capital Employed; perhaps 8 per cent in one case and 15 per cent in another. To determine this relationship for any given company a fairly complicated calculation must be made. Nor is there any direct relationship between Return on Capital Employed and return on capital required from new projects. A company showing 10 per cent Return on Capital Employed may think that by investing $1 million in a new project that yields $120,000 (i.e. 12 per cent return) it will improve its overall return of 10 per cent. Not a bit of it! This will be discussed again in Chapter XI.

Computer Models

Although great accuracy is not required in setting the company's targets, the complexity of the finances of some companies is very considerable. Taxation, loans, depreciation, trade investments, overseas subsidiaries (each with their own taxation complexities), do make for severe difficulties. Furthermore, corporate planners may wish to test the effect of altering one or more of the assumptions underlying their targets. A good example of such an exercise is to see what is the total amount of tax paid by shareholders and company together for any combination of dividend and growth making up the d.c.f. return (e.g. 3 per cent and 7 per cent or $3\frac{1}{2}$ per cent and $6\frac{1}{2}$ per cent or 6 per cent and 4 per cent). To make even these simple calculations by hand, especially if he wanted to extend the study over many combinations or over many years, would be tedious. It is possible to make a mathematical model of a company's financial structure including the shareholder's dividends, loan stock, tax, capital employed, depreciation and so on, and to use a computer to study the effects of any changes. Such models are not difficult to prepare using one of the high-level computer languages such as Algol. However, except for large or complex companies it is not necessary to prepare such a model at least in the early stages of corporate planning. The use of computer models is mentioned again in later chapters.

Revising the Targets

We have been discussing two targets in this chapter. A d.c.f. target return to shareholders and the company's profit target that is derived from it. The first had to be set in order to calculate the second but it is the second one, profits, that is going to be used by the company in all its planning. It is necessary to review the appropriateness of these targets from time to time. Let one thing be made absolutely clear: a company need not review its objective. This, it will be recalled, was something permanent and unalterable: it will become inappropriate only when profit itself becomes undesirable. But the *target* may be altered when it is seen to be at a level that is no longer appropriate in current conditions. The objective was 'to make that profit which enables the company to give a return to shareholders that would satisfy them'. The target is a numerical measure of what would satisfy them at any given moment: this figure may well change in changing circumstances.

A target of 10 per cent d.c.f. would be appropriate for the average company over the next ten years only so long as other average companies are giving 10 per cent d.c.f. return to their shareholders and this in turn depends on the general level of business activity, the rate of inflation, the social climate towards capitalism, and so on. It would obviously be sensible frequently to review a target that depends on such important assumptions. It is suggested that the review should take place once a year – in other words, once a year the company should ask itself whether its shareholders would still be satisfied with the returns set as a target the previous year.

It is also necessary to review the profit target once a year. It was assumed, it will be remembered, that if dividends were to grow at 7 per cent per annum then, other things being equal, the company's profits would also have to grow at 7 per cent in order to maintain dividend cover, and thus the profit target was set almost automatically. However, if company taxation rates were changed, if the proportion of loan stock to ordinary shares changed, if dividend cover requirements changed, then it is quite possible that the profit target would have to be

TABLE 1

Deriving a Profit Target for a Company from a Shareholders' Return of Ten per cent d.c.f.

		1967 (Actual)	1968	1969	1970	1971	1972
Net Dividends paid to Ordinary Shareholders. (Net yield of 3 per cent)	$	64,800	69,400	84,200	79,400	85,000	91,000
Gross Dividend (Rising at 7 per cent per annum)	$	108,000	115,200	123,600	132,000	141,400	151,200
Gross Dividend Yield	%	5	5	5	5	5	5
Stock Exchange Valuation of Ordinary Shares (Rising at 7 per cent per annum)	$	2,160,000	2,304,000	2,472,000	2,640,000	2,827,200	3,024,000
Dividend Cover	%	1.4	1.4	1.4	1.4	1.4	1.4
Net Profit	$	151,200	161,300	172,800	184,800	198,200	212,200
Corporation Tax at 40%	$	100,800	108,000	115,200	123,600	132,200	141,400
Gross Trading Profit (The Profit Target)	$	252,000	269,300	288,000	308,600	330,500	353,500

Note: Loan stock interest has been omitted for the sake of simplicity. Figures are rounded to the nearest hundred dollars.

changed even if the target return to shareholders was not changed. How the company's profit target can be calculated from the return to shareholders target can be seen in a much simplified form in Table 1.

There is one thing a company must never do. It must never revise a target downwards just because the company is finding it difficult to achieve. If the target was set at an appropriate level originally then either it is still appropriate or it is not. If it is not then it should be revised for that reason and no other. If it is still appropriate – that is to say the shareholder's level of satisfaction has not altered, then it must not be reduced, if it is then the company runs the risk of aiming not to satisfy them.

This point is made with some force because some books on management clearly state that if a target proves to be too difficult it should be reduced. They do not often add the important caveat that a target is not set at a particular level because it is easy or difficult but *because it is appropriate*. If it is reduced just because it is difficult it may then cease to be appropriate. It is not always easy to do the right thing, but there is no licence for doing the wrong thing just because it is easier.

Summary of Chapter VI
Having agreed that the company exists to satisfy the owners, and having determined who these owners are, the corporate planner has to find out what level of return will satisfy them and then calculate what profits the company will have to make to allow it to give them this return. It was discovered that 'maximize profits' is a meaningless exhortation and that the traditional Return on Capital Employed is so flexible a yardstick as to be useless. In any case it purports to measure return on the *company's* capital which is less apposite than a measure of return on *shareholder's* capital.

The discounted cash flow method was found to be an ideal concept. The average company over the past ten years or so has yielded a d.c.f. return of about 9 per cent (many have done no better than 8 per cent, a few better than 16 per cent) but in view of the economic outlook, the social climate against capitalism, and so on, shareholders may be lucky to get as much as 8 per cent over the next few years.

Privately owned companies can probably arrange to make the return to their owners to suit the owner's convenience or to minimize the combined incidence of tax. Companies owned by members of the public, however, are more closely constrained by tradition so that if a target is set at 10 per cent d.c.f. this will probably take the form of a 3 per cent after-tax dividend yield and a 7 per cent per annum growth in dividends and Stock Exchange valuation.

From the shareholder's target it is usually a simple matter to calculate a profit target for the company for if dividend cover, taxation and loan stock in proportion to equity remain constant, a growth of 7 per cent in dividends means a growth of 7 per cent in Gross Trading Profits.

This brings the corporate planner to the end of Step 1, except that, from time to time, he must reconsider whether the target still reflects the level at which shareholders would be satisfied and whether the profit target still allows the company to meet it.

(See also Outline of the Five Step Process in Appendix 1.)

CHAPTER VII

STEP 2   PREPARE A FORECAST

The necessity for a forecast – a forecasting procedure – stage 1, analysis of revenues, costs, volumes – stage 2, the projections – stage 3, the factors affecting profits – stage 4, the forecasts.

CONSIDER the position now reached; the corporate planner has prepared a long term profit target. This set of figures represents the level of achievement that the company is now aiming at – these are the profit figures that it would like to see in its Company Accounts over the next ten years. If it achieves this record it believes that it will have slightly more than satisfied the shareholders and also, incidentally, the directors and senior executives would have demonstrated their competence as managers. Few companies in Britain set themselves a profit target in this way so the vast majority may not really know what they are aiming at: they cannot therefore know on what scale to lay their plans.

Consider an average company such as Hypothetics Ltd., mentioned in the previous chapter, which has decided to set itself a profit target based on 7 per cent per annum growth taking the current year's (1967) profits of $252,000 as the datum. It is looking forward to profits of this order:

	$		$
1967	252,000	1973	376,800
1968	269,300	1974	403,200
1969	288,000	1975	432,000
1970	309,600	1976	463,200
1971	331,200	1977	496,800
1972	352,800		

It can see at once that it has got to take action to lift its profits by about $19,200 a year for the next few years and by the end of the ten year period it must try to lift them by about $31,200 per annum. Put it another way: its present profits are

$252,000 and by 1972 – only five years ahead – its profits should be up to about $352,800. This is an increase of over $96,000. Knowing this the company's executives will at once start thinking of schemes and projects designed to yield this extra profit. Unfortunately if they think that all they have to do is to find ways of generating an extra $96,000 in the next five years they may be in for a rude shock! What they have forgotten is that the present business, now yielding $250,000 profit will almost certainly not continue to do so. To swim at 3 mph relative to the bank may mean having to swim at 5 mph if there is a 2 mph current against you. Most companies are swimming against a tide: it is known as the profit squeeze.

Consider what would happen if a company did nothing from today onwards other than do what it had already decided to do – in other words if all the executives froze into their current decision-making posture, if all the decision-making machinery stopped leaving the company running like a train without an engineer. Costs would continue to rise just as they have done in the past, selling prices would remain at their present levels. Margins would fall. Sales volume might continue to rise as it had in the past but perhaps not fast enough to offset the fall in margins. Profits will fall, unless the company does something about this – but we have postulated that they will not take any action other than what they have always done before. Sooner or later profits from the existing business will die away. The fire will go out unless more logs are thrown on.

It may be thought that this is a ridiculous assumption – of course the company will do something to stop the rot. And of course they will – but how much they will have to do and what this action should be is just the question we need to answer. It must be remembered that they have not only to stop the rot, they have to do this *and* improve profits by 7 per cent per annum.

Suppose the company decides not to try to bolster up the existing business but to launch out into a new direction entirely. How much extra profit must this new venture yield? Clearly it must yield the extra $96,000 profits by 1972. But it must in addition yield a further profit to make up for the falling profits from the existing business that they have chosen to neglect. Only in this way will the company profits – from the new and the old business together – attain the 1972 target. If it is objected that no company would totally forsake its existing business when launching a new venture one may or may not agree: this assumption was made only to clarify the argument which remains valid even if the company does not neglect its existing business. The salient fact – and one so often forgotten – is that the profits of most existing businesses are being eroded by the profit squeeze (costs rising due to inflation, selling prices constant or even falling due to competition). If the company's profits are to grow then action has to be taken that is powerful enough both to counteract this squeeze and to add new profits. Most companies have to run pretty fast up the 'down' escalator in order to progress upwards.

A company's profit target can be drawn on a graph:

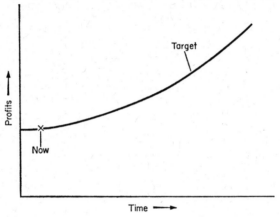

The falling away of profits on the existing business can be shown thus:

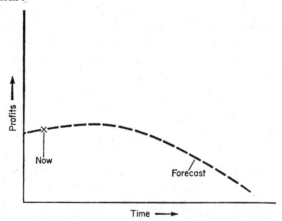

These two graphs can be superimposed.

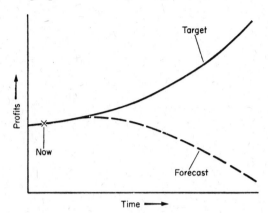

It is the widening gap between these two lines on this last graph that represents the task facing a company. This is the gap between the target and the forecast – the difference between what the company *wants* to happen and what it *expects* will happen if it does nothing. It shows how much it has to do.

The corporate planner has to determine what this gap is for his company so that the size of the task of achieving the target can be gauged. In the last chapter we saw how he set the target. In this chapter we must follow him through the process of forecasting future profits. In the next chapter he will measure the gap and spell out the task.

A forecasting procedure
There are probably a dozen ways of making a forecast. The method used here is somewhat complex, in that it involves four stages, but the value of proceeding in this way goes beyond the resulting forecast as will be seen. The four stages of forecasting are:

1. Analysis of Revenue, Costs and Volumes.
2. The Projections and Errors.
3. The Factors Affecting Profits.
4. The Forecasts and Errors.

Briefly, the first stage is to analyse what is to be forecast, and in what detail. Then it is necessary to project past trends into the future, i.e. simply to extrapolate the past into the future making no adjustments of any sort. The third stage is to list all those factors that might or could possibly affect profits in the future, whether or not they were present in the past and whether or not they actually affected profits in the past. And finally, using this as a check-list one modifies the projections; i.e. instead of assuming the future will be identical to the past as when making the projections, one attempts to determine in what way the future will be different. To give a simple example: imagine the analysis in stage 1 indicates that a company's total salary bill is one of the elements to be considered in making a profit forecast. Suppose it is seen that in the past the company's salary bill has risen at the rate of 6 per cent per annum. The second stage merely requires that this trend be projected into the future – an extremely simple thing to do. In the third stage any factors that may affect the salary bill in the future must be considered and it may be felt that due to these factors the salary bill will rise at some other rate than 6 per cent – that new rate is the forecast. At the same time the limits of likely errors must be noted.

Now this appears at first sight to be unnecessarily complex. Why not just forecast the future salary bill straight away without going through the other stages? There are several reasons why this roundabout route is recommended.

(1) The corporate planner may or may not be brought into the company from outside. If he is he will need to know a good deal about its past– he learns this in the first and second stages of forecasting. But even if he has been with the company for many years, his knowledge of the company's past may not cover every area in equal depth. The more he does already know the better, but he is unlikely to have enough knowledge without at least refreshing his memory over the whole field of the company's past activities.

(2) If one makes a simple projection of past trends one frequently discovers anomalies. One might find, for example, that the projected salary bill rises at a lower rate than the projected wages bill; an odd circumstance when one considers the trend towards higher overheads and increased automation on the shop floor. This may indeed be a valid prediction for a particular company in unusual circumstances but it would certainly be necessary to examine it with more than usual care before accepting it. In other words such anomalies act as a

warning signal to the corporate planner that here may be a case where the past may not be a good guide to the future.

(3) In making a projection the corporate planner gains a useful insight into the possible future of the company, it gives him a rough guide against which he can judge the credability of the statements made to him by the company's executives about the future. He will frequently seek the opinion of these executives but if he has no idea himself of what the future may be he is not in a good position to challenge or question their opinions: one must not ignore the possibility that their opinions may be tinged with optimism or pessimism.

(4) The Factors Affecting Profits are of enormous value to him later on in Step 4 of the corporate planning process (Deciding the Means) as well as in this forecasting stage where their systematic use is essential.

(5) One advantage of making a simple extrapolation from the past to the future is that the past records of costs and revenues include inflation; a simple projection will therefore, also include inflation. It will be realized that if inflation is included in the target it must also be included in the forecasts; unless the corporate planner starts by making a simple projection, which automatically includes inflation, there is a danger of it being inadvertently left out.

These forecasts are intended as a prediction of future profits if the company's decision-making machinery froze as from the present. The assumption is that the company will do nothing in the future that it is not already in the habit of doing. If labour productivity has risen by 2 per cent per annum in the past then we will assume that it will go on doing so. If the company has made a particular product for years then it will be assumed that it will go on doing so. If research costs represent 1 per cent of turnover then this will continue unaltered. These forecasts are intended to show what would happen if the executives did nothing new. Then, when the forecasts are compared with the target, the company can see what it *has* got to do.

The assumption is made that research costs, labour productivity etc. continue as they have done, that no new plant will be installed, no new product introduced, no attempt made to increase share of the market. Decisions to change any of these must come *out* of the calculations, not be put in. A position of

minimum assumption about the company's future behaviour must be reached – i.e. that the company will
do nothing new. The only changes that may be allowed
to enter the forecasts are those decisions recently made
and to which the company is committed. Nothing else is
assumed.

Each of the 4 stages of forecasting must be considered in some
detail.

Stage 1: Analysis of Revenues, Costs and Volumes
It is necessary to break down the company's past performance
into its constituent revenues and costs. Immediately the
corporate planner has to ask himself to what extent he needs
to go into every detail. If a company has a turnover of $2.5
million per annum from twenty-seven different products it is
perfectly possible that the top five of these account for perhaps
as much as $2 million and the smallest accounts for only
$2,000. Should he analyse the past trends for all the products
or only the top few? The answer will be different for each company and each corporate planner but, as has been mentioned
before, the corporate planner is concerned with overall company strategy and it would seem inappropriate to delve into
too much detail. As a guide it is suggested that any revenue or
cost that could affect profits by more than a few percent should
be considered. Thus if a company's profits were $250,000 per
annum it is most unlikely that a product accounting for a turnover of only $12,500 could affect profits by as much as 3 per
cent under any imaginable circumstances. It would be sensible to ignore factors of this size.

Similarly, it would be sensible to break down the company's
costs into relevant headings but the process should not go so far
as to isolate items that could not affect profits by more than a
few percent. Thus for a company with a turnover of $2.5 mil-
lion and a profit of $250,000 it would be sensible to consider
any item costing $125,000 but probably not any item of
$12,500 since it is unlikely that such a small item would change
so much as to affect profits by more than a few percent. This
suggestion is intended as a guide only; it is sometimes possible
for the cost of a small item to increase explosively. A much
simplified list of the revenue and cost items that a corporate
planner might choose to study is shown opposite:

Major Revenues and Costs 1967

Revenues	$000	Costs	$000
Product A	1200	Salaries	432
B	624	Wages	497
C	288	Materials	504
D	130	Transport	130
E	55	Fuel	98
F	29	Rent	173
21 Others	74	Depreciation	262
		Selling costs	24
Total	2500	Others	40
		Total	2160

In practice there will probably have to be more items in both lists and the corporate planner may wish to subdivide some of the larger items – materials, for example, could well be broken down into their various major types. However, at this stage at least, the corporate planner should resist the temptation to examine every detail until he is sure that he will have to do so in order to obtain a meaningful level of accuracy in the forecasts. There is one subdivision he must make. This is the split between 'fixed 'and 'variable' costs (or 'overheads' and 'direct' costs as they are often called). This is difficult to do realistically because few variable costs are truly variable and few fixed costs are immutably fixed. Variable costs are defined as those that vary directly with the volume of sales or production: thus if a motor car producer pays the supplier of the tyres $12 per tyre, then for every extra car produced the *total* cost of tyres goes up by $60 (assuming they are 4-wheel cars with a spare of course!). The company's material costs, as far as tyres are concerned, will vary directly with the number of cars produced. Unfortunately this very seldom happens in practice with any 'directly variable' costs since the more cars the company produces the more likely is it that the tyre supplier will allow his customer a quantity discount. So up to, say, 500 cars a week the tyres may cost $60 a car but above that they may cost only $57 due to a quantity discount per tyre. It is even more complicated than this sometimes. If the car producer has an exceptionally successful season he may find that his usual tyre suppliers cannot meet his orders and he may have to buy elsewhere at $15 per tyre. So directly variable costs are not always directly variable with volume.

Nor are fixed costs always fixed. The company producing cars may be paying rates to the local council of, say, $25,000 per annum on the factory site. No matter how many cars he produces this figure remains the same. It is fixed. But suppose the company has an exceptionally bad year and closes down part of the factory, it may be possible to de-rate this part of the premises. Therefore this fixed cost is 'fixed' only until it becomes variable! Similarly the salary of their Design Engineer, for example, is fixed in that it does not vary with output. However, if output fell disastrously the company might declare him redundant. And so on through almost every 'fixed' cost imaginable.

Fortunately for the corporate planner he does not have to make his profit forecasts with minute accuracy – he knows it is not possible to achieve this and he does not waste time trying – so the fact that these are not-so-direct and not-so-fixed need not cause severe problems: he need only separate them out into the two broad categories. Usually salaries, rent, depreciation and most of the wages bill will be fixed within quite wide variations of output while materials, transport, fuel and power, and some wages will be found to vary in proportion to output. Since output is the factor that determines the level of these variable costs to a large extent, the corporate planner must examine the volume of sales for those products that seem to him to be the most important – this list will normally therefore contain the same products as that for the major revenues above:

Sales Volume of major products in 1967

	units
Product A	400
B	200
C	300
D	70
E	40
F	10
G	40
21 others	140
Total sales volume	1200

Having determined which are the major revenues, costs and volumes at the present moment of the company's history the

corporate planner needs now to learn how these have varied
over the past few years. In making this study he will probably
find that the lists of revenues, costs and volumes are not
in sufficient detail and, as the study progresses he will find them
becoming progressively longer and more detailed. Again, he
should bear in mind that extreme accuracy is not called for and
should resist the temptation to obtain it. Taking each major
product[1] in turn he will first prepare an historical schedule showing how its volume and revenue have altered in the past. How
far back he should go in his researches depends upon the relia-
bility of the figures he obtains – but the best answer to this
question is to go as far back as possible. If the corporate
planner intends making his forecasts for ten or more years
ahead it would be sensible to look back at least ten years.

Consider a five-year record of the volume and revenue
relating to Product A for an imaginary company:

Revenue and Volume for Product A – Five years

	1963	1964	1965	1966	1967
Revenue, $000	1416	1464	1464	1392	1440
Volume, units	350	370	390	380	400

Several conclusions spring from these simple figures. Sales
volume has increased by about 15 per cent over the five-year
period (about 3 per cent per annum), revenue has remained
very roughly constant, hence the selling price per unit must
have fallen: in fact from $4,046 to $3,600, an average drop of
about 3 per cent per annum. The corporate planner may feel it
is unnecessary to look any further back in the records in this
case since a fairly steady, consistent pattern of trends is shown.
However, if the records are available he should certainly use
them: a ten-year record may give a somewhat different picture.

Revenue and Volume for Product A – Ten Years

	1958	1959	1960	1961	1962	1963	1964	1965	1966	1967
Revenue $000	—	—	336	1008	1440	1416	1464	1464	1392	1440
Volume units	—	—	70	220	350	350	370	390	380	400

Evidently Product A was introduced in 1960 at a selling price
of $4,800, rapidly gained favour (possibly due to price reduc-
tions in the next two years) and they are now selling a little more

[1] Or group of products.

each year, but each year the average selling price is falling. This is typical of the first part of the life-history of a product. The story told by the five-year record was one of gradual and fairly steady growth, which if projected into the future would have suggested a continued gradual steady growth. The story told by the *ten-year* record is quite different – one of rapid growth reaching a plateau and if projected forward might well suggest a picture of gradual or even rapid decline in conformity with the normal second half of a product's life-history. Obviously the moral of this experience is that the corporate planner must look as far back as he can in the records lest he sees only one misleading fragment of history.

This ten-year record for Product A raises a teeming mass of new questions. Which product was the biggest seller before Product A was introduced? When was it introduced and how long was *its* life? Did the company have to cut the selling price of that product too? Which other products were affected by the rise of Product A? Answers to all these, and more, will be revealed as the corporate planner searches systematically through the records. For next he will study the record of Products B, C and so on. He will note their rise and fall, the price movements, their interactions on each other. Such exercises are rarely carried out in industry; he may well know more about the company's past by the time he has finished than anyone else in the company. Such a study should be carried out for any services a company sells as well as for the physical products, of course.

It is important for the corporate planner to be able to identify the point at which he need pursue any study no further. When can he claim to have done enough work on the history of Product A and turn to a study of Product B? When can he claim to know enough about the past trends exhibited by a particular cost item to entitle him to turn to the study of the next item? The answer is provided by a combination of two considerations: (*a*) The importance of the item in terms of its likely effect on profits. If an item is a really vital one to the company – Product A for example – then he must be more sure of his knowledge than for Product H. If labour costs are a large proportion of total costs then he must be more confident of the explanation behind past variations than if it was a very small item. (*b*) It also depends on the extent to which the record he is

studying is consistent and coherent. If it is consistent with the
records of other similar items then he may not need to try to
understand this item in particular but should try to understand
all these items collectively. Thus if Product A's volume record
was the same as all the other products:

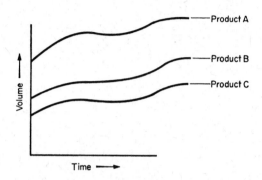

then he can reasonably assume that if he knows why the total
sales volume moved like this then he also knows why Products
A, B, C individually behaved like this. But if the record shows:

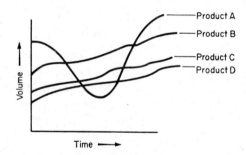

then of course he must admit that the forces behind the sales
record of products B, C, D are not sufficient to explain the record
of Product A. Only when he has discovered what these special
forces are can he end his study of Product A.

He will know when this point has been reached when the
pattern of the graph for Product A can be derived from a graph
of the forces affecting it. In the example above the record of
Product A was shown as:

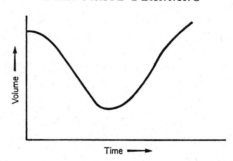

Now if the sales of this product are proportional to its selling price compared with the selling price of a competitor's similar product and if the graph of these two prices is as shown below:

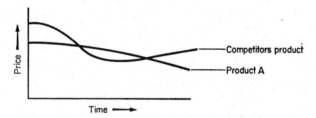

then a rational explanation has been achieved and the corporate planner can claim that he probably understands enough to explain the past behaviour of the sales volume of Product A. (He may then have to try to understand the forces behind the price relationship).

He must make the same systematic survey for *costs*, where the analysis is more difficult due to the problem of distinguishing between fixed and variable costs. However, let us start with a relatively straightforward fixed cost item – rent and rates. Suppose the records show the following rent and rates for a company's offices and factory:

Rent and Rates – Ten Years ($000)

1958	1959	1960	1961	1962	1963	1964	1965	1966	1967
60	62	79	82	82	91	94	98	98	103

This item increased dramatically in 1960 (due to an extension to the factory), but has also risen by approximately 4 per cent per annum on an average over the period. Quite a simple picture. Similarly, salaries have risen by about 10 per cent per annum after allowance has been made for the dramatic rise in 1959:

Total Salary Cost – Ten Years ($000)

1958	1959	1960	1961	1962	1963	1964	1965	1966	1967
146	197	216	240	242	293	322	348	384	432

But when the corporate planner turns to consider labour costs he may find a much more confused pattern to sort out.

Total Labour Costs – Ten Years ($000)

1958	1959	1960	1961	1962	1963	1964	1965	1966	1967
376	352	400	468	540	560	592	676	712	714

Now this looks like a fairly straightforward rise of 7 per cent per annum at first glance – one might easily explain it by mere wage inflation. However, on second thoughts it cannot be due to this factor alone since he knows that the number of men employed in 1959 was 180 whereas in 1967 it was 200. In any case the corporate planner will have discussed these figures with the Production Director and would have learnt that about eighty of the men in 1967 were employed on maintenance, cleaning and general duties largely unrelated to the level of output – i.e. a 'fixed' cost. Wages per man has risen by about 5 per cent per annum, according to statistics kept in the personnel department. Output per man has improved by 30 per cent in the past ten years. The number of units produced has risen by 50 per cent in the past ten years. All these trends acting together have produced a fairly steady rise of 7 per cent per annum in the total wages cost. It takes a considerable effort of analysis to reconcile all these conflicting figures and trends – an effort that would not be worth making were it not for the fact that labour costs usually represent a large proportion of a manufacturing company's total costs and any trend in this item can have a significant effect upon their profits. In the example given above the explanation for the upward trend of 7 per cent per annum in the total wages bill was as follows:

Fixed About eighty men (in 1958–59 it was sixty) were required for general duties, their wages per man rose from an average of $2,000 per annum to $3,600 over the ten years and there was no improvement in labour productivity. This part of the wages cost, the fixed element, totalled:

($000)

1958	1959	1960	1961	1962	1963	1964	1965	1966	1967
120	120	180	192	204	220	240	256	280	288

and, making allowance for the increase in the labour force in 1960 the total fixed labour costs had increased at the rate of 6 per cent per annum.

Variable The number of men required to produce 100 units fell steadily from thirteen in 1958 to ten in 1967 but the wages per man steadily increased from \$2,200 to \$3,800. Since the number of units produced rose from 820 to 1200 a year during this period the variable wages increased as follows:

(\$000)

1958	1959	1960	1961	1962	1963	1964	1965	1966	1967
256	232	220	276	336	340	352	420	432	456

This last set of figures is of little interest, however. What really matters when considering variable costs is the cost per unit of production. This has been as follows:

(\$)

1958	1959	1960	1961	1962	1963	1964	1965	1966	1967
312	280	276	288	312	316	320	360	360	380

Clearly the costs per unit rose only slowly for the first six years or so but rapidly in the past four. Over the whole period the rise was at 2 or 3 per cent but in the past four years at the rate of over 4 per cent.

The example discussed above illustrates a point made previously in this chapter: if a cost item is an important one the corporate planner must make substantial efforts to understand its past behaviour. In the case of total labour costs there are usually many forces combining together to produce any given pattern. In the above example the *total* wages bill showed this pattern:

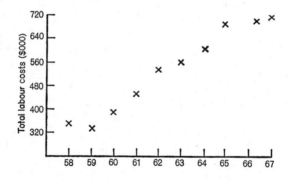

but it was due to no less than five factors:

(1) Expansion of the factory in 1960.
(2) No rise in productivity of eighty men on general duties.
(3) A rise in productivity from thirteen men per 100 units produced to ten.
(4) A rise in output.
(5) A rise in wage rates.

It might be necessary to study this item in even greater depth – for example to analyse the rates at which wages for each type of workman rose – it depends how important an effect on profits this item has for any given company.

Many other costs may have to be analysed: material costs being a large item in most industries would certainly require analysis and it would usually be found that these are almost entirely variable: Research (fixed), Electricity (mainly variable but part, the standing charges, for example, fixed), Fuel (mainly variable), Telephones (fixed), Computer Rental (fixed), Maintenance (mainly fixed,) Transport (variable), and so on. Each cost item being of major importance in one company, minor in another; fixed under some circumstance, variable in another. Always the corporate planner aiming to avoid unnecessary detail and excessive accuracy but always striving to achieve an understanding of the way in which the company's profits depend upon volume, revenue, variable cost and fixed costs. Always asking himself which items of cost really matter, which do not. Asking which are really likely to affect profits by more than a few percent and which can safely be relegated to a 'miscellaneous' category without detailed analysis.

It is surprising how few companies have made this type of analysis – as the reader can easily verify by asking himself or his colleagues the question, 'which are the ten (or five or twenty) main factors that have affected our profits over the past few years?' If the answers do not come readily one cannot see how the company can claim to be trying to make a profit since if a company's profit depends largely on ten main factors and the executives do not know what these are . . .![1]

---

[1] A few companies have identified these major items and have gone to the length of nominating one senior executive to maintain a constant watch over them. Not at all a bad idea!

Stage 2: The Projections

Having identified the trends exhibited by all the important revenues, volumes and fixed and variable costs in the past few years the corporate planner will have no difficulty in simply extrapolating these over the next five, ten, twenty years. Exactly how far ahead he needs to project will be considered later.

Take the simple case of rents and rates. It was seen above that this item – (which in many companies would not be of sufficient importance to be treated as a separate item. This is only being done here to provide an easy example before discussing the more complex ones) – this item stood at $103,000 in 1967 and had grown at the rate of about 4 per cent per annum. So in 1968 it will be $107,000, in 1969 $111,600 and so on until in 1977 it would be about $151,000 and in 1987 about $216,000.

Again, take another simple fixed cost such as Research. If in 1967 it was $25,000 rising at 20 per cent per annum then in 1977 it would be $155,000 and in another ten years it would have risen to $957,500. And so on for all the fixed costs, including the fixed portion of those that are also variable.

The variable costs cannot be calculated until a projection of the volume of sales has been made. Sales in 1967 were 1200 units and had risen by, say, 4 per cent per annum over the past ten years. So, by simple projection sales will be:

1968	1969	1970	1971	1972	1973	1974	1975	1976	1977	1987
1250	1300	1350	1400	1460	1520	1580	1640	1710	1780	2640

Now if the cost per unit is known then the total cost of each variable item can be calculated. If materials cost $250 per unit in 1967 and if, over the past few years the trend had been for material prices to fall by 2 per cent then the total cost of materials can be estimated for each year. Similarly the revenue can be calculated.

Perhaps the best way to derive a profit projection from all these calculations is to use the 'gross contribution' method. 'Contribution' is the amount of money that each unit of sale would contribute towards paying for the fixed overheads and the profits. If each unit brought in $100 in revenue and if the variable costs of producing this unit was, say, $60 then each unit sold would contribute $40 to help to pay for the fixed overheads. If these fixed overheads cost, say, $40,000 a year then the company would have to sell 1,000 units to pay for its overheads before it made any profit at all. So if 1,100 units were sold the contribution from the extra 100 units would all be sheer profit – $4,000 of course. These four components must always be kept in mind. They are:

Selling Price per unit   (SP)
Variable Cost per unit   (VC)
Sales Volume in units   (SV)
Fixed Costs   (FC)

It will be appreciated that the contribution that each unit sold makes towards the company's profit and overheads is SP–VC. The total contribution made by all these units sold is:

$$SV \times (SP-VC)$$

And the profit that the company makes is:

$$SV \times (SP-VC) - FC$$

This is an extremely useful approximation to the fundamental mechanism of how profit emerges from a company's activities. (It is also an invaluable tool for evolving a Pricing Policy for one's products, and for evaluating the *real* effect on profits of one course of action against any other.) The study of contribution is sometimes known as Contribution Analysis but so useful is the mechanism described above that these main items also deserve a title: we will call Selling Price, Variable Cost, Sales Volume and Fixed Costs – 'The Four Components of Profit'.

Imagine that a company expects to sell: 1,000, 1,200, 1,400, 1,600, 1,800 units respectively in the next five years. Assume it expects the selling price of this product to be $10, $9.50, $9, $8.50, and $8 per unit respectively in these years and the variable costs to remain constant at $6 per unit, then the contribution per unit will be $4, $3.50, $3, $2.50, $2. The contribution to fixed costs and profits will therefore be:

Year 1   1,000 × $4.00 = $4,000
Year 2   1,200 × $3.50 = $4,200
Year 3   1,400 × $3.00 = $4,200
Year 4   1,600 × $2.50 = $4,000
Year 5   1,800 × $2.00 = $3,600

Let it further be assumed that the total fixed costs of this company are expected to be $2,000, $2,200, $2,400, $2,600, $2,800. Then the profits it expects to make will be:

Year 1	$2,000		Year 4	$1,400
Year 2	$2,000		Year 5	$800
Year 3	$1,800			

Thus the end point required has been reached – a profit projection has been obtained. The examples given have been somewhat oversimplified compared with real life figures but the method described can be used in practice. The aim is not to achieve accuracy but to give the corporate planner a chance to understand how the company's financial mechanisms function, what is important and what is not, what outstanding trends and events have occurred and how all these have affected profits. The profit projection just produced is useless as a forecast; its value lies solely in providing the corporate planner with a very rough guide to the future on the assumption that the future is exactly the same as the past. He knows it will not be, but until he has made these projections does not know how it will be different, how much the future might affect each item or which items really matter if they are affected.

He has already learnt much from making these projections but he can learn still more. He has so far dealt with each individual item on its own: he has, for example, examined salaries and then, quite independently, wages. Now he should examine the inter-relationships between these items.

Are total wages rising faster than total salaries? If so, is it credible? Surely automation on the shop floor will restrain the rise in total wages while the tendency to increased overheads, transfers of wage-earners to staff status and so on would tend to accelerate the rise in total salaries? Again, does the total amount spent on research rise faster than the rate at which new products are being introduced? If so why? Do product selling prices fall faster than the purchased prices of raw materials and components? If so, why?

A further source of knowledge is to project each item until it becomes an absurdity. For example, if research costs have been rising at 20 per cent per annum and the rest of the costs for the entire company have been rising at 2 per cent per annum then, however small research costs may be today compared with the total they will become an unbelievably large proportion of the company's total costs in twenty years time: therefore, one can conclude, research costs will not continue to rise at 20 per cent per annum or, alternatively, the rest of the company's costs will rise faster than 2 per cent – furthermore this change in past trends must occur quite soon. How soon? Well, if research costs are now $25,000 per annum and all other costs are $2,500,000 per annum then in ten years time research costs will no longer be in this ratio (1 – 100) but in the ratio $155,000 to $3,100,000 or 1 – 20. In twenty years the ratio will be $957,500 to $3,830,000 or 1 – 4. Which of these ratios is credible bearing in mind the nature of the company's business? Other anomalies will be found if these examinations are made. Do the figures suggest that labour productivity will rise so slowly that it will be hundreds of years before a completely automatic factory is in action? If so the corporate planner should be sceptical of them. If labour productivity is rising by 1 per cent per annum then if the company employs 1,000 men now it will still employ 600 men for the same output in fifty years time! Surely by then their processes will be nearer than this to complete automation – if not their competitors' might be!

Again, in his search for anomalies he can calculate the company's Return on Capital Employed over the next ten or twenty years assuming the company ploughs back the same proportion of profits as in the past. Does this show a ridiculous figure? If so can he identify which of his projections cause the anomaly – is it in the costs, the revenue, the volume or the scale of capital expenditure? When does the return on capital figure start looking ridiculous – if it is within the next few years then the corporate planner must expect a violent change compared with his projections, if not for many years, then perhaps the projections are not ridiculous: the future may not be too unlike the past.

He can compare some of the projections for his company with projections for other companies or other published data. If his company's sales are rising at 10 per cent per annum and the total market only by 2 per cent then if they now have 30 per cent of the market by the tenth year from now their share will have risen to nearly 65 per cent. Is this likely? A mass of statistics is now available for this type of study from such sources as the Board of Trade, Trade Associations, Trade Journals, Professional Societies, Inter-Firm Comparison, etc.

Let it be clearly understood what the corporate planner is doing here. He wants to know what will happen to the company's profits over the next ten years or so. The best guide to the future is what has happened in the past – it is a poor guide, but it is the best we have. A company's past is full of complexity. What he has been doing, then, is to examine the company's past performance in order to identify which parts of its past may be reliable guides to its future profits and which are not. To be a reliable guide an item has to be one that materially affects the profits, has a past history that is reasonably steady, and is not inconsistent with other trends.

The corporate planner probably now knows more about the company's past than any other member of the company. He knows

(1) which items of volume, revenue and cost are important to the company's profits and which are negligible;

(2) which trends may be carried forward from the past to the future and which trends must change;

(3) how soon some of these trends must change. Some that lead to absurdities in the near future must change in the near future, others perhaps not for decades;

(4) what events have occurred – and may occur again – and what effect they had on profits.

He is now armed with some knowledge of the future and can discuss intelligently and critically any opinions concerning the company's future that are offered to him.

To conclude this stage 2 of the forecasting process he should draw up a systematic report of his findings. This will be for his use only; it is his ladder to the next stages in the forecasting process. It should be methodically constructed, perhaps on the following lines:

Profit Projections for Company 'C' ($000)

1968	1969	1970	1971	1972	1973	1974	1975	1976	1977	1987
4,800	4,968	5,112	5,232	5,328	5,232	5,136	4,968	4,412	3,768	– 39,240

Conclusion

Profits will rise slowly for five years then fall with increasing severity leading to a loss early in the 1980s.

Assumptions made

The profit figures above are based on a projection of the past trends in Selling Price, Variable Costs, Volume, Fixed Costs each shown in total opposite:

		1968	1969	1970	1971	1977	1987
Selling price per unit	$000	240	235.2	230.4	226.1	200.6	161.3
Variable cost per unit	$000	120	122.4	124.8	127.2	143.3	178.1
Contribution per unit	$000	120	112.8	105.6	98.9	57.4	−16.8
Volume units		100	112	125	140	277	964
Total contribution	$000	12,000	12,600	13,200	13,800	15,912	−16,200
Fixed costs	$000	7,200	7,632	8,088	8,568	12,144	−23,040
Profits	$000	4,800	4,968	5,112	5,232	3,738	−39,240

Major Factors noted during the study
Selling prices Selling prices have fallen (by about 2 per cent per annum) in recent years.
Variable costs Direct wages per unit for all products have increased rapidly in the past seven years (approximately 4 per cent per annum). This is due to labour productivity rising at only 3 per cent and wage inflation of 7 per cent per annum.

Fuel costs have risen by 15 per cent per annum and, although this is at present a small item of cost ($96,000) at this rate of increase it will rapidly rise to a significant factor in production costs.
Volume The volume of sales of all products has risen by about 12 per cent per annum for many years. Product P has risen at a very slightly greater rate.
Fixed Costs Salaries are a large proportion of fixed costs (30 per cent), they have risen only by 1 per cent per annum in the past six years.

Research costs are rising at 12 per cent per annum and are now 15 per cent of fixed costs. They will rise to 25 per cent of fixed in ten years time.
Detailed projection of each item (Here the corporate planner would list each of the items – selling price for each major product, costs, volumes, etc. – that he has investigated, showing the expected figure for each item and drawing attention to the major reasons for the trends shown).

Stage 3: The Factors Affecting Profits
The corporate planner is now ready to consider what other factors could seriously affect the company's profits in the future. He has already isolated many from his study of past figures and the projections; for example, selling prices, direct wages, fuel costs, sales volume, salaries and research costs, but there may be many more. In fact there are certain to be.

He should now search, therefore, for all those factors, in the company and outside it, that may, might or could affect profits by more than a few percent. His projections showed what the profits would be if the future was exactly the same as the past. He knows it will not be, but in what way he should alter any of his projections he does not yet know. He must search for those trends and events in the future that will make it different from the past. There may not be as many of these as one might at first think. He is not looking for every tiny change – only for those that are really going to make a significant difference to profits. The sort of event that, in five years time, the company's staff will remember as one of the ten highlights of this year. The sort of event that would come to the notice of the Board and might be mentioned in the Chairman's Report to shareholders. Really, there are two types of factors affecting profits: one is the long slow trend of the sort that was described in the previous section on the projections but which, over a period of years can, if not controlled, insidiously erode away the profits. The other is the sudden, often unexpected and unpredictable event that ensures that the future is going to be very different to the past.

For most companies there are probably only a few trends or events that could affect profits by 30 per cent – to do such damage it would indeed have to be momentous. There may be millions that could affect profits by 0.0001 per cent. The corporate planner is looking for those – probably only a few dozen – that might or could affect profits by 3 or 4 per cent.

The corporate planner should draw up a list of all factors that might affect profits by more than a few percent. It might appear as follows: –

Factors Affecting Profits

Section 1: Inside the Company

A.	People	1.	Prolonged absence of 1 or more key executives.
		2.	Strikes.
B.	Plant and Equipment	1.	Damage by fire, flood, etc.
		2.	Breakdown.
C.	Sales	1.	Faulty products.
		2.	Damaging publicity.
D.	Research and Development	1.	Failure of scale-up or
		2.	Delayed start up of new process.
E.	Trends in Costs		
F.	Others		

Section 2. In the Environment

A.	Suppliers	1. Price trends of materials and components.
		2. Availability of materials and components.
		3. New sources of supply.
		4. New types of material.
B.	Customers	1. Total market.
		2. Top 10 per cent
		3. Loyalty
		4. Quality.
		5. Service.
		6. Selling Prices.
C.	Competitors	1. Share of market.
		2. Products and product obsolescence.
		3. Research and patents.
		4. Larger competitors.
		5. Smaller competitors.
		6. Foreign competitors.
D.	Government	1. Taxation.
		2. Subsidies.
		3. Tariffs.
		4. Legislation.
E.	U.K.	1. Social trends.
		2. Economic trends.
		3. Political trends.
		4. Climate.
F.	Foreign	1. Tariffs and quotas.
		2. Political, economic and social trends.
		3. Size and share of markets.
		4. Competitors.
G.	Technology	1. Substitutes for products.
		2. New products.
		3. New processes, plant, equipment.
		4. Scale of operations.

The list is not intended to be exhaustive, merely indicative of the type of factors that must be considered. The purpose of this list is as follows: the corporate planner has identified trends in the past and, with intentional blindness, has projected them into the future to determine the resulting profits. Thus for each main item of volume, revenue, costs he has taken the past trends:

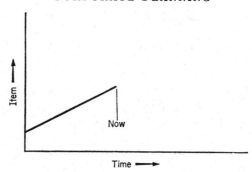

and simply extrapolated:

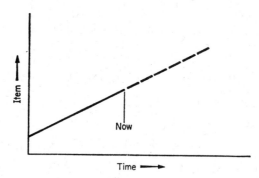

But the future may not be like the past and this item may behave in any number of ways, such as

How the future will be different, which of these patterns might emerge, depends upon the influence of the Factors Affecting Profits.

With the 'four components' – selling prices, variable costs, volume and fixed costs – in mind, the corporate planner should work through the list of Factors Affecting Profits. For each factor he must ask whether it might apply to the company and if so by how much might it affect profits. If it is either highly unlikely to occur or, if it did occur, would not affect profits by more than 3 or 4 per cent then he can ignore it, otherwise he must consider its effects on one or more of the four components.

Take Factor $1A_1$, 'prolonged absence of key executive'. Is there any executive whose prolonged absence (illness, resignation, retirement or death) would affect profits by more than 3 or 4 per cent? That is to say, in a company earning profits of $2,500,000 is there anyone whose absence could affect profits by $75,000? The corporate planner's colleagues may agree that there are several but all have suitable understudies except the Production Director who is forty-five, in good health, and has been with the company nearly twenty years. They agree that this factor is so unlikely to apply that it can be ignored. The corporate planner makes no modifications to his projections therefore but does note, for use later, that there is no replacement at present for the Production Director.

As for item $1A_2$, 'strikes', the company have never had a strike and human relations are good. However, they calculate that a two-week strike would lose them $125,000 (i.e. they could lose this contribution to fixed costs and overheads) if it did occur – 5 per cent of profit. The factor is so unlikely to apply that no alteration is made to the projections but, again, the corporate planner makes a note for use later on.

Consider item $1B_1$ 'damage to plant by fire and flood' the company is presumably insured for the damage but perhaps not for the consequential loss of profits. Is this a contingency to be reckoned with?

And so on through the list – two items in Section 1 require further explanation. The first, 'Trends in costs' (1E) includes all those items examined by the corporate planner in stage 2 when he made his projections and he would certainly ask the company's executives whether in their opinion any items that should have been included have not been. The second is 'others' (1F). The executives should be asked to search their experience to identify any factor inside the company that might affect profits by 3 or 4 per cent that had not been included: it is possible, for example, that only the Chief Engineer knows that if a certain special machine failed the whole factory would close down because it would take six weeks to obtain a replacement from Japan!

Consider some of the factors outside the company. Take item $2A_1$ – 'price trends of supplies'. The Chief Buyer may have much to say about the future trends in prices of certain components: almost certainly he will disagree that the trends of the past are appropriate to the future and the corporate planner will alter these projections, noting the alteration and its rationale. Thus whereas the projection may have been:

Materials Projection   Prices of materials L, M, N, will rise at 2 per cent per annum and of P and Q by 6 per cent per annum as in the past.

it may now read

Materials Forecast   Price of materials L, M, will rise by 2 per cent per annum, as in the past. Material N will rise by 4 per cent per annum due to increased home consumption in its country of origin. Materials P and Q will fall by 3 per cent per annum due to the comissioning of a new producing plant in Brazil.

Many of the Projections made in stage 2 will be approved by the company's executives as being reasonable attempts to predict the future – these Projections will become Forecasts without the need for any change; for these the future is expected to be very similar to the past. In the example above, however, the Chief Buyer did not believe that the projections were an accurate assessment of the futre.

It will often happen that the corporate planner's projections will be deemed to be inappropriate and instead of

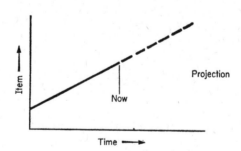

an executive believes the future will be more like:

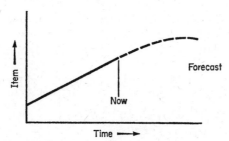

But the difference between the Projection and the Forecast should be clearly explained – for example

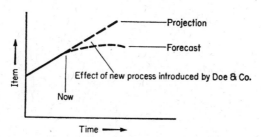

Whenever a projection is felt not to be an adequate estimate of the future the corporate planner must do three things:

(1) He must alter the projection.
(2) Estimate the effect on profits of the alteration.

In the case of the materials quoted above the effect would have been — $10,000 per annum for the alteration to material N and + $70,000 for materials P & Q. He will not need to double-check the Chief Buyer's estimate for material N but for the much more important changes to P & Q he will have to ask the Buyer for a detailed rationale behind this opinion.

(3) He must go through the entire list of projections and the list of Factors to see whether any change (e.g. the major one to materials P & Q) affects any other items. Clearly it might affect the selling prices of those of the company's products that contain P & Q since if these products can be produced more cheaply by his company, other companies can do so as well and this cost reduction may appear as price cuts.

It is possible to construct an Interaction Chart indicating which Factor affects any other Factor. Thus a change in selling prices may affect Profits, Volume, Customers, Competitors, Subsidy (if any) and so on. For some of these the interaction is a two-way one – thus a change in the Factor headed 'Competitors' will probably affect selling prices just as a change in selling price affects competitors. But not always; a change in 'Volume' can take place without any consequent change in selling price. A section of such a chart might appear as follows:

Interaction Chart

Key: 0 = no interaction, 1 = weak interaction,
2 = strong interaction

Factors	Absence of Employees	Strikes	Flood, Fire	Breakdown	Price of Materials	Availability	New Sources	New Processes	Scale	Variable Costs	Fixed Costs	Capital	Profits
Absence of Employees	−	1	1	1	0	0	0	1	0	0	0	0	2
Strikes	2	−	0	1	0	0	0	0	0	2	2	1	2
Flood, Fire	0	0	−	2	0	0	0	0	0	2	2	1	2
Breakdown	0	0	0	−	0	0	0	0	0	2	2	0	2
Price of Materials	0	0	0	0	−	2	2	2	1	2	0	0	2
Availability of Materials	0	0	0	0	2	−	2	2	2	2	0	0	2
New sources of Supply	0	0	0	1	2	2	−	2	1	1	0	0	2
New processes	0	1	0	1	1	0	0	−	2	2	2	2	2
Scale of Operations	0	2	0	1	2	2	1	1	−	2	2	2	2
Variable costs	0	0	0	0	0	0	0	0	0	−	0	0	2
Fixed costs	0	0	0	0	0	0	0	0	0	0	−	0	2
Capital	0	0	0	0	0	0	1	1	0	2	−	2	
Profits	1	0	0	0	1	1	0	0	0	1	1	2	−

(Notice that some of the entries are not symmetrical. For example a breakdown can affect profits, but a rise or fall in profits is seldom likely to cause a breakdown. Similarly, a strike will have no effect on the size of factory, but the greater the size of the factory the more prone it will be to strikes.)

The value of an Interaction Chart is largely as an *aide-mémoire*, for throughout the corporate planning process from this stage onwards the corporate planner will be considering change. A change in one sector of the environment will sometimes affect only one item in the company – but most changes will have a multiplicity of effects on it. When considering what effect the appearance of an entirely new competitor will have on the company, for example, one would naturally think of such matters as price and volume of one's products – one does not always think of some of the other possible effects such as the new opportunity for employment that this new competitor may offer to one's employees. An Interaction Chart, containing all the important areas in which events might occur and how the company could be affected by them, is frequently of great value.

Continue to study the list of Factors Affecting Profits. Is there a customer whose loyalty is in doubt? Is he one of the big ones? ($2B_2$) If he took his custom to a competitor would it affect profits by 3 or 4 per cent – this is not a difficult question to quantify: knowing his usual volume of business and the price he pays one can quickly calculate the loss of contribution to profits and overheads. If this is more than 3 or 4 per cent he is a factor to be recorded as of major importance.

Again, which competitor has the power to affect prices to the extent that it could affect the company's profits by more than 3 or 4 per cent? Will he use this power and if so, how? What products might each competitor be researching? ($2C_3$). How would their introduction affect this company's profits?

Will the government increase company taxation? ($2D_1$). If so, on all companies or selectively – if so then which companies will be selected? Will the tariff on imports come down? ($2D_3$). But stop here, and consider this one further. Assume there is a U.K. tariff of 10 per cent against imports of products of the same type as those the corporate planner's company produces. If the tariff comes down then prices in U.K. may fall nearer to the level prevailing in Europe. To take an example, imagine these were 3 per cent below U.K. prices and that, if they fell to this level, it would cut a company's profits by $450,000 per annum – an enormous percentage of their current $2,500,000 profit. Clearly this is something of immense importance to the company's future. Certainly it must be taken account of in the forecasts if it is likely to happen. Will the tariff be removed; if so, when? Either the company must guess the answer or it could seek advice from the appropriate Government Department; an estimate having been obtained the projection must be revised. And again the corporate planner must search through the Interaction Chart to identify any consequential changes: one such will be the cut in profits of all the company's U.K. competitors, some of whom might go out of business. If they do what would happen to their share of the market – would it go to U.K. producers, fall prey to foreign competitors, be bought up by a large company? How would any of these events affect our company? These are difficult questions but in each case an informed estimate can be made. It may be objected that one cannot possibly predict when a Government will reduce a tariff or by how much. This is true, but one can place bounds around their likely action. At present there is a trend in the world towards freer trade – several international bodies are working to that end. It should not be impossible for a company's executives to know within a margin of a few years when all these international efforts will succeed in reducing the particular tariff in which they are interested. Nor should it be entirely beyond them to estimate when each competitor will introduce a new product. Nor whether a customer is loyal. Such estimates are never accurate but they can be sufficiently so to be well worth making.

To continue briefly through the list of factors. How will social, political, economic trends in U.K. affect profits? Will there be a boom or a recession next year and how might it affect us? ($2E_2$). How will Bank Rate move and could it affect profits by 3 or 4 per cent. Will the trend towards staff status alter salary and wages costs in some way not reflected in mere projection from the past? Will the GNP of U.K. ever grow at more than about 3 per cent? Does the trend towards wetter, milder winters affect the company? ($2E_4$).

If the company exports, does the country it sells to intend setting up its own factory to produce these products? Is it politically stable? If there was a *coup d'état* could it affect profits by 3 or 4 per cent? ($2F_2$).

What will the next generation of products be like and who will be first on the market? ($2G_2$). By what year will some revolutionary product or process render our plant obsolete? Can a small company obtain sufficient economy of scale in production costs to survive against the international giants?

(2G₄). Many of these questions involve the analysis of very long term trends and events far into the future. An interesting and important concept in keeping the discussion on such faraway topics firmly on the ground is known as the S-curve. This curve illustrates the typical pattern in the rates of growth of many goods and services. To illustrate: in the early days of a product its sales will increase slowly –

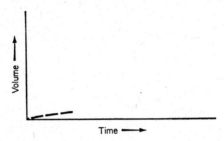

Then it may catch on and grow rapidly:

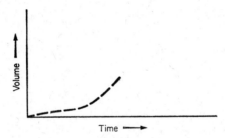

Then it may continue to grow at a fairly steady rate depending upon the rise in population, for example,

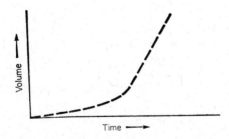

Finally its popularity will wane due perhaps to a better product being introduced or the product becoming inappropriate

to the new era or even to it becoming socially, morally or aesthetically undesirable:

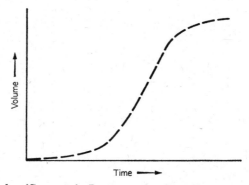

This is the 'S curve'. It not only describes the life cycle of many products but many other phenomena as well: it describes the rate at which the size of oil tankers grows (sooner or later the trend towards bigger tankers must reach a technical or practical limit and slow down as it reaches the top of the S-curve). Or it describes the rate at which crop yields per acre grows (sooner or later the trend to higher yields must slow down). Or the speed at which a computer can calculate (sooner or later the trend towards faster machines must reach a technical limit). And so on. Now this S-curve concept is useful in deciding whether a future trend is likely to be similar to the past trend. For if one can identify where one's product is on the S-curve the rest of its life cycle can be predicted. The best way to determine this is a 'reduction to absurdity' method. Imagine a community in which there is one car to every 4 adults and the history of the industry is:

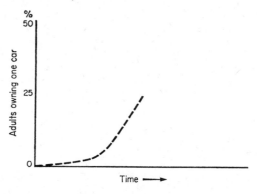

One can see clearly the first part of the S-curve. But is the product approaching the point when the curve bends over and the rate of growth declines? Or will it continue steadily up for many years before this happens. That is, are we at X or at Y:

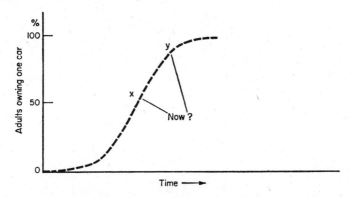

A good guide can be obtained by considering when the curve might start to bend over. If one assumes this would only happen when every adult owned one car (a few will then have none, a few will have two – but not many people will ever want *two* cars for his own exclusive use), a simple calculation will show in how many years time this might happen at the present output of cars. If it looks as though it will be another eighty years before this happens the corporate planner can confidently assume that 'now' is nearer to X than to Y. If it is felt to be nearer to Y then, in making a forecast he must declare that there may be some slowing down.

The use of the S-curve illustrates again the desirability of studying records as far back as possible – preferably right back to the very start of the S-curve of the factor under consideration. It also illustrates the value of projecting forward as far as possible until a point of absurdity is reached – for one can be fairly confident that a change will take place before that point: if the rate of production of baths exceeds the rate of growth in population how long can this go on? If the rate of increase in the consumption of bananas per head is x, how soon does that imply that we each eat several a day? And so on.

Many, many questions are provoked by this list of Factors Affecting Profits. Most are vital to the future of any company and they must be asked and answered sooner or later if the company is to flourish. The corporate planner chooses to ask them now, systematically, at this stage of his work, rather than haphazardly at random intervals. When each question is asked it may not be known if it is an important one or not, only the answer can show that. Some of the questions may turn out to be irrelevant for a given company – not all companies operate behind a tariff barrier, for example – but they may be crucial ones for some other company.

Now consider what the corporate planner has been doing while asking these questions. To each question the answer is either. 'This Factor will not occur' or 'this may occur'. Only if it is the latter answer is a second question put: 'if it does occur by how much *might* it affect profits?' Either the answer is 'by less than 3 or 4 per cent of profits' or 'by more than 3 or 4 per cent of profits'. Only if it is the latter answer is a third question put: 'Is it sufficiently likely to occur as to warrant altering the projections?' If the answer is that it is not likely to occur then the corporate planner need do one thing only at this stage: make note of it under the title 'Less Likely Events and Trends' to which reference will be made later. If it is likely to occur then he must do three things:

(1) Alter the relevant 'projection' to become the 'forecast' and note why the alteration was made (as in the 'materials P and Q' example).

(2) Note what affect this alteration has on profits.

(3) Alter any other projection affected by this alteration noting the reason here also.

Notice two things about this procedure. Firstly the corporate planner is altering the 'projection' to 'forecast' on the assumption that the company is not going to take action to counteract any of the events that might affect its profits. The forecasts reflect what might happen to profits if the company's decision-making procedures were frozen. Of course the company will take action but what it is will be left for a closer study later in the corporate planning process. The whole purpose of this stage is to see whether action is going to be necessary, not to decide what that action should be.

Secondly, the assumption that the company's decision-making machinery is frozen also implies that the company, while continuing to take day-to-day action as before, will take no action that will commit its resources irrevocably for any length of time. It will sign no long-term contracts, approve no capital expenditure, break·into no new markets, close down no factories. To assume that it is going to do any of these things is quite unwarrantable at this stage; decisions of this sort should come out of the study, not be put into it.

Stage 4: The forecasts
The corporate planner will now draw together all his forecasts into a systematic format headed 'Forecast O' (zero) – so called because it is made on the basis of the company doing nothing new.

Profit Forecast for Company C

Forecast O   Date 7.6.67.

PROFITS ($000)

1968	1969	1970	1971	1972	1973	1974	1975	1976	1977	1987
4800	5184	4630	4272	4080	3840	3960	4080	2640	1800	−8112

CONCLUSIONS

Profits will rise rapidly until 1969, fall rapidly until 1973, remain level until 1975 when they will fall very rapidly to reach a loss position by about 1980. Forecasts for the four components of profit are:

1. SELLING PRICES

Prices have tended downwards for the past seven or eight years and no end to this trend, which is due to competitive forces, can be assumed over the next ten or even twenty years. Assuming tariffs are removed in 1970 prices will fall sharply from 1969 to 1972, thereafter the normal downward trend will continue. The effect of the normal trend is to reduce profits by approximately $480,000 per annum at 1967 volumes. The price fall due to the removal of tariffs may reduce profits by about $1,680,000. Prices are forecast to move as follows:

($000)

1968	1969	1970	1971	1972	1973	1974	1975	1976	1977	1987
240	235	226	216	211	209	204	199	194	192	151

2. VARIABLE COSTS

Variable costs have risen slowly for many years. Direct wages per unit have risen because wage inflation has not been counterbalanced by similar improvement in productivity. This trend will reduce profits by approximately $120,000 per annum. Materials prices have remained steady overall. Total variable costs per unit are forecast to be as follows:

($000)

1968	1969	1970	1971	1972	1973	1974	1975	1976	1977	1987
120	120	122	122	122	125	125	125	127	127	137

3. VOLUME

The reduction in selling prices of our products forecast above will ensure that sales volume will continue to rise as in the past. No end to the present rate of increase in sales is foreseen in the next ten or even twenty years. However, the capacity of our factory (210 units a year) will be reached in 1976 and this will preclude further expansion of sales, affecting profits by $1,440,000 per annum. Volumes forecast are:

1968	1969	1970	1971	1972	1973	1974	1975	1976	1977	1987
100	112	124	138	153	169	186	206	210	210	210

4. FIXED COSTS

Fixed costs have risen due to inflation exceeding the rate of improvement in efficiency and due to the expansion of the company's business. In 1976, when this expansion ceases due to the limitation of present production facilities fixed costs will rise with inflation less the improvement in efficiencies, reducing profits by $240,000 per annum. Fixed costs are forecast to be:

($000)

1968	1969	1970	1971	1972	1973	1974	1975	1976	1977	1987
7200	7680	8136	8640	9600	10,320	10,800	11,280	11,520	11,760	14,160

The above sections of a typical, if somewhat simplified, corporate planner's forecast shows only five sets of figures – Profits and the Four Components – and six of the really important Factors Affecting Profit, with their effect on profit –

Competition	(−$480,000 per annum)
Tariffs	(−$1,680,000)
Wages	(−$120,000 per annum)
Volume	(+$1,440,000 per annum)
Production Limit	(−$1,440,000 per annum)
Fixed Cost inflation	(−$240,000 per annum)

He will also have to list the other major Factors Affecting Profits that, while not being quite so crucial in their effects as the six above, will affect profits by at least 3 per cent or 4 per cent in any year. Here he will follow the same pattern as above, that is to say, record the forecast figures for each year and add some explanatory notes. Finally, he must not forget the 'Less Likely Events and Trends' which are thought to be so unlikely to occur that they have not been taken account of in the forecast but which, if they did occur, could have serious consequences. A list of these with their possible effect on profits should be included in his forecast report, and, at a later stage, 'contingency plans' drawn up to meet them.[1]

Thus the report consists of:

A. Profit forecast for each of the next ten or twenty years.

B. Forecast of each of the Four Components for the next ten or twenty years with brief notes on those few Factors that are of outstanding importance.

C. Forecast and notes on the other major Factors.

D. Notes on some of the Factors which, though unlikely to occur, could be important if they did.

The corporate planner might also wish to show other calculations in addition to those above, such as loan interest and so on. This alternative or additional layout of the information is shown in Table 2, not for Company C but for Hypothetics Ltd., whose profit target was shown in similar detail in Table 1. Notice, incidentally, how clearly the contribution method brings out how the value to the company of its two products declines over the years, how the contribution from Thetix declines faster and further than from Hypon. Notice also how the fixed overheads themselves increase; remember that this is in spite of the fact that the company's turnover increases only very slowly.

Two more comments are necessary before ending this long chapter. The first is to draw attention to the fact that the corporate planner is searching for factors that may affect profits *either way*. He is looking for good news as well as bad. One example of good news among the bad (a silver lining to a cloud in fact) is the possibility, mentioned above, that if import tariffs are removed from a product the subsequent fall in price in the home market will affect competitors' profits as well as one's own company's. Perhaps one of these competitors will become ripe for take-over. This may present an opportunity, but the forecasts do not assume that the company takes advantage of it – its decision-making machinery is frozen, remember.

Secondly, although the end of the forecasting procedure has been reached, these forecasts will need constant revision. It will be recalled that the Profit Target should be revised only once every year or so. The forecasts must be revised whenever

[1] See page 199.

TABLE 2

Forecast of Profits for Hypothetics Ltd.

(Assumes no capital expenditure or other long-term commitments)

		1967 (Actual)	1968	1969	1970	1971	1972
Hypon	Selling price per unit	$ 240	240	235	235	233	228
	Directly variable costs per unit	$ 192	197	197	199	202	204
	Therefore contribution per unit	$ 48	43	38	36	31	24
	Sales volume in units	5,000	5,300	5,600	5,800	6,000	6,000
	Therefore total contribution	$ 240,000	228,000	216,000	208,800	187,200	144,000
Thetix	Selling price per unit	$ 2,400	2,400	2,400	2,400	2,352	2,304
	Directly variable costs per unit	$ 1,920	2,016	2,047	2,076	2,093	2,107
	Therefore contribution per unit	$ 480	384	353	324	259	197
	Sales volume in units	500	525	550	580	600	620
	Therefore total contribution	$ 240,000	204,000	168,000	187,200	156,000	122,400
Total contribution from Hypon and Thetix to fixed costs and profits		$ 480,000	432,000	384,000	396,000	343,200	266,400
Fixed costs (including depreciation, and interest on loans)		$ 228,000	240,000	252,000	264,000	276,000	288,000
Therefore Gross Profits		$ 252,000	192,000	132,000	132,000	67,200	−21,600
(Turnover from Hypon)		$ 1,200,000	1,272,000	1,320,000	1,368,000	1,392,000	1,368,000
(Turnover from Thetix)		$ 1,200,000	1,260,000	1,320,000	1,392,000	1,416,000	1,428,000

it is plain that a new trend has emerged or an event has or may occur that could affect profits by 3 or 4 per cent. Thus if it has been assumed that labour costs would rise by 6 per cent per annum, and it becomes apparent that they are really rising by 8 per cent then the forecast for this item, *and* any others with which this might interact (such as salaries), should be revised. Again; if it has been assumed that no replacement for the Production Director would be needed for fifteen years and he falls seriously ill then this forecast needs revision. There is no set time for revising the forecasts – it must be done whenever it is necessary.

Summary of Chapter VII

Having obtained a profit target the corporate planner needs to prepare a profit forecast. This entails a four-stage procedure involving a careful study of the company's past performance to identify trends in the four components of profit – selling prices, variable costs, volume and fixed costs. These trends are projected into the future. In consultation with the staff of the company he modifies these projections to take account of any events and trends that may occur in the future but which may not have been evident in the past. He uses a check list to ensure that he makes a methodical study of all possible Factors Affecting Profits. His forecast includes notes on the few dozen really important trends and events in the past and the future – certainly all those that might affect profits by as much as 3 or 4 per cent. The forecast will need to be revised continuously as new trends emerge and events occur.

(See also Appendix 1.)

CHAPTER VIII

STEP 2 . . . AND DECLARE THE PROBABLE ERROR

All forecasts are wrong – Reducing the errors – Estimating the errors.

IT is often said that one cannot forecast the future. This is nonsense; anyone can forecast the future, what one cannot do is to forecast it accurately! The reader may think this distinction is so obvious that it is the height of naïvety to mention it all, let alone start a chapter with it as though it was a new discovery of great moment. It may not be new, it is of great moment. Anyone who makes a forecast must know it cannot be accurate but only very, very seldom does this admission appear alongside a forecast. The sales director says 'sales will reach 10,000 units in 1970' – he hardly ever is heard to say: 'sales will be between 9,000 and 11,000 units in 1970 – I cannot claim to forecast so far ahead with any greater accuracy'. One often sees forecasts for several years ahead stated in terms implying extreme accuracy – 'sales will rise to 10,162,731 units'.

It is understandable that people called upon to make a forecast like to give the impression that they really do have a mysterious ability to see into the future with great precision. They must not be believed, for it cannot be done. All forecasts are inaccurate to a greater or lesser extent.

If this is so then it is a fact that must be taken into account. Unfortunately taking errors into account is difficult and that is probably why it is so seldom done. It is probably true that more plans fail because of this omission than for any other reason, for, if a plan is based on an assumption that turns out to be false, then the plan itself may fail.

One thing is certain, the corporate planner of all people in industry must never claim that his forecasts are accurate – he should know better.

The inaccuracies in a profit forecast derive from two main sources. In the first place it will be recalled that the projections were made by extrapolating past trends. But the past trends may be difficult to discern: take the example below:

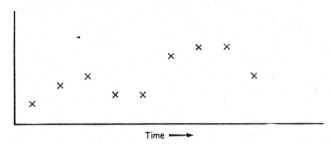

Time ⟶

Is there a trend at all? Perhaps it is merely cyclical:

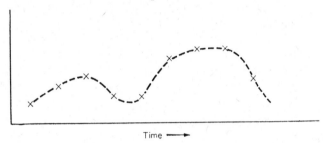

Time ⟶

or 1967 is exceptional:

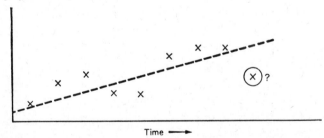

Time ⟶

Perhaps one could see the true trend more clearly by taking figures from much earlier years as well. But there may be no such records. Suffice to say that there are severe problems in making the projections and many will be inaccurate.

The second source of inaccuracy comes in when the company's executives try to predict how the Factors Affecting Profits might operate. Both the timing and the extent are liable to severe error. Even if it is agreed that competitor Y is likely to introduce a new product in the next few years no one can say in which year this will take place nor precisely what effect it will have upon the sales volume or price of existing products.

There are several ways of dealing with errors arising from these two sources.

Some ways of reducing the errors

(1) Statistical techniques. An armoury of mathematical techniques exist with which it is possible to identify trends and extrapolate them correctly. Regression Analysis, curve fitting, analysis of variance, correlation and many others. The corporate planner may use them – in some cases, perhaps he must use them – but in general they represent an excessively fine instrument for the rather coarse operation he is performing. By their use he may well improve the forecast of some items by a few percent but even so this would leave many other forecasts just as bad as they were. And on top of the errors in the projection much larger ones may be superimposed when the executives attempt to forecast future events. In general then, it is recommended that the corporate planner relies on his industrial experience to guide his forecasting rather than using refined techniques.

(2) A more practical way of reducing error is to cross-check the forecasts in much the same way as one cross-checked a projection. There are two checks the corporate planner should make.

(*a*) Check that the forecast for each item is consistent with that for other items with which it has a relationship. That the forecast for fuel prices, for example, shows a trend not too dissimilar to the price trend shown for electricity (unless it is thought that these will be different for some reason.)

(*b*) Test for absurdities. Again this test is similar to the one suggested in the last chapter. By projecting the forecast trends forward the corporate planner may discover an absurd conclusion – such as that by 1990, the price of a raw material will fall to zero – and this will indicate either that the forecast is suspect or that a dramatic alteration in trends will take place long before 1990.

Generally speaking, there is not a great deal a corporate planner can do to reduce errors beyond a certain point. It is often more sensible to spend less time on reducing errors and more time on understanding the true nature of the company's profit-making mechanism, on estimating what the errors are and on taking account of them.

Estimating the extent of errors
Consider an item that has fluctuated in the past by 10 per cent either side of the trend line:

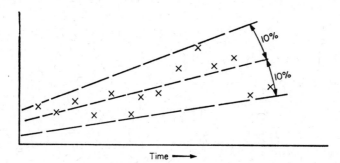

This item will probably go on varying in the same way in the future so at any given moment it may be 10 per cent above or below the predicted figure. If it is predicted that the selling price of a product is going to be $100 in 1978, the actual price could be anything from $90 to $110. By studying the variability of each past item the corporate planner can obtain a fairly good idea of the width of the band of errors in his projections.

The more closely he has studied past trends, the deeper his analysis of the mechanisms responsible for them, the more confidence will he have in his forecasts. If he has analysed a trend such as

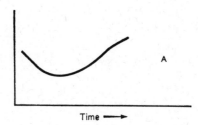

into two components each showing a reliable and consistent past history, such as these:

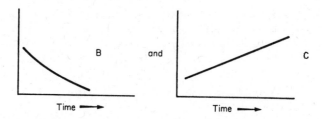

and if he understands how these two trends combine to form A then, by forecasting B and C he can forecast A with some confidence. On the other hand a curve such as

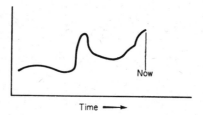

can be forecast only to a rather wide degree of accuracy:

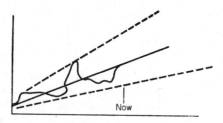

In the same way, it may be quite impossible to say when an event will occur. But it should be possible to set some bounds to this: if it may occur between 1970 and 1973 then one must recognize that the forecast of profits will be wrong by a certain amount over these years. Imagine a profit forecast for five years:

	1968	*1969*	*1970*	*1971*	*1972*
$000	1000	1100	1200	1300	1400

Now imagine that the company hears that a competitor is building a new factory and that they could take 5 per cent of sales off the company, reducing profits by $100,000 per annum. The full effect could hardly be felt in 1968 but may be felt in full by between 1969 and 1972. Thus the best forecast may be between these two sets of figures.

	1968	1969	1970	1971	1972
$000	1000	1100	1200	1300	1300
	1000	1000	1100	1200	1300

A profit forecast will contain many errors. Each component of each major cost item, for example, will contain its own error. Thus if the total fixed cost of a company is forecast to be £2,500 made up of four sub-headings and if the error on each is as shown:

$200	error ± $50
$400	± $100
$900	± $100
$1000	± $300
$2500	± $550

then the likely error on the total will be between + $550 and − $550. However, it is unlikely that all the errors will go the same way – they are unlikely all to conspire together in the same direction. To take account of the fact that some of them will cancel out one can estimate the most probable range of error on the total by squaring the individual errors, adding them up and then finding the square root:

errors		squared =	
	50		2500
	100		10000
	100		10000
	300		90000
		Total	112500 of which the square root is 335

Therefore the most likely range of errors on the total fixed costs of $2,500 is ± $335.

The error on almost any profit forecast will, in practice, be at least ± 10 per cent – for a forecast that looks five years ahead it might well be ± 20 per cent. That is to say if the profit forecast for 1970 is $100,000 one must recognize that this could be wrong by as much as 20 per cent either way – down to $80,000 or up to $120,000, and for forecasts for further ahead – say twenty years – the error could be 50 per cent either way.

The corporate planner should try to place 'confidence limits' upon his errors: the most practical level of confidence being 10 per cent or 1 in 10. That is to say, when he claims 'the error on this item of $10,000 is ±10 per cent' he means that this item is likely to be down to $9,000 or up to $11,000 one year in ten – the 1 in 10 level of confidence. This is fairly simple to do when looking at past figures for one can see whether for more than one year in ten the value was more than ±10 per cent:

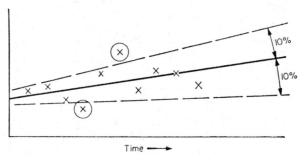

Time ———▶

It is much more difficult in the case of future events: even so it does make sense to ask 'Is there a 10 per cent chance of a strike lasting two weeks?' if by that one means 'will there be one two-week strike every ten years?'

There is nothing surprising or reprehensible about an error of up to 10 per cent or 20 per cent or 50 per cent once in every ten years in profit forecasts – the profit records of almost any company will show fluctuations of 10 per cent about the trend line – and these inaccuracies should not be swept under the carpet but brought firmly into view. They should be declared in the corporate planner's forecast of each major item. The errors expected in Hypothetics profit forecast are shown in Table 3.

Summary of Chapter VIII
All forecasts are subject to error and no forecast should be made that does not have, prominently displayed, an indication of the

TABLE 3

Errors in Forecast for Hypothetics Profits

	1967	1968	1969	1970	1971	1972
Forecast $	252,000	192,000	132,000	132,000	67,200	−21,600
Errors $	±0	±24,000	±28,800	±36,000	±48,000	±60,000

range of errors associated with it. Although this extra information renders the production and the use of forecasts more difficult and complex its absence can make a forecast grossly misleading.

The corporate planner should always indicate the probable extent of the accuracy of his forecasts. For a five-year-ahead forecast it could well be as much as 20 per cent. For a twenty-year-ahead forecast, it could be at least 50 per cent.

(See also Appendix 1.)

CHAPTER IX

STEP 3 CALCULATE THE GAP AND DECIDE THE TASK

Calculating the gap – Taking account of errors – Review of Steps 1 to 3.

IN principle Step 3 is extremely simple. All that is required is to compare the profit target with the profit forecast for each year, and by subtraction, calculate how great the difference is. Taking the case of Hypothetics Limited whose profit target was shown in Table 1 and whose profit forecast was shown in Table 2 the calculation is as follows:

Hypothetics Ltd. Profit Gap

	1968	1969	1970	1971	1972
Target $000	269	288	310	331	352
Forecast $000	192	132	132	67	−22
Gap $000	77	156	178	265	374

This Table indicates that for the company to achieve its target each year it must earn an *extra* cumulative profit of $76,800, $156,000, $177,600 . . . from the actions that it takes from now on, assuming the profits from the existing business are made according to the forecast. This forecast, it will be recalled, was made on the assumption that the company's existing business would be run on exactly the same lines as in the past few years and that no changes in policy and no new commitments would be made. The implication then is that the changes and commitments that *are* made will have to yield the extra profit indicated by the Gaps. This is the essential meaning of the Gaps – they represent the extra task facing the company and which its actions must be designed to close: if the company's executives can find ways of earning $76,800,

$156,000 . . . over and above its 1967 level then their profits will reach the target figure each year – subject to one proviso.

Taking Account of the Errors
Unfortunately closing the gap will only result in achieving the target if profits from the existing business are in line with the forecast – and, as was emphasized in the last chapter, they may not be in line with it. Far from it; the forecasts are almost certain to be inaccurate. To the best of his ability the corporate planner has estimated what the profits might be but he has had to admit that this forecast may be inaccurate by quite a wide margin. He is not even sure what the margin of error will be but as best he can he has estimated the errors he expects to be associated with the forecast figure for each year. Table 3 showed that he thinks there is a one in ten chance of the errors being as much as:

	1968	1969	1970	1971	1972
$000	±24	±29	±36	±48	±60

Now this implies that if the company aims to add $76,800, $153,600 . . . extra profit each year, then if their actions do indeed yield this extra profit, there is a one in ten chance of missing or exceeding the target by as much as $24,000 in 1968, $28,800 in 1969, $36,000 in 1970. . . . To simplify the discussion consider the situation in one of these years only – say, 1970: assume they do actually succeed in finding ways of making an extra profit of $177,600 – the amount of the Gap for that year. If they also made a profit of $132,000 in that year from the existing business then they would hit their target of $309,600. But the profits from the existing business might turn out to be $36,000 above or below the $132,000 that was forecast and the total profits might therefore be $36,000 above or below the target figure. There is only about a 1 in 10 chance of profits being as low as $273,600 or as much as $345,600 but the risk is there.

Obviously the executives and the shareholders will be delighted if they exceed the target by $36,000 and make $345,600 – it represents a rate of growth from 1967 of about 11 per cent per annum compared with their target of 7 per cent per annum growth in profits. But they will not be so pleased if it goes the other way and they make a total profit of only $273,600 – and there is a 1 in 10 chance of this happening. This represents a rate of growth from 1967 of only 3 per cent per annum. How seriously does the company take this risk?

Consider this rate of 3 per cent growth against some of the others that were considered in Chapter VI.

0 per cent: represents a decline in real profits of about 3 per cent per annum.

3 per cent: represents no growth in real profits: they would keep pace with the anticipated rate of inflation of money value.

5 per cent: the rate at which Hypothetics expect the profits of an average company to increase in the next ten years.

6 per cent: the rate at which Hypothetics profits have risen in the past ten years, and also the rate at which the average company's profits have risen.

7 per cent: the rate at which they are aiming – this is their target rate.

Seen against this background the Board of Hypothetics may well conclude that 3 per cent per annum would be a thoroughly disgraceful performance and that they are simply not prepared to risk such an eventuality. They may agree that 5 per cent per annum is tolerable since this is what they expect an average company to achieve in the next ten years and since Hypothetics have in the past done no better than average there would be no severe reaction from the shareholders if they merely continued this performance. The point being made here is this: if the company aimed to close a gap of $177,600 in 1970 there is a 50–50 chance of achieving and even exceeding the target. But there is also a 50–50 chance of profits turning out below the target level and, much more serious, there is a 1 in 10 chance of a really poor profit outturn representing a rate of growth over the 1967 profits level of 3 per cent per annum – i.e. no growth at all in real money terms. The company cannot accept this risk. They are prepared to accept a 1 in 10 chance of achieving a profit representing a growth of 5 per cent per annum but to ensure that profits do not turn out worse than this they must aim to close a gap, not of $177,600 but something higher. How much higher can easily be calculated. A growth of 5 per cent per annum from 1967 implies a profit of $290,400 in 1970 and since there may be an error of $36,000 in this year the figure to aim at is $326,400 not $309,600 which was the target for that year. Put it another way; if they aim at

$309,600 there is a 1 in 10 chance of a profit outturn of $273,600 representing 3 per cent growth; if they aim at $326,400 there is a 1 in 10 chance of a profit of $290,400 representing 5 per cent growth. They will not tolerate $273,600 but will tolerate $290,400, therefore they must aim at $326,400 in 1970, not at $309,600 which was the target for that year. The gap they must aim to close, then, is not $177,600 but $194,400.

The gaps for the other years can be calculated in the same way. The lowest rate of growth the company will tolerate is 5 per cent per annum which implies profits each year as follows:

	1967 (Actual)	1968	1969	1970	1971	1972
$000	252	264	278	290	307	320

The errors expected in each year are

$000	0	24	29	36	48	60

and therefore the target to be aimed at each year in order to have a good chance (9 in 10) of doing better than a 5 per cent per annum growth record is

$000	—	288	307	326	355	382

and the gaps to be closed are:

$000	—	96	185	194	288	403

Compare these with the gaps calculated on page 119 before the errors in the forecast were brought into consideration.

Taking errors into account in this way is confusing and perplexing to some people. It certainly means a lot of hard thinking and is seldom done. However the need to do it is undoubted since, without taking this precaution now, the company will later be bitterly disappointed when profits do not turn out as forecast – as may very well happen. If this were a text-book on corporate planning a large and highly mathematical section on risk analysis, probability, decision theory and utility theories would have to be included here. But in a practical guide this would be out of place since these techniques are probably not sufficiently developed to be used in practice in this type of problem. However all the fundamental concepts underlying these techniques have been employed in the discussion above. To illustrate again the points being made consider a quite different example:

A man wishes to catch a train at 10 o'clock – he must not miss it if he can possibly help it. Fortunately he knows that the time his journey takes to the station is subject to error – in fact on the last ten occasions when he travelled there from his home he arrived five minutes late on one occasion and five minutes early on another (i.e. it is subject to an error of $\pm$ five minutes on one in ten occasions). At what time should he aim to reach the station? Clearly if he aims to get there at 10 o'clock he will have a 1 in 10 chance of having to wait more than five minutes but he does not mind this (nor did Hypothetics mind the possibility of exceeding their 1970 forecast by $36,000 or more). But he simply cannot tolerate the other possibility – of arriving more than 5 minutes late which there is a 1 in 10 chance of him doing. (Nor could Hypothetics tolerate the 1 in 10 chance of a profit as low as $273,600 in 1970). So he aims to arrive at 9.55. (So Hypothetics aim at a profit of $326,400 instead of at their target of $309,600 for 1970).

Hypothetics have not altered their profit target. They are still aiming at 7 per cent growth each year, but, to make reasonably sure of achieving it and, more important, to make reasonably sure of not disastrously undershooting it, they have decided to try to find ways of earning extra profits over the next ten years in case profits from the existing business fall short of the forecasts.

Three points must now be mentioned. Firstly it has so far been implied that errors will be symmetrical about the central forecast figure; e.g. Forecast: $240,000; plus $36,000 or minus $36,000. This may not always be the case, for the corporate planner may estimate that some of the events that will improve profits if they occur are more likely to occur than some of the events that will depress profits (or vice versa) and the errors may therefore be: Forecast: $240,000; $+$40,000 or $-$28,800. This does not involve any change in principle from what has been said in this chapter and the point is raised only to draw attention to the fact that this sort of thing does happen.

The second point is that it is psychologically unwise to decide on a company's profit target *after* calculating the profit forecast, i.e. taking Step 1 in the corporate planning process *after* Step 2. This is because these two things, target and forecast, are not only distinct but also independent of each other: a target is what one wants to happen, a forecast is what one expects will happen and these may be, indeed usually are, quite different and have no reaction upon each other. If the forecast is made before the target is set there is a danger that the target will be set with the forecast in mind. If the forecast indicates a bleak and difficult future ahead for the company then there is a danger that the target will be set lower than is appropriate. A company has a definite, unalterable function – to make that profit which enables it to pay a satisfactory return to share-holders – and this is true whatever the future holds for it. Either it will succeed in this or it will fail, but this is what it must aim for whatever the difficulties. Thus it is being suggested that the forecast is irrelevant to the target setting procedure and that to set a target with the forecast in mind may result in a target not related to satisfying shareholders and therefore one that is inappropriate to the fundamental nature of a company.

In the same way, having set a target it is wrong to reduce it merely because the future looks bleak. The only justification for reducing a target is that it has become inappropriate: a company that aims to give a return to shareholders that is average and aims at 8 per cent d.c.f. in the belief that this is what would satisfy an average shareholder may find, after a few years, that the average shareholder is satisfied with 7 per cent – then and only then may the targets be reduced. Even so, great care must be taken when adjusting a target to ensure that the risks of and the consequences of not achieving the new target are taken into account – i.e. the forecast errors must be considered.

Thirdly it will be appreciated that whenever the target or the forecast is revised a new gap must be calculated and whenever the company feels its confidence in the errors as currently stated has altered then, too, a new gap has to be calculated.

Summary of Chapter IX

Having determined the company's profit target and forecast the likely profits for each year the corporate planner calculates the gap between these two figures. This gap represents the extra task facing the company over and above the mere continuation of the existing business – it indicates how much extra profit has to be yielded from the decisions and the commitments that will be made over the next few years.

If the company were to aim to close the gap indicated by comparing the target and the forecast without taking account of the errors that will surely be associated with the forecast it may run the risk not only of failing to achieve the target, but of failing to do so by an unacceptably wide margin. Taking account of these errors is often difficult but is essential. The real size of the task ahead is shown by the profit gap calculated so as to avoid an unacceptable profit result.

(See also Appendix 1.)

Review of Steps 1 to 3

It will be recalled that corporate planning is intended to help companies decide two basic questions: what to do and how to do it. The first of these two tasks is now complete: the company knows exactly what it is trying to do. This fact alone places it in a class by itself for many companies, perhaps most companies, have given the matter very little thought. Of those that have thought about it many have determined upon a target in terms of growth of sales, asset value, employees, turnover, or return on capital employed: all of them are irrelevant to the real purpose of a company which is to make a profit that is sufficient to allow shareholders a satisfactory (d.c.f.) return on their money. The return that meets this requirement can be determined whoever the shareholders may be although the level that would satisfy some categories of shareholders is more difficult to measure and predict than others.

The profit target would completely define the task facing the company's executives were it not for the fact that profits from the existing part of the business may not continue at their present levels – thus, although the target tells the executives where they want to go it does not tell them how fast they will have to run to get there. This is calculated by forecasting the profits likely to be made by the existing business assuming no new actions were taken, no new commitments were made.

Unfortunately this forecast is inaccurate, as all forecasts are liable to be, and the probable errors have to be taken into account before finally specifying the task.

Now, what is the point of all this? The first one of overriding importance is that organizations are created by people to benefit them in some quite definite way: organizations are not like organisms whose purpose is known only to God. It is not the aim or purpose of any organization merely to survive, but to benefit someone. Only when an organization clearly knows what benefit it is supposed to be providing, and for whom, can it set about the job of providing it. Few companies seem to have identified their purpose in these terms. Only those that have identified it can achieve it.

To know the size of the task is to know much about how to tackle it. If the profit gap is likely to be $240,000 in three years time then it is no use the company's executives relying on a project that is designed to yield $96,000. Only if the task is known will the scale of their efforts, their thinking and their actions be geared to it. If they do not know the size of the task they cannot judge if the measures they are about to take are adequate. What may be even worse is when the target has been set in the wrong terms altogether; if, instead of setting a profit target, the company set a target in terms of share of the market, for example. For all the time and effort the company spends striving to increase its share might have been better spent entering a different market with a new product.

A method of deciding the task has been described. Now it is time to consider how it is to be carried out.

CHAPTER X

STEP 4 DETERMINE THE CONSTRAINTS

The difference between objectives and constraints – constraints can overshadow objectives – constraints and means – companies must decide where they stand on moral issues – some examples of constraints.

IN Chapter IV the conclusion was reached that the objective of a company was to make a profit. All the subsequent chapters have been devoted to describing how a profit target for a company should be set. The conclusion in Chapter IV went further than this, however, for it was decided not merely that the objective was to make a profit but that this was the one and only objective. None of the other objectives that were considered passed the test of the three questions which were designed to identify genuine objectives and to reject any that did not meet the definition – i.e. 'the permanent, unalterable *raison d'être*' of the company.

This conclusion might be considered to be at variance with the present day moral and political climate. Indeed, as was pointed out in Chapter IV, some people deny the morality of profit however it has been made, and so for them this conclusion was indeed an immoral one. The great majority of people, however, hold the view that profit is a perfectly moral and respectable goal provided that it is not obtained by immoral means. This is the view taken here but an attempt is made in this chapter to define it more precisely than is usual, to take it to its logical conclusion and to draw practical results from it. One further reminder of a statement made before: in Chapter IV it was stated that there were two sections of the corporate planning process that depended largely on philosophical considerations; one was found in Step 1 'Determine the Objective.' The other is here, in this part of Step 2. We are dealing with part of the subject known as ethics.

One of the suggested objectives that failed the three-question test was 'to be good employers'. The questions and the answers obtained were :

1. 'Under what circumstances would the company *not* try to be good employers?' Answer: None.
2. 'Why does the company want to be good employers?' Answer: To improve profits; or because it is the right thing to do, etc.
3. 'If the company failed to be good employers, would it fail as a company and therefore cease to exist?' Answer: No.

It may or may not be true that by being good employers the company would improve its profits – there does seem to be evidence to suggest that it is true. But imagine that it was not true, imagine that new research showed that the worse a company treats its employees the greater are the profits: would a company, faced with this incontrovertible evidence, start to treat its employees badly? Surely the answer is that it would not. The reason that it would not is that the company's executives believe it would be morally wrong to do so. It is wrong and that is the end of the argument. When moral questions are raised it is pointless to bring consequences into the argument. Thus, whether treating employees well improves profits or depresses them is irrelevant. If it is morally right to treat them well then one does this regardless of the consequences on profit or on anything else.

Thus the company may feel bound, restricted, constrained by its own moral sensitivities from treating employees badly even if this might have improved profits. Similarly it might feel constrained from planting electronic recording devices in its competitor's Boardroom although, if it did so, the secrets that it learnt in this way could certainly be used to improve its profits. One can improve profits by selling insurance policies with let-out clauses in small print. By switchselling. By selling products that fall to bits the day after the travelling salesman has left the district. By knowingly selling panaceas that cure nothing. By dismissing employees when they are ill. People who cheat at cards win more money than those who do not. Athletes who take pep pills win more races. Many people and many companies do succeed handsomely by the use of these methods.

It is very much up to each company to decide where it stands on the moral scale which extends from the deliberate but cunning infringement of the law to the highest level of courtesy and consideration for others.

Constraints can Overshadow the Objective
Let it be quite clear: to treat one's employees well is not an objective, it is a constraint. It is something the company will do even if to do so makes it more difficult to achieve its profit target. In the same way the objective of an expedition may be to climb Mount Everest, it is not one of its objectives to treat the porters well. But, clearly to state the objective as 'to climb Mount Everest' does not imply that one intends to maltreat the porters – it says nothing about how they are to be treated. Even if it could be conclusively shown that it would make the objective easier to attain if the porters were beaten from time to time, the climbers may have decided that they will not do this: but this decision is separate from and unrelated to, the objective. In the same way the company's decision not to do certain things that it considers immoral may make its profit task more difficult: but the decision as to this constraint is made separately to the decision as to what the company's objective is to be.

One can take this line of argument further. It is possible to quote examples of companies who have prefered to go out of business rather than infringe their moral codes. They have said to themselves 'our objective is to make a profit but we will not permit action x, y, or z even if that makes our objective more difficult, or even impossible, to attain'. They have then found that only by taking actions x, y, or z could a profit be secured and, having forsworn their use, have gone into voluntary liquidation. As an example, consider a variety theatre whose business was threatened by the increasing popularity of strip-clubs; the owners could have followed this trend but either because they objected to strip-shows on principle or because of the need to employ a type of variety artist of which the owners disapproved, they prefered to close down.

In fact both the objective and the constraints are decided on moral grounds. Anyone who founds a new organization must know what the purpose of that organization is and whether its aims are in accord with his moral, political, religious, aesthetic, etc. creed. In the same way the constraints are decided on moral, political, etc., grounds. Thus these two, the objectives and the constraints, have this much in common: that both are decided on moral grounds. But there are other similarities as well, and, perhaps, these similar qualities have led to the mistaken belief that constraints are objectives, that 'to treat employees well' is as much an objective as 'to make a profit' or that 'to treat the porters well' is as much an objective as 'to climb Mount Everest'. The confusion is understandable but it is a confusion nevertheless. One of the other similarities between objectives and constraints is that no help can be obtained from Science as to what objective or constraint should be chosen. There is no science, nor can there ever be one, that is capable of pronouncing upon the validity of an organization's objective or on its chosen constraints. Many sciences can help to determine the *consequences* of a decision to choose this objective or that constraint but no science can say whether the decisions were right.

This being so, objectives and constraints will not lose their validity whatever the progress of science, they will lose it only as a result of a change in moral attitudes. Perhaps this thought has implications for the membership of Boards of companies since it is the Board who will determine the objectives and the constraints.

Constraints and Means
Constraints are those actions that the company will take or will not take on moral grounds regardless of the consequences to profit.

Means are those actions that the company will take *only* if they may improve profits and will not take if it is thought that they will not improve profits. Thus a company that has decided not to give short weight will not do so even if its profit position is perilous, but a company that has been exporting will decide to stop doing so if it finds that it is no longer profitable – no moral issues are involved in this decision which is based solely on its effect on the profits.

Now it is clear that if a company has set itself an ambitious profit target, if it has also set itself a high moral standard in deciding its constraints, if in addition business enters a difficult phase, then the means by which the company hopes to achieve its target must be extremely powerful. The interplay between profit, constraints, means and business climate is continuous and closely linked. Moral pressures on the company are increasingly imposed by society, public opinion, and, through legislation, by the government. When profits are also under pressure the incentive to reduce the moral constraints is considerable. The need for companies to decide where they stand on these issues is increasing as public opinion presses from one direction and the need for profit presses from the other.

Companies must decide where they stand on moral issues
There are four reasons why a company must decide what moral attitude it is going to adopt:

(1) As was mentioned above, moral constraints are being increasingly dictated by public opinion, the press, the government, the unions, consumer organizations and so on. The greater the number of constraints imposed on companies the fewer are the options available for making profit and the more difficult does it become to make a profit at all. A company must decide which constraints are valid in its opinion and which are not, so that it can gauge just how difficult it is going to be to make a satisfactory profit.

(2) Only when it has decided what constraints to adopt can it give instructions to its executives to guide their course of action when faced with a moral problem. Almost any plan may involve a proposed action that could be foreign to the company's ethics; it would be sensible to make these constraints known.

(3) Only when it has decided what its moral attitudes are can it select suitable staff. If it has decided to use high-pressure selling then it is necessary to take on a particular type of sales staff. If it has decided to sail as close to the wind as possible then it needs a certain type of legal adviser. If it is determined to treat its employees with consideration then it needs executives who are by nature considerate of others.

(4) The employees need to know what sort of company they are working for so that they can decide whether to go on working for it. Customers and suppliers need to know so that they can decide whether to trust it. Sooner or later everyone who deals with the company will find out what sort of company it is so it is as well for the company to decide what it wants them to think of it.

Some example of constraints

It is part of the job of the corporate planner to help the company to decide what sort of company it wishes to be. In addition to all the other elements that make up a company – its products, its factories, its employees – there are also its moral attitudes. A set of statements describing these should be prepared. It may be very brief, covering only those few constraints that the company will honour right to the point of going into liquidation. Or the list can be long and detailed covering almost every possible moral decision ever likely to have to be made by an executive: on the whole this seems unnecessary unless its moral code is of variance with that currently accepted as normal.

Some of these decisions are:

Will the company knowingly break the law?
Will it deliberately mislead employees, suppliers, customers or government officials?
Does it believe that the 'closed shop' is immoral?
Will it practice racial discrimination?
If it could make more profit by selling shoddy goods would it do so?
How far will it go to beat its competitors – industrial espionage? – denigrating their products?
Under what circumstances will it dismiss an employee?
Will it take more safety precautions in the factory than is called for by legislation?
Will it export at a loss out of a sense of patriotism to help the Export Drive?

In most of these examples the need for a decision springs from purely practical considerations as well as philosophical ones. If a coloured man asks for a job the foreman needs to know whether to take him on or not. The works manager needs to know how to reply to a union demand for a closed shop – and he needs to know whether the company's views are so strongly held that they are prepared to resist even against a strike. The Board needs to decide whether any of their moral convictions are held so strongly as to justify a reduction in profit of 1 per cent or 10 per cent or even 100 per cent.

A statement of the constraints might consist only of one sentence such as:

'*Constraints*: In all respects this company will follow the lead of the top few British companies and nationalized industries.'

This would imply that if British Railways run a welfare scheme, if British Petroleum does not bar coloured job applicants, if I.C.I. take more safety precautions in their factory than called for by the legislation, if the National Coal Board approve the closed shop, then it is the intention of this company to do the same. Such a policy has one advantage: if anyone in the company is uncertain how to react to a moral issue they can go and ask some of these organizations what their policy is, and although they may not all react in the same way there will usually be one policy that is pursued by the majority of large organizations. This simple statement also has one disadvantage: it implies very considerable expense. Most large organizations spend considerable sums of money in maintaining their high standards of behaviour and if a smaller company wishes to maintain this standard it must realize that this will cost it a great deal of money: constraints make profits more difficult to achieve.

At the other end of the scale are the companies that decide to cheat, lie, and mislead all who deal with them, who use their monopoly position to the full, whose immorality is taken, quite deliberately up to, but not beyond, the point at which they might be found out.

Somewhere in the middle are the majority of companies who aim neither so high as the moral code of the major companies, nor so low as those run on criminal lines. It is sensible for these to state where they stand on at least five major issues: their proposed relationships with employees, competitors, customers, suppliers and government officials of all sorts. Merely as an example, the Policy Statements might appear as follows:

'*Attitude to employees*: the company will treat all employees with respect and consideration; however it will not employ – indeed it will dismiss – any employee who endangers the safety of another employee, jeopardizes valuable property, fails to reach the required standard in quantity or quality of work. The company does not recognize the union's right to resist such dismissals. It does not permit a closed shop but does admit the right to bargain for pay and conditions and it recognizes the union as sole negotiator on behalf of wage earners. It would prefer to enter into individual contracts with all employees as it does with staff members.

'*Attitude to competitors*: the company will not purchase trade secrets from unauthorized sources. It will not enter into 'understandings' as to price fixing or market sharing whether legal or not: it considers that competition should be free and vigorous.

'*Attitude to suppliers*: the company will buy on merits. It will not allow employees to receive personal gifts from suppliers. It will purchase 'dumped' imports.

'*Attitude to customers*: the company recognizes that its products could be harmful if misused and will take every precaution to limit this possibility even to the extent of not selling to customers who may use the product irresponsibly. The product will be sold on its merits which may be exaggerated by the salesmen but not up to the point where this exaggeration misleads the buyer. Salesmen will not make personal gifts to prospective customers.

'*Attitude to officials of local and national government*: the company recognizes the need for officials to ensure that the company is meeting the requirements of the law and will co-operate fully with them. It does not recognize the right of officials to interfere with the company in any other way.'

These examples are not intended as model constraints, or even ones typical of any type of firm: they are intended merely to show the sort of problem to be considered and decided upon at this stage of the corporate planning process. (Incidentally, it should be noted that companies who operate internationally may have to add modifications to its constraints to take account of the differing moral codes of the various nations – e.g. compare the attitude of North Europeans to the work that women may do, with the attitude of South Europeans.) Having made these decisions these constraints guide the behaviour of the employees, constrain their plans, determine the selection and employment of the staff – and to some extent limit their profits.

Summary of Chapter X
Although a few people believe profits to be inherently immoral most people take the view that profit is a perfectly permissible

objective providing the means by which it is obtained are not immoral. Many company directors share this latter view and would not wish their company to take certain types of action to improve profits – that is to say the company imposes certain constraints upon itself in the pursuit of profit.

It is important, for purely practical reasons, to know what constraints a company has chosen to impose so that its relationships with its employees, customers, suppliers, competitors and government officials can be defined. If these are not defined the company's executives may not know how to react to a problem involving moral decisions. The greater the number and severity of the constraints the more difficult will it be to achieve the profit target: however, every firm will hold a number of moral convictions which it will not abandon under any circumstances whatever.

(See also Appendix 1.)

CHAPTER XI

STEP 4 . . . AND DETERMINE
THE MEANS

This long and important Step is divided into six Stages –
Possible Means – Possible areas of business – Which means
can be applied in the Existing Business Area – and in the
New Business Areas – Voluntary Liquidation.

Two out of the three elements that together completely describe
what sort of company it is to become have now been examined –
the Objective and the Constraints. They describe what the
company is aiming at and some of the things it is *not* going to do
to achieve its aim. Now it must decide what it *is* going to do.

This is probably the most difficult and complex section of the
corporate planning process and the one in which a thoroughly
systematic approach is vital. The first step is to make it clear
what this part of the process is intended to do, and this can be
stated quite simply: it is to prepare a list of actions that the
company might take in order to achieve the profit target bearing in mind the limitations imposed by the Constraints.
At this stage what is required is not so much a detailed statement at the tactical level but a more general statement of the
strategy that will remain largely valid over the following few
years. It is a process roughly parallel with designing an army's
weapons that will be appropriate for the battles it will probably
have to fight in the next few years – it is not yet time to decide
exactly when these armaments will be used, or where, or by
whom. At this, the second part of Step 4 in the 5-Step process
then, the concern is with strategy; tactics are left until Step 5.

The Six Stages
This second part of Step 4 – determining the means – is carried
out in six stages. Before turning to these, however, consider what
these Means are for. It will be recalled that the company has

given itself a very clear and distinct task to perform – to achieve a given profit figure in each of the next few years. The means by which *part* of this task is to be performed already exists in the business already being operated by the company. The corporate planner knows that even if the existing business is carried on in just the same way as in the past and even if no new capital expenditure is made and no new commitments are entered into, quite significant profits will continue to be made. What these might be he has shown in the profit forecast. But now it is necessary to find ways and means of adding to these profits to bring the total profit up to the target level, that is, to find ways and means of closing the profit gap. What changes in the present way of running the business, what new capital expenditure is required, what new commitments should be made in order to close the gap – that is now the problem. By assuming that the company would do nothing new, the corporate planner made the profit forecast on a position of minimum assumption so that no action to improve profits – however obvious any such actions may have seemed – was assumed to be taken. Now it is necessary to examine the merits of each possible action, obvious and less obvious, to see which of them are most likely to close the gaps.

The six stages of Step 4 are as follows:

Stage A Review the possible means:
  (1) Invest capital
  (2) Overcome obstacles
  (3) Exploit opportunities
  (4) Use of strengths
  (5) Overcome weaknesses
  (6) Institute profit improvement plan
  (7) Use of management techniques

Stage B Review possible business areas:
  (1) Existing business to be
      (*a*) Reduced
      (*b*) Maintained
      (*c*) Increased
      (*d*) Forced
  (2) New business
      (*a*) Integration forward
      (*b*) Integration backwards

    (*c*) Diversify: new products in existing markets
    (*d*) Diversify: new products in new markets
    (*e*) Diversify: existing products in new markets.
    (Note: 'products' means goods or service.)
  (3) Liquidation

Stage C Test the effect on profits of the use of these seven possible means on the existing business.

Stage D Test the effect on profits of the use of these seven possible means on new business.

Stage E Test the effect on shareholders of liquidation.

Stage F Draw up Policy Statements.

The procedure, in brief, is to note what types of action one can take to improve profits (Stage A) and to note in which areas of business activity (Stage B) these actions might be effective. Then in Stages C, D, E, test how effective each of these actions might be on each area of business. It will be noted later that although all seven possible means can be used to improve profits from the existing business, only some can be in the case of new business, and very few in the case of liquidation. It should be said now that the most fruitful place to start looking for extra profit is usually in the existing business, the next best is in new business, and, if these fail, then the only way of satisfying the shareholder may be by going into liquidation and returning his money to him. The final stage (F) is to draw the conclusions reached from these studies together into a Policy Statement setting out the proposed strategy by which the profit gap is to be closed.

Each of these stages must now be considered in detail.

Stage A. POSSIBLE MEANS

In this stage the corporate planner should make a list of all those actions by which companies in general and his in particular might be able to generate profits. How do companies make profits? By investing capital, by exploiting opportunities, by improving efficiency and so on. They can probably best be classified into seven main categories that are each briefly described below.

(*1*) *Investment of Capital.* Very little has so far been said about capital expenditure in this book, not because it is not of much importance – it is almost certainly the most important generator of profit there is – but because it was specifically excluded from consideration in the forecasts. This was to avoid making any unwarrantable assumption as to what the company would do with its cash flow until Step IV was reached: it is in this Step (at Stages C, D, E) that a decision must be taken as to how much capital should be invested in which projects.

The corporate planner needs to know whether the company he works for relies heavily on capital expenditure for its profits, as in the oil, chemical and other capital intensive industries or not, as in many of the service and retail industries. In broad terms he must know how much capital is available currently, whether the current cash flow will add to the reserves, what short and long term loans are outstanding, to what extent they can be increased or must be reduced, what is the company's total capacity for debt, what return on capital can be expected from projects in their industry, and so on. At present he need only note these facts and figures and conclude whether capital expenditure is likely to be a significantly useful means of increasing the profits. In most businesses it will be.

(*2*) *Overcoming Obstacles*. It will be recalled that when the corporate planner had completed the profit forecast he prepared a report in which he recorded all the trends and events that might be expected to affect profits by more than a few per cent. Those that tended to reduce profits might be termed obstacles. They will be of two types: those that the company has the power to overcome and those that it has not. A very large company has more power than a small one. It might even be possible for a large company to alter the determination of a government to abolish an import duty that was restraining the foreign competitors of that company from competing with it in its home market: a small company could probably not do this.

Broadly speaking, the more obstacles there are that a company is powerless to overcome the more effectively does it need to look for profit from new ventures. A very obvious example of this is when a company is operating in a declining market and is forced to diversify.

(*3*) *Exploit Opportunities*. In his analysis of the company's future the corporate planner also noted down any trends or events that might represent an opportunity for the company to exploit. The example was cited, in Chapter VII, of the case of a company facing a difficult period ahead realizing that its competitors might also be facing a difficult time and that the possibility of one of them becoming ripe for a merger should be borne in mind. However at that stage the corporate planner was engaged in forecasting and not specifically in searching for opportunities. Now he is specifically searching for them. He should work through the Factors Affecting Profit and the Profit Forecast to identify any more there may be. (Some examples are given later in this chapter.) Having identified them, he will probably use the technique of Market Research to investigate them more thoroughly.

(*4*) *Exploit Strengths*. (*5*) *Overcome Weaknesses*. These two categories should be distinguished from 'obstacles' and 'opportunities': obstacles are trends or events in the environment of the company that tend to reduce profits, and opportunities are trends or events in the environment that might be turned to the company's advantage. Strengths and Weaknesses on the other hand, are to be found inside the company itself. Very often they spring from the quality of the staff: there may be three first-rate marketing executives in a marketing department who together have given the company a leading place among its competitors. Or there may be a staff of 100 scientists in a research department not one of whom is capable of bringing a good idea to fruition.

Strengths and weaknesses also spring from the geographical position of the company's factory, the type of plant it has installed, its standing in the City, and a dozen other factors, some due to historical accident, others the result of years of solid endeavour and cultivation.

The corporate planner should attempt to list all those characteristics of the company that seem to him to be unusually valuable or unusually useless to it. It would have been better, perhaps, to have made this list while preparing the forecast during which he needed to probe deep into the company's past and future. However, classifying a characteristic of a company as a strength or weakness is a somewhat subjective activity and it is unlikely that the corporate planner would have had sufficient experience of the company to be able to do this then, in the early stages of Step 2, when he may only have been with the company for a few weeks.

He must do it now, however. The lists might appear as follows:

Strengths	Weaknesses
(1) The only producer within seventy miles of London.	(1) Factory not connected by rail; roads poor for fifty miles.
(2) Research Department prolific in new ideas.	(2) Onerous contract for a major component still has eight years to run.
(3) First-rate labour relations. Low staff turnover.	(3) Four of the nine executive directors are over sixty.
(4) Patent for main product has seven years more to run.	(4) We only have a 2 per cent share of the total market.
(5) Our company is the largest buyer of material M in Europe.	(5) We are excessively reliant on one major customer and two major suppliers.

It is worth making three further points under this heading. The first concerns take-over bids. There are of course a great many reasons for taking over or merging with another company; it will extend one's share of the market more rapidly than one can achieve by other means, it can provide a rapid entré into a new field of business, it can be a source of tax losses, and so on. One of the most important motives for this type of action, however, is that it can provide a company with some ready-made strength that it needs but lacks. A company wishing to find an outlet for a by-product which can only be sold into an industry in which it has no experience, can buy up a company in that industry and can dispose of the by-product through it. In this way the outlet is obtained far more rapidly than the company could have achieved on its own. Bids may be an expensive means of overcoming a weakness (because no Investment Grants are payable) but it is a rapid and reliable one.

The second comment concerns research. Few companies appear to have decided why they feel it necessary to do research or how much to spend upon it: some companies do no research at all. This is a weakness from which many companies appear to suffer. The purpose of scientific research and development for most companies is to prepare new products or processes for the future. It is thus linked, and subservient to, the product development plans of the company. One spends whatever is necessary to allow one to launch a new product or bring on stream a new process and in deciding whether to introduce these products or processes one takes account of the cost of the research necessary. Nor does one ignore the possibility of buying know-how or simply imitating as opposed to innovating.

The third comment concerns marketing. Many companies have still not realised the distinction between selling and marketing: the first concerns the act of persuading a customer to buy one of your products. Marketing is a far wider concept including the entire process of *creating* a market for a product – making people think they need it, desiring it and welcoming it. Many authorities extend the meaning of marketing to include market research, design, packaging, distribution, promotion, advertising, after-sales service, franchising and so on. Marketing in this, wider sense, is probably another common weakness in industry.

(6) *Institute Profit Improvement Plan.* A profit improvement plan is one of the names given to a deliberate, systematic, long term improvement in profitability across the whole field of operations. Another name for it is 'Management by Objectives', but this term appears less apposite than profit improvement since the objective is, after all, profit, and it seems right to emphasise this in the title.

The procedure normally adopted is to break down virtually every activity into minute detail – such things as gasoline consumption of the trucks, lines of type per typist per day, output per machine hour and so on – and to set targets for improvement to the executive responsible for each one. This procedure has the merit, especially if financial incentives are linked to success, of focussing the executive's attention on the need to improve efficiency as well as to solve day-to-day problems. It has only one possible disadvantage, namely that great energy may be expended by an executive on improving the performance of his section, while it might have been better spent in closing down the section altogether and substituting something more appropriate to the needs of the future.

However, the concept of management by objectives is valid. Unfortunately it is often not appreciated that results do not come quickly or dramatically. One seldom achieves a 10 per cent improvement in labour productivity in the despatch department, for example, in one year: what one may achieve is a 2 or 3 per cent improvement every year. If this sort of performance can be repeated throughout the company, year after year, then the benefits mount up impressively. It must be appreciated that a profit improvement plan must be treated as a long term measure; it cannot help the company who, finding its profits lower than expected in the current year, need to make immediate cuts in cost: to do so under these conditions will often result in panic cuts that do more harm than good – not always (sometimes it is useful to review costs stringently), but usually.

Such profit improvement plans, covering almost every part of the company can make a valuable contribution to profits: expecially if one is looking systematically for improvements in revenue as well. It should be a profit improvement plan, not merely a cost-reduction plan.

(7) *Management Techniques*. There are now well over 100 separate and distinct management techniques such as those shown in Appendix 2. As with the profit improvement plan, swift results are seldom achieved by their use. Much painstaking work, extending for months or even years, is required before their effects are felt, for many of them are designed to help solve long-standing problems. Each technique can be used to solve one type of problem – Linear Programming is useless in human relations problems, discounted cash flow is valueless as a means of reducing factory bottlenecks – and the corporate planner probably by now knows enough of the main problems facing the company to be able to identify which techniques will be most useful to it and which will not be appropriate at all.

These last two possible means, the profit improvement plan and management techniques, have several features in common: they cannot be used to improve profits immediately; indeed neither are likely to yield results within a year. Both should be used in a systematic and continuous search for profit over a long period, relying on a gradual but eventually an impressive cumulative effect. Both call for specialist training and super-vision. Few companies have yet appreciated their value or have obtained even a fraction of the benefits that they can yield. One has only to consider for a moment the effect on morale, let alone on profit, of challenging the company's technical staff to improve fuel efficiency by 4 per cent per annum for the next five years or the work study department to improve labour pro-ductivity by 5 per cent per annum for the next ten years or the production department to reduce waste by 3 per cent per annum to realise the potential of this approach. When one realises also that there are over 100 management techniques available to assist these executives achieve these targets, then the scale of the benefits that are practical begin to be understood. It should certainly be possible to improve profits by 1 per cent of turnover by these means alone.

These seven categories represent the tools in the company's garden shed. It next has to consider the possible fields in which they might be effective.

Stage B POSSIBLE BUSINESS AREAS

There are three main areas of business in which a company may operate:

(*1*) *The Existing Business.* If a company sells oranges in Bristol it can either: stop doing so; aim to sell about the same volume in the next few years as currently; aim to sell more or aim to sell much more. It must decide which of these four things it is going to do. The main factor in its decision will be the future prospects, as it sees them, of selling oranges in Bristol compared with doing something else. If the prospects apppear to be dismal then it might stop doing this and try something else or give the shareholders their money back. If the prospects are moderate it may continue to sell the same number or more oranges in Bristol but, at the same time, try something else as well. If prospects are really excellent it might throw all its resources into increasing its sales – it cannot do something else as well for it will have committed all its resources to its present business.

(*2*) *New Business.* The company may decide to search for new business in any of these areas (*a*) integrate forwards (find out what oranges are used for and sell that – marmalade for example). (*b*) Integrate backwards (find out where oranges come from and grow them or transport them). (*c*) Diversify by selling a new product in the same market (sell apples in Bristol). (*d*) Diversify by selling a new product in a different market (sell apples in Bath). (*e*) Diversify by selling the existing product in a new market (sell oranges in Bath).

Its decision to do one or the other – or several or all – will again be determined by its estimate of the prospects for each.

(3) *Liquidation.* This is hardly a 'possible area of business'. It is included here, however, because the decision to go out of business is one that does sometimes have to be taken and 'do nothing' is as legitimate a decision for a company as 'do more' or 'do something different'. A company decides to go out of business when to continue would probably yield a lower d.c.f. return to the owners than would satisfy them.

Stage C POSSIBLE MEANS IN EXISTING BUSINESS

Stages A and B were preliminaries. In them the corporate planner need do no more than review possible means and possible business areas to make sure nothing had been forgotten. Now in Stage C he must examine how effective these means are likely to be in extracting extra profits from the *existing business*. Then in Stage D repeat this examination in possible *new business* areas.

Take the case of a company whose profit gap is calculated to be:

$000	1968	1969	1970	1971	1972	1977	1987
	24	96	192	264	360	1440	3360

The question now being asked, then, is can these gaps be filled by capital expenditure, by overcoming obstacles, by exploiting the company's strong points, by the use of management techniques, and so on, in *existing* area of business? Does it look hopeful or hopeless? Are there reasonable grounds for thinking that extra profits of the same order of magnitude as these gaps can be found by the use of one or some or all of these measures?

Let us make the first, and for some companies, the most important test: can capital expenditure in the existing business area alone close the gaps?

Stage C (1)
CAPITAL EXPENDITURE IN THE EXISTING BUSINESS AREA

Imagine that the company whose profit gaps are shown above had available from the previous year's earnings (after paying the dividend) $120,000 for reinvestment in 1968. Assume that in the past the average return on capital realized on projects connected with its existing business is 20 per cent. Now this suggests that if the available $120,000 was invested in the existing business it would yield a profit of $24,000 per annum. This would close the $24,000 gap in 1968 – and, since this type of project usually continues to yield a return of this order over a period of ten years, the gaps now remaining to be filled are reduced by $24,000:

	1968	1969	1970	1971	1972	1977	1987
$000	0	72	168	240	336	1416	3360

By the end of 1968, partly due to the increased profits resulting from the investment of this $120,000 in 1968, the capital available might be $132,000. Reinvested in a further project at 20 per cent would increase profits by $26,400. But the 1969 gap is $72,000 – and a glance at the gaps for the following years is enough to see that there is no chance whatever of closing these with capital sums of this order of magnitude yielding 20 per cent. Even if the company could find projects to yield double this return – an outrageously optimistic assumption – this would still not close the gaps. Can it find double the amount of capital, perhaps? So far it has considered reinvesting only retained profits and perhaps it can obtain loans, realise underused assets, resort to leasing or hire purchase. There is no need to illustrate this example with figures any further – the principle being put forward is that a company can calculate how much capital it has available from all possible sources and how much extra profit this might yield if invested at a realistic return. The calculation involves only simple arithmetic but is somewhat tedious to carry out over many years since in real companies as opposed to imaginary examples, financial matters are somewhat complex: Taxation, Preference, Debentures, depreciation and many other things have to be considered. An example showing some of these factors is given in Table 4, but even this example would be an oversimplification for many companies. It shows what return on capital a company would have to achieve to close the gaps: if this return was thought to be achievable by the company then the corporate planner would merely note this and pass on to the other possible means – he might, however, be suspicious of so easy a victory over the gaps. In the example in Table 4, however, it is quite clear that this company, accustomed to projects yielding only 20 per cent return, cannot close the gaps by this means alone since the return required to do so is over 50 per cent. The corporate

TABLE 4

Calculation of Capital available for investment and hence the Return on this Capital needed to close the Gap

	1967	1968	1969	1970	1971	1972
Capital available for investments ($000)						
1. Previous year's depreciation (at 10 per cent of fixed capital) available for investment		96	120	144	170.4	199.2
2. Previous year's retained profits (after Tax)		144	153.6	165.6	177.6	192
3. Hence cash flow for investment (1+2)		240	273.6	309.6	348	391.2
4. Loan capacity of company (assumed to be 50 per cent of written down fixed assets in previous year)		480	600	720	852	996
5. Loans already outstanding		360	480	600	720	852
6. Hence loan capital available (4−5)		120	120	120	132	144
7. Hence total capital available for investment (3+6)		360	393.6	429.6	480	535.2
8. But additional working capital required		24	26.4	26.4	28.8	31.2
9. And capital required for non-profit-making purposes		48	48	60	60	72
10. Hence total capital available for profit-making projects (7−8−9)		288	319.2	343.2	391.2	432
Extra Profit required ($000)						
11. Profit gap		62.4	180	424.8	576	746.4
12. Profit gap already closed		0	62.4	180	424.8	576
13. Profit gap still to be closed		62.4	117.6	244.8	151.2	170.4
14. Interest (at 8 per cent) on loans taken up		9.6	9.6	9.6	9.6	12
15. Effect of capital expenditure on forecast		24	28.8	33.6	38.4	43.2
16. Total extra profit required (13+14+15)		96	156	288	194.4	225.6
Return on Capital necessary on new capital invested (%)						
17. Therefore return on capital needed (Traditional method of calculation)		79.2	117.6	199.2	120	124.8
18. D.C.F. return on capital needed (assumes constant income for ten years)		48	84	144	86.4	88.8
Fixed capital employed	960	1200	1447.2	1706.4	1987.2	2292
Working capital		240	264	290.4	316.8	345.6
Total Capital Employed		1440	1711.2	1996.8	2304	2637.6

planner's notes, which would include a schedule similar to Table 4, might read as follows:

'Effect of Capital Expenditure on Profit Gaps
The company is most unlikely to close the gaps merely by investing capital in the existing business area. This remains true even when all possible loans, realization of under-utilized assets, leasing, etc. have been accounted for – it is not recommended that loans outstanding should exceed 50 per cent of the written down value of assets. A return of over 50 per cent on this maximum available capital is required to close the gaps: at the more normal 20 per cent return, the gaps would be reduced to approximately:

	1968	1969	1970	1971	1972
$000	36	96	276	360	456

which indicates that other measures in addition to capital expenditure will be needed to close the gaps fully.'

Before following the corporate planner through the next part of his search for other means of closing the gaps, it is necessary to comment more fully on some of the more technical aspects of the capital expenditure calculations made above.

Notes on capital expenditure calculations
Computer models. It has been mentioned before that the calculations that a corporate planner has to do involve only simple arithmetic but are of a tedious and repetitive nature. This was true of the calculations for arriving at a profit target, for arriving at a forecast and, now again, for the effect of capital. Ideally all three sections – target, forecast and capital, should be amalgamated into one schedule which should also show the various traditional features of the balance sheet – fixed assets, working capital, return on capital employed, dividend cover, and so on, for each of the years of the forecast period. This schedule can then be programmed for a computer. Once this has been prepared it is a simple matter to alter one of the variables to see the effect throughout this amalgamated long term financial and accounting description of the company – one could see the effect over ten years, say, of a change in Capital Grants, or return on capital, or altering the limitation on loans, or a rise in fixed costs, etc. etc. It would take a

reasonably intelligent assistant two days to learn a suitable computer language and perhaps two to three weeks to prepare the fairly detailed model of the company's financial and accounting amalgam.

Return on Capital. This expression has four different meanings, two of which were discussed in Chapter VI. These were (1) discounted cash flow return to shareholders, (2) Return on Capital Employed, which, it was explained, involves written down assets and working capital taken together – rather a hotch-potch of real money and 'written down' money of a kind not met with in real life. The third meaning of 'Return on Capital' refers to capital invested in a project. Thus if a machine costs $100, this is the cost of the machine in real dollars (as opposed to written down dollars!); and, if, by installing this machine a company believes its profits will rise by $10 a year compared with what its profits would be if it did not install it, then the return on capital of this project is 10 per cent. Since meanings No. 2 and No. 3 refer to different 'Capital', one is hardly surprised to discover that a company that invests all its money in projects yielding 10 per cent return, will *not* end up with a Return on Capital Employed of 10 per cent for the company as a whole. If it does do so it is due to a purely fortuitous combination of financial factors: capital grants, depreciation, working capital and so on.

The fourth meaning of Return on Capital is the d.c.f. return on a project. This is conceptually exactly the same as the calculation made for a shareholder in Chapter VI in which $100 is invested (by a company in a machine or – the same thing – by a shareholder in a company) and the net, after tax, cash flow is discounted. Many executives (and indeed many financial experts, too) believe that if a company is aiming to give 10 per cent d.c.f. return to shareholders (i.e. if the cost of capital is 10 per cent) then it must aim to invest in projects yielding not less than 10 per cent. This is incorrect. Some companies would fail to give shareholders 10 per cent d.c.f. even if they invested in no project yielding less than 20 per cent d.c.f. There are many reasons why this is so and why the cut-off (i.e. minimum acceptable) rate of return for a project is different to the cost of capital and has to be calculated for each individual company, but briefly these are:

Not all capital invested yields a profit (e.g. neither working capital nor capital spent on a canteen).

Not all a company's profits are generated by capital expenditure.

The company has many expenses (e.g. the auditor's fees etc.) that are not related to any particular capital expenditure project. These expenses are not usually included in the return on capital calculation made to justify individual projects.

One company may have a millstone round its neck, another has a pot of gold at the end of a rainbow: the one has to work harder to give shareholders the same return as the other. Its capital has to work harder too.

Unfortunately the correct cut-off rate has to be calculated separately for each company and this can only be done in a way similar to that shown in Table 4. Incidentally the target that the imaginary company in this Table was aiming at was 10 per cent d.c.f. (notice row 2 – retained profits – rising by 7 per cent per annum) but the cut-off rate would have had to be around 40 per cent d.c.f. to achieve this! Companies not aware of this phenomenon must be in some danger.

If a calculation similar to Table 4 is done there is in fact no need to calculate the return on capital required from new projects at all. One simply notes the two profiles of capital available and profit required and fits one's choice of projects to meet them both. Thus if the capital available is:

$000   240   264   288   331   360

one aims to find projects costing this amount of capital provided the expected yield of profits fits the profile of the profit gaps which may be:

$000   48   96   156   192   288

This is a somewhat ideal situation and some form of ratio Capital/Profit would be a sensible calculation to do. Nevertheless, the aim is to close these gaps and, as far as it is practicable to do so, this is what one should choose the projects to do, rather than to choose them because they yield a particular return.

Side-effects of Capital Expenditure

It will be remembered that when forecasting the company's profits over the next few years, the assumption was made that no capital would be spent, an assumption that has been completely abandoned in this stage of Step 4. One effect of this, obviously, is that the profits would rise compared with the forecast. However many other changes must also follow. For example, if one assumes that a company will approve no capital projects then it needs no projects department – a fact that would have been reflected in the total salary forecasts for the company. If one now assumes that the company *will* approve such projects one must expect a change in items such as fixed costs and working capital compared with 'forecast o' – changes like these are noted in the example given in Table 4 (rows 8, 14, 15). The point being made is that these are central costs that are related to the size and activity of the company and not capable of being allocated to any particular project.

One particular item in Table 4 deserves mention: row 9 refers to capital required for non-profit-making projects. These are such things as canteens, offices, recreation areas, effluent disposal equipment and so on. In effect expenditure on these items represents part of the cost of the constraints; a company that has decided not to provide attractive facilities for their employees, or not to worry too much about the effect of their waste products on the countryside, would not incur such expenditure.

Much more of a technical nature could be said – but it is hoped that the principles involved at this stage have been sufficiently described to allow any company's accounts and finance departments to combine together to assist their corporate planner to carry out this part of the study.

Stage C (2)
OVERCOMING OBSTACLES IN THE EXISTING BUSINESS AREA

Whether the previous study showed that capital expenditure alone might be sufficient to close the gaps or not, the corporate planner should study each of the other six possible means in both the existing and new business areas – after all, there may be a better way than capital expenditure. Leaving the new areas until later, consider now the specific question of overcoming

the obstacles that may be found in the future that would reduce
the company's profits from the existing business.

Most of the work in identifying these obstacles has already
been done in Step 2 – forecasting the profits. At the end of that
Step the corporate planner drew up a report including all those
Factors Affecting Profits that were likely to affect profits by
more than a few percent. At that stage in the corporate planning
process no suggestions as to how to deal with them were made.
Now they must be made. But, again, a systematic approach is
called for. It is suggested that each factor is considered in turn
and for each (a) the reason behind the factor is identified,
(b) every possible way of overcoming its harmful effect on
profits is considered and (c) suitable actions are listed. To give
some examples:

EXAMPLE (1)
Description of Obstacle: Demand for our products is expected to
fall by 1 per cent per annum in the next few years and to fall even
faster after 1970. (Effect on profits: $96,000 per annum and up to
$240,000 per annum after 1970).
Reason behind this: The total market for our type of product is
falling (our share of the market is steady) due to the rise in pre-
fabrication methods of house-building.
Possible Actions:
 Increase our share of market.
 Improve our product to compete with prefabrication methods.
 Adapt our product to prefabrication.
 Merge with prefabrication company.
 etc. etc.
Selected Actions
 Our product cannot compete with, or be modified for prefabri-
 cation by its very nature.
 As a short term measure, increase our share of the market, *or*
 consider a merger with a company exploiting prefabrication
 methods.

EXAMPLE (2)
Description of Obstacle: Demand will exceed productive capacity of
the factory by 1969. If nothing is done this could reduce profits by
$960,000 per annum.
Reason behind this: The Chief Engineer states that, having recently
surveyed the factory no amount of minor modification or re-
arrangement can increase throughput beyond the 1969 demand.
Possible Action:
 Buy products from competitors for resale.
 Build small extension to factory.

Build large extension.
Modify product mix.
etc. etc.
Selected Action:
The margin on bought-in product is likely to be nil.
No alteration to the product mix is likely to improve throughput
A small *or* a large extension seems most appropriate.

It will be noticed that even at this stage the corporate planner is not prepared to recommend one unequivocal course of action. He is prepared only to eliminate some of the less acceptable suggestions. It will be found later on, when he has considered all the possible means, that the best course of action to take in each case emerges with remarkable clarity. Notice also that not only does he not choose one best action, he does not even start to consider what actions are suitable until he has determined what lies *behind* the obstacle. For example; had he merely described an obstacle as, say, 'Our share of the market is expected to fall by 1 per cent per annum', he could not then have gone on to propose suitable actions to counter this, for he would not have known *why* the company's share was likely to fall. Only when a cause has been identified to account for an effect can any *appropriate* action be taken. Unfortunately it is a common mistake in industry not to take this difficult but vital step first before taking action. All too often the executives in a company whose share of the market is falling rush round taking every action they can think of in the hope that something that they do will do the trick. It is no use, however, improving the quality, cutting the price, reinforcing the sales team, changing the advertising agent, if what is really wrong is that the company invariably fails to deliver on the promised dates.
Consider one more example:

EXAMPLE 3
Description of Obstacle: A further rise in purchase tax possibly to 20 per cent by 1970. (Effect of this, if selling prices fall by amount of tax increase: $168,000 per annum).
Reason behind this: Government's belief that our products are not socially desirable.
Possible Actions:
Alter Government's opinion, perhaps by publicity campaign through Trade Association.
Modify product to eliminate or reduce that element considered undesirable.
etc. etc.

Selected Actions:
The product cannot be so modified.
Publicity campaign most unlikely to succeed.
It is virtually certain that nothing can be done to overcome this obstacle.

It must be recognized that there are some obstacles that cannot be overcome! (The smaller the company the fewer are the obstacles it can overcome.) When this happens the best action can be to dispose of that part of the business – divestment is more appropriate than investment in some cases.

The corporate planner, then, works through each of the Factors Affecting Profits that were mentioned in his forecast report to determine (*a*) what lies behind them, (*b*) how they might be overcome and (*c*) which of these possible actions can be ruled out and which look promising. Thus all the factors that could affect profits by 3 or 4 per cent will be considered, including those events that were thought to be unlikely to occur (and were not therefore included in the forecast calculation) but which, if they did occur could have serious results.

Stage C (3)
EXPLOITING OPPORTUNITIES IN THE EXISTING BUSINESS AREA

Exactly the same pattern is followed in this part of Stage C. The corporate planner searches through his forecast notes for any item that hints of an opportunity to exploit: he then goes through the same procedure as for the obstacles.

EXAMPLE I
Description of Opportunity: The virtual certainty that six of our smaller competitors will go out of business in the next two years. (Their business in our hands could improve profits by $300,000 per annum.)
Reason behind this: Margins have been falling for years and one or two competitors are taken over or go into liquidation every year. The next two years could be much more difficult and five competitors (Companies F, G, P, T, and Z) are known to be in serious difficulties.

Possible Actions:
Do nothing and pick up our share of their trade.
Take them over.
Supply them with our product for resale.
etc. etc.

Selected Actions:
> To do nothing is not recommended since, if instead of going into liquidation these companies are taken over by a competitor, then this competitor's strength will grow at our expense. Suggested action is to take them over or supply them with our products.

No further examples need be given here, but it is certainly worth mentioning that in all these studies the 'Possible Actions' list should be as long as possible: perhaps one should use the Brainstorming method described in Appendix 2.

Opportunities and obstacles occur in the environment of the company. Similar possible advantages and disadvantages may be found inside the company itself and these are called strengths and weaknesses to which we may now turn.

Stage C (4)
USE OF STRENGTHS IN THE COMPANY IN THE EXISTING BUSINESS

Here the corporate planner studies the list of the things the company is good at or in which it has some natural advantage over its competitors in order to suggest ways of exploiting them further. He may use the same procedure as for obstacles and opportunities:

EXAMPLE
> *Description of Strong Point:* The company's research department has proposed several very advanced and highly successful products. (Together they may have contributed $480,000 per annum to profits.)
> *Reasons behind this:* Success due largely to Dr F's leadership of the team which includes the nationally recognized experts Mrs S and Dr N.
> *Possible Actions:*
>> Strengthen this team.
>> Ensure it is not weakened.
>> Sell know-how.
>> etc. etc.
>
> *Selected Actions:*
>> No disadvantages can be seen in selling know-how to those foreign competitors who do not trade in our markets.
>> The team could be strengthened; care should be taken to see it is not weakened in any way.

Notice one more feature of this type of study: at the heading of each study, where the obstacle or opportunity or strength or weakness is described, an attempt is made to indicate its importance to profits. If the corporate planner has decided to limit his examination to those factors that might affect profits by more than 10 per cent then the subjects of study in this section will be limited to those that might affect profits by that amount – in most companies there will only be about twenty or thirty of them. If he has decided to go into more detail, down to factors affecting profits by 3 or 4 per cent as is recommended in this book, then there will be several dozen of them for the corporate planner to list, analyse and note.

Stage C (5)
OVERCOMING WEAKNESSES IN THE COMPANY

Notice the following features in the example given below for it illustrates the comments made so far concerning the way in which these studies should be carried out:

Firstly, in the *Description* an attempt is made, using the Contribution method, to evaluate the importance of the item to the company's profits.

Secondly, the *reason* for the existence of this weakness is identified.

Thirdly, a list, as long as possible, of *all actions* that could conceivably be taken is recorded.

Fourthly, most of these are ruled out leaving only *one or two* that are selected as the most likely to succeed. Incidentally some Possible Actions might have to be ruled out on the grounds that to take this action, while being practicable, would run counter to a Constraint.

EXAMPLE I

Description of Weakness: The company is prone to strikes. (Each one that lasts four days, as many do, costs $108,000 in lost contribution to profit.)

Reason behind this: Almost certainly due to poor relations between foreman and the wage earners they supervise. Not due to wage levels or working conditions which are good for the area. Not due to unions since most strikes are unofficial.

Possible Actions:
Replace foremen.
Retrain foremen.
Introduce no-strike bonus.
Dismiss strikers.
Lock-outs.

Dismiss trouble-makers.
Call in consultants.
Demand stronger action from unions.
Avoid quoting firm delivery dates.
Send letter to the strikers' wives.
Put the company's case to the local newspaper.
etc. etc.

Selected Actions:

All these actions are possible but the company does not feel that its influence over its employees should extend beyond the factory gate – for this reason, it is decided not to provide leisure-time facilities for them. By the same token it feels it would be morally wrong to involve the strikers' wives in the company's affairs.

It is suggested that where necessary some foremen should be replaced but all should first be trained in human relations.

Stage C (6)

PROFIT IMPROVEMENT PLAN

Here the corporate planner should attempt to evaluate whether a systematic attack with cost reduction and revenue increasing measures would significantly help to close the gaps. In most companies it would. Referring to the forecast report again he will be able to see which items of cost and revenue are the most significant and which are barely worth consideration.

Some companies when installing 'management by objectives' give every manager, section head, supervisor and foreman an objective to aim at in terms of efficiency. This certainly is a worthy aim, but it takes many man-years to set realistic targets to everyone. It seems sensible to start with those items that really matter. For example if labour costs are 40 per cent of the total expenses of a company it seems sensible to give labour productivity targets to everyone responsible for a department, section, team in which labour is used. If labour costs are 4 per cent of the total then it does not seem sensible to start with labour productivity targets for each executive, but instead by all means give them a target in an area that does matter to the company. Similarly, if by incompetent packaging the packing department could affect profits by 10 per cent then certainly set a target to the managers responsible for packaging. If it barely matters how the packaging is done then leave the setting of this target until later.

Having studied the company's costs and revenues one would prepare reports on the following lines:

'*Fuel Costs* represent 20 per cent of the total cost of the company's operation. It seems reasonable to challenge the Furnace Manager and the Fuel Technology Section of the Research Department to improve fuel efficiency by 4 per cent per annum over the next ten years. The effect on profits would be $50,000 per annum.'
or

'*Secretarial Costs* amount to 15 per cent of the total cost of manning the company. It seems reasonable to challenge the Office Manager and the O and M Department to reduce this by 10% per annum. If successful this could improve profits by $125,000 per annum.'
or

'*Transport Costs* account for 40 per cent of company's operating costs. The Transport Manager. . . .'

And so on through all those items that really matter to the company. Naturally these targets must be pitched at a realistic level and this could only be done after discussion with those most concerned and most knowledgeable in each field – i.e. the managers, technologists and experts who will be responsible for achieving these targets.

Stage C (7)
USE OF MANAGEMENT TECHNIQUES

By using management techniques of the sort described in Appendix 2 the company may be able to improve its profits substantially. The corporate planner should search through the forecast report and the studies made above to identify areas where these techniques could be used. It must be clearly understood that each of these techniques is designed to tackle a specific type of problem. Identify the problem and the appropriate technique can be chosen. Again, however, as in all cases quoted above, only those problems that really matter to the company should be considered. If capital expenditure represents a small part of the company's activities then those techniques relating to capital expenditure (d.c.f. for example) can be given a low priority. A report on similar lines to the examples below should be made out:

'The Company's diverse interests, each administered by a Subsidiary, may lend itself to analysis by Portfolio Selection techniques. (Effect on profit not known.)'

or

'The Company's complex network of distribution may lend itself to analysis by Linear Programming methods using a large computer. (This could reduce cost of distribution by several per cent – perhaps improving profits by $96,000 per annum).'

or

'The Company's assembly shop lends itself to a Method Study approach followed by a soundly based incentive scheme (together these could cut labour costs by up to 25 per cent or $960,000 per annum).'

or

'If it is proposed to introduce a new product in 1970 as has been suggested, the use of Critical Path Methods could be useful. (This could obviate a delay in launching of several weeks – perhaps improving profits by $125,000.)

This study of the applicability of management techniques ends Stage C of Step 4. In it the corporate planner has been asking himself and his colleagues, 'what weapons have we got and which could we most effectively use to improve our profits in the same area as that in which our business is now carried on. Can the gaps be closed by these means?' He may already have formed a very good idea of the answer to this question for merely by inspecting his study notes he can see how many measures he has been able to list and what effect on profits each might have. He may for example have the following:

	1968	1969	1970	1971
Stage C				
(1) Capital.				
Could contribute $000	24	96	168	240
(2) Overcome obstacles				
Could contribute $000	12	24	48	48
(3) Exploit opportunities				
Could contribute $000	0	0	72	24
(4) Use strengths				
Could contribute $000	24	24	24	24
(5) Overcome weakness				
Could contribute $000	0	0	12	12
(6) Profit improvement plan				
Could contribute $000	0	24	36	48
(7) Management techniques				
Could contribute $000	0	12	36	48
TOTAL POSSIBLE $000	60	180	396	444

If the profit gaps for this company were rather less than these total figures the corporate planner might be tempted to think that his problems were over. They may not be for two reasons: firstly, there is a danger of double counting – perhaps some of the obstacles can only be overcome by the expenditure of capital, in which case the effect on profit will not be the effect of overcoming the obstacle *plus* the effect of the capital spent in overcoming it, but the effect of overcoming it alone. In a similar way if part of a profit improvement plan calls for the use of a management technique then the effect on profits will not be that of the plan plus that of the technique but only that of the plan.

The second reason why the corporate planner should go through *all* these six steps, even though he may think the gap can be closed by action in the area he has just considered, is that there may be even better ways of doing it.

Before turning to consider the possibilities of profit in New Business Areas a few practical suggestions concerning attitude of the mind that is appropriate in this Step of the corporate planning process might be made here. Firstly, obstacles to profit take little finding – they usually stand out for all to see. Opportunities, on the other hand, have to be sought out diligently. It is helpful if the corporate planner has this firmly in mind throughout these studies.

Secondly, it is helpful if he thinks less of the product that the company produces and more of the function that the product performs. Thus a company making electric light bulbs can usefully be thought of as a company not so much concerned with bulbs as with illumination. Not so much 'ships' as 'transport.' Not so much 'movies' as 'entertainment.' Indeed he can go further still and think not of ships or even of transport but of 'transport systems'. In this way he is less likely to attempt to make forecasts, diagnose problems, propose actions that are narrowly relevant only to ships. He is more likely to appreciate the problems of a shipping company if he sees it in the context of 'transport' or even of 'transport systems' (a complex of types of transport including loading and unloading facilities all considered together as a transport system). Within this wider framework he is more likely to see new opportunities, new products and services, new markets that are relevant to the company's strengths.

Thirdly, he should never ignore the possible responses to his company's actions of other competitors, customers, the government and all the other factors listed in the Interaction Chart. Nothing his company does is done in a vacuum; everything it does will affect someone in its environment and they may react to it. This must not be forgotten.

Fourthly, it is becoming increasingly true that it is possible to achieve almost any technical feat. One has only to specify what is to be done for a science or a technology to produce a way of doing it. The importance of research is becoming even greater for every company. Science has overtaken science fiction, or, if not quite, then sufficiently nearly for one to be very, very sceptical of any scientist or technologist who says 'it can't be done'. He may mean by this that it would be expensive to do it, or it would take time, or there are difficulties in the way; these are things to be evaluated in any project. But to say that something can't be done is, these days, an invitation to someone to do it.

In all his studies, a wide view, a tendency to believe that obstacles are there to be overcome, that opportunities are there to be sought out and that almost anything is possible, is, within the bounds of realism, a useful attitude to take.

Stage D
NEW BUSINESS AREAS

Many companies, peering into their futures, cast envious eyes at the greener grass over the hedge. The grass may only look greener from a distance and before leaping over it is worth having a closer look. It is worth doing this systematically by testing each of the seven categories of possible means against each of the possible new business areas. These, it will be remembered, were as follows:

(a) Integrate forwards
(b) Integrate backwards
(c) Diversify: new products in existing markets
(d) Diversify: new products in new markets
(e) Diversify: existing products in new markets

(Note: 'products' means services as well as goods.)

Stage D (1)
CAPITAL EXPENDITURE IN NEW BUSINESS AREAS

The question to be asked here is whether it seems likely that the profit gaps are any more likely to be closed by capital expenditure in any of these five business areas than in the existing one. If the company's usual rate of return on projects in 20 per cent, is it likely to do better than this by investing in a project to introduce a new product in a new market, for example? The corporate planner can attempt to find out what return companies operating in these areas expect but it is the return on capital for *new* projects that is of interest, not Return on Capital Employed, which although freely published by many companies, is a very misleading yardstick as has been pointed out. Unless the company has some reliable information on the return to be expected from capital spent on new projects in some of the new business areas in which it might be interested this study – Stage D (1) – is likely to be rather barren.

Stage D (2)
OBSTACLES IN THE NEW BUSINESS AREAS

Here more facts will be available. A company making furniture, for example, must be aware of the obstacles likely to be met by its timber suppliers and by its retailers so it can fairly readily list what these would be if it decided to integrate backwards into timber or forwards into retail respectively. Again it must have some knowledge of the obstacles in the way if it decided to sell ironmongery (i.e. new products) through its present wholesalers (i.e. in existing markets) or though French wholesalers (new markets). And it must have some idea of the obstacles in the way of selling furniture through retailers in Greece (existing products in new markets).

These obstacles should be studied in the same way as those for the existing business in Stage C (2): that is to say the obstacles should be described, the reason behind them noted, possible action to overcome them listed and a selection of actions made. This should be done for each of the new business areas that look even remotely promising or relevant. Nor must one neglect the possibility of a manufacturer selling a service or a service industry selling goods: a car manufacturer might well consider selling insurance and a laundry might consider selling second-hand clothes.

Stage D (3)
EXPLOITING OPPORTUNITIES IN NEW BUSINESS AREAS

Remarks similar to those made above can be made here. The company will have some idea of the opportunities available to companies in the new business area. It will know, for example, how many companies there are already who can supply it with a particular component and what their future outlook might be. It will know also a great deal about the opportunities that may lie ahead for its customers if it is thinking of integrating forwards. The more closely associated with its existing business is the intended field of diversification the more the company will know about it.

Perhaps this is an appropriate moment to remark upon the greater popularity of diversification in the U.S.A. than in England. Many of the American books on management contain large sections on this subject. It should be noted however that this trend is prompted by a feature of the American economy that is not yet so evident here, namely the Anti-trust legislation. As soon as a company obtains a significant share of one market it begins to worry that the ever-watchful Administration will interest themselves in their affairs. Hence the need to diversify. A similar trend, much less powerful as yet, can be seen here but not yet in the rest of Europe. Broadly speaking it is true that one should not diversify if one can achieve one's profit targets in one's existing area since diversification inevitably carries a risk born of one's lack of knowledge in a strange business area.

It is also an appropriate moment to reiterate the importance of Market Research techniques in evaluating opportunities in both the existing and the new business areas.

Stage D (4) and (5)
USE OF STRENGTHS IN NEW BUSINESS AREAS
WEAKNESSES RELEVANT TO NEW BUSINESS AREAS

Perhaps these are the most important studies in Stage D. In searching for suitable new areas of business the company must have in the forefront of its mind what its own strengths and weaknesses are. If it is strong in the technology of stainless steel it would probably not be appropriate to launch a new product made of wood. If it is strong in retail marketing then it may not matter what new product is added to the range, it might have a good chance of succeeding with it in existing markets. In general success in diversification is less likely if the new business is not closely related to either the existing technology or the existing customers.

In this study therefore the corporate planner will test each strength and each weakness to determine whether it might represent a significant advantage or a serious hindrance in each possible new area of business.

Stage D (6) and (7)
PROFIT IMPROVEMENT PLAN AND MANAGEMENT TECHNIQUES

Little scope exists for a detailed examination of the value of these two possible means of increasing profits in a new business area. This is because the company may have insufficient knowledge of these areas. Nevertheless it is sometimes possible to identify obvious inefficiencies in an industry and if it did decide to enter this new area it might, for example, use some particular management technique in which it was highly skilled, thus gaining some advantage over the companies already operating in this area who were not using it.

Finally the corporate planner must consider under what circumstances the company would go into liquidation.

Stage E
VOLUNTARY LIQUIDATION

If a company's future is so bleak that there is little chance of achieving a profit that is sufficient to give the shareholders a satisfactory return, then it should go into liquidation. Many companies go on struggling against impossible odds to remain in business under the impression that their objective is to survive. Meanwhile the shareholders receive no dividend and the value of their holding ebbs away. At Stage E the company should decide whether it agrees to go into liquidation if, in spite of every possible means that could be used to close the profit gaps, it manifestly will fail to do so. If it does agree this in principle then the level of profit below which this will be done must be decided. One would expect it to be set at the level at which shareholders would not be satisfied – in the case of Hypothetics this was 8 per cent d.c.f. equivalent to 5 per cent per annum growth in profits.

So important is Stage F in which the Policy statements are drawn up that it warrants a chapter of its own.

Summary of Chapter XI
Having decided what profit gaps the company should aim to close and having decided what constraints apply, the company needs to know what strategy will succeed in closing the gaps.

There are seven categories into which nearly all possible action to earn profits can be divided: invest capital, overcome obstacles, exploit opportunities, use of strengths, overcoming weaknesses, profit improvement plans and the use of management techniques. At this stage the corporate planner should work systematically through each of these to determine what chance there is of closing the profit gaps by applying these, first in the area of business in which the company is currently engaged and then in those areas of business which the company might realistically expect to enter.

At this stage, which in effect is a study of the feasibility of closing the gaps, the corporate planner eliminates those means which do not appear to be of significant value or which are contrary to the constraints. He notes those that may be useful but does not yet complete the process of choosing any particular course of action. This is left to Stage F of Step 4.

CHAPTER XII

STEP 4 DRAW UP THE POLICY STATEMENTS

What happens in Stage F – Combined Actions – the Policy Statements – some comments on the Policy Statements.

THE corporate planner has already prepared two of the three sections of the Company's Policy Statements that will describe completely what sort of company it proposes to be and the strategy by which this will be achieved. These first two were, of course, The Profit Target and The Constraints. Now a statement is required showing The Means.

Up to Stage F, the corporate planner has been noting those means by which the company could reasonably expect to close the profit gaps each year. There may be as many as two hundred perfectly practical and effective actions in this list, but a final selection has to be made because it would be beyond the resources of the company to take them all, and of course, some of them might be more effective than others. More important, perhaps, is the fact that if several were combined into one single action, the effectiveness of this combined action might be greater than the sum of the separate actions on their own.

It is at this stage, then, that the company must decide between expanding its scale of operations in the current area moderately, greatly or not at all, between integrating forwards or backwards or diversifying or merging or introducing a new product or breaking into a new market. It must decide how it is going to do these things. And it must decide whether it can do them so effectively as to close the gaps.

What happens in Stage F
The corporate planner now needs to stand well back from the company at this stage and review the notes he made in Stages C and D when he was examining possible actions in the existing

and new business areas. Having analysed every corner of the company and its environment for many years past and future, he now has to synthesize the parts into a coherent whole. The jigsaw puzzle is scattered on the floor; which pieces fit together? Which are from some other puzzle? Are there any pieces missing?

As he goes through his notes he will certainly see some items that form naturally interlocking groups, others that are contradictory, some that stand on their own and fit with no other items. Consider a few imaginary notes taken from a corporate planner's studies in Stages C and D. Take Company N where, amongst other things, he noted these possible actions:

'Increase our share of the Market' and
'Call in consultants to improve our weak Marketing Department'

Now these were two of the actions selected as a result of a prolonged study of the obstacles, strengths, weaknesses and so on. Do these two actions fit neatly together or do they clash? Surely they clash? There is little hope of improving one's share of the trade if the marketing department is one of the company's weak spots. So if the corporate planner was hoping that 'increase our share of the market' was one way of overcoming an obstacle he will now have to reject it in the light of this further (and presumably later) conclusion – at least until the consultants have done their work.

Take another example. A corporate planner's notes on P may contain, amongst others, the following possible actions:

'Increase our share of the market' and
'Further use should be made of the excellent marketing department'.

Now, needless to say, these two do fit together and suggest a useful and practical course of action: 'The marketing department should employ their skills to increase our share of the market'.

Take another selection of notes – from Company Q:

'The contraction in the demand for our products can almost certainly not be halted' and
'One possible action is to integrate backwards into the manu facture of components'.

But surely these do not fit: if demand for the product is falling, one might expect that demand for the components of which it is made is falling as well – not, perhaps, a very promising field to enter!

Or take R's case:

'Introduce Work Study to improve the efficiency of the factory' and 'Labour relations are poor and should be improved by T.W.I.' (T.W.I. is a management technique – see Appendix 2.)

Here again, these two actions are antithetical since the introduction of Work Study can severely exacerbate poor labour relations.

These few examples also incidently illustrate what can happen to a company if each department makes its own plans – the actions of one department can very easily fail to fit in with the action of another. The ideal is that each action that a company takes should not only fit in with all other actions but should reinforce them. Only when the corporate planner has examined *all* possible actions can he be sure that he will be able to select the best combination from them.

Combined Actions

While it is often sufficient to solve problem A by taking action A and to solve problem B by taking action B, great economy in effort and in cost would be achieved if one could take action C to solve both problem A and problem B at the same time – two birds with one stone, as it were. It is hardly possible to believe it, but it has been known for one department of a large company to buy a $200,000 computer for accounting work and another department to buy a $100,000 computer for scientific work. Neither knew what the other was doing. Had they known they might have bought a computer for, say, $250,000 and both used it.

In much the same way two departments taking action to solve their problems independently can easily miss an opportunity to kill two birds. If the corporate planner studies all the company's major problems in one period of intense discussion and enquiry he may be able to identify several problems that can be solved by one action rather than by several. In Stages D and E of Step 4 he was only looking for individual actions to solve individual problems: now, in Stage F he is not only making the final selection of individual actions but should also look for these combined actions of the sort that kill two birds with one stone. Consider some examples of possible actions that fit together and reinforce each other is this way taken from an imaginary corporate planner's notes:

For Company S, for example, the corporate planner may have noted these possible actions:

'Increase our share of the market'
'Cut production and declare some employees redundant'
'Strengthen our marketing department'

Now it is just possible that none of these actions are necessary for one might be able to find one action that solves all three problems at one blow, for example:

'Take over a small competitor whose marketing methods are good, close down his plant and use our own spare capacity to make his products'.

This action might (a) increase the share of the market for S, (b) obviate the need to cut production and (c) strengthen their marketing department.

Take a quite different example – T:

'Take on 20 more sales representatives'
'Purchase more delivery trucks'
'Obtain long term loan'
'Tighten up credit control'.

Now it is just possible that all these actions are unnecessary and all the problems which they are designed to solve can be solved by one, quite different, action:

'Maintain level of retail selling, sell more through wholesalers'.

One must not over-emphasize the number of occasions when such combined actions are possible – suffice it to say that the corporate planner would be failing in his duty if he was not always on the lookout for them. Very often no such combined actions can be found and one is back to the 'action A to solve problem A' situation. The pieces of the puzzle do not always fit together – indeed some pieces may stick out like sore thumbs and do not seem to belong to the same puzzle. Perhaps they don't. It is perfectly possible for a company to have acquired a machine, a factory or a section of its business that is no longer appropriate. Divestment is as much a part of management as investment and it makes sense to dispose of an asset that is no longer useful. But it *only* makes sense if the company is better off without it than with it: just because an asset yields but little to the company's profits that is not a good reason for disposing of it – its disposal must yield more than its retention.

The corporate planner, then, is searching in Stage F for a combination of actions which, because they interlock and are consistent, suggest a strategy for the company that will allow it to close the profit gaps. He is searching for a course to steer that will employ the company's strengths to overcome obstacles and exploit opportunities, that will make full use of the capital available, challenge the employees to exercise their skills, draw upon powerful management techniques, allow full scope for a profit improvement plan and yet will not be jeopardized by any of the weaknesses inherent in the company. He is ready to fit together the pieces, complete the synthesis and demonstrate how, by the use of this coherent long term strategy, the company stands a good chance of achieving its objective.

A completed Policy Statement for an imaginary company is given below: before considering it, however, it is necessary to interpolate a few comments concerning the role of this book in the context of this discussion on the Means. This is a book on corporate planning and is particularly intended as a practical guide to a highly systematic version of it. The emphasis is inevitably, therefore, on the *system by which* a corporate planner can handle the facts and figures, problems and ideas relating to his company. The facts and figures given in this book are quoted only for the purpose of illustrating the system, not for the value or validity of the facts and figures themselves – indeed since most of them are imaginary they have little value. The problems and ideas are imaginary and, except by chance, are not likely to have any useful relevance to any particular company. The examples are quoted merely to illustrate the system, to clarify how it can be used in real-life companies, for, although imaginary, the examples given are typical of business situations.

The purpose of the book is to show a company's corporate planner how he could go about his task, not actually to do it for him. This word of warning is necessary here because, in quoting specific examples above – and in the equally imaginary policy statements below – one runs the risk of incurring the criticism, 'I wouldn't have done it that way'. For example, in the problem quoted above of a company with a weak marketing department, the suggestion made was that consultants should be called in to propose improvements. This, it is recognized, was just one possible solution and if a reader felt inclined to solve it by 'sacking the lot and starting again', that is a quite legitimate alternative: these examples are merely intended to illustrate the *system by which* solutions can be found to a company's problems, not to propose ideal solutions to specific problems met within a particular company.

Again, a reader may fail to find any example referring to a particular problem he may have: most of the illustrations quoted have been concerned with manufacturing industry, little has been said about commerce or the service industries. No example has been given of the problems encountered by a Coal Factoring and Shipping Company, nothing has been said about an Insurance Company's need to search for 'new products', no reference has been made to Merchant Banking, or the Gambling industries or a hundred more. It is not difficult to see how the system being described can apply to all types of business (indeed to all types of organization – see Chapter XVII). Just as a manufacturer of machine tools needs to think ahead to identify what tools industry will need in ten years time, so a company selling insurance needs to ask itself what cover the man in the street will need (or can be persuaded to need) in a few years time. A Merchant Bank needs to consider what service its customers will want it to perform for them in a few years time.

The Policy Statements
The examples given then, are intended as illustrations of the system of corporate planning: no other significance should be read into them, they are not intended as ready-made solutions to any particular problem: this is a book on corporate planning, not on management. With these remarks firmly in mind consider now the Policy Statements of an imaginary company; these

Statements show what the company intends to achieve (the Objective), some of the things it is not going to do even if that makes the Objective harder to attain (the Constraints) and some of the things that it *is* going to do (the Means). It is its long term Strategy:

POLICY STATEMENTS FOR HYPOTHETICS LTD.

OBJECTIVE

Our aim is to make sufficient profits to allow our shareholders to receive a 10 per cent d.c.f. return on capital – i.e. 3 per cent net dividend yield and 7 per cent per annum growth.

CONSTRAINTS

We will behave in the same way as the top twenty British companies towards our employees, customers, competitors, suppliers and Government. We do not, however, consider that our duties or our obligations towards our employees extend beyond working hours.

MEANS

Existing Business. Much of the existing business will continue as at present and this is expected to contribute the following profits:

	1968	1969	1970	1971	1972
$000	192	132	132	67	−22

These figures, suggested by Forecast O, leave a gap between the 7 per cent per annum growth target. This the strategy proposed below is intended to close.

Hypon Sales

Sales of Hypon are rising slowly: the size of the market is falling by 2 per cent per annum and this rate of decline will accelerate to approximately 10 per cent per annum by 1972 – by 1980 products similar to Hypon will probably no longer be made in Britain. The share of the market achieved by Hypon has been increasing rapidly due to its unrivalled quality and price: its share is now 30 per cent rising at 6 per cent per annum. Demand will exceed capacity in 1970, but soon after the decline of the market size itself will cause a reduction in demand for Hypon and productive capacity will then increasingly exceed demand.

It is proposed not to increase productive capacity for Hypon, due partly to the anticipated decline in demand after 1970 and partly to the current political attitude to monopolies – for this reason also no attempt will be made to increase the share of the market after full capacity at the existing factory has been achieved. Two actions will be taken: first, demand for products similar to Hypon is rising rapidly in Southern Europe and will continue to do so for many years. It is proposed to enter into agreements with several of the continental competitors who have applied to us for licence to manufacture Hypon. The agreements will involve a joint venture in which Hypothetics provide 50 per cent of the capital and production know-how and our partners provide 50 per cent capital and marketing outlets in Southern Europe. Secondly, it is proposed that as the market in the U.K. falls, agreement will be sought with any U.K. competitors whose plants become uneconomic. These agreements will provide for our surplus capacity to be used to produce Hypon for these competitors at a guaranteed margin to them and sold under their brand names through their outlets.

Studies and discussion with foreign and U.K. competitors suggest that these actions will have the following cumulative effect on profits compared with Forecast O:

		1968	1969	1970	1971	1972
Foreign	$000	—	—	36	84	96
U.K.	$000	—	—	—	24	31

and will require the investment of the following capital:

		1968	1969	1970	1971	1972
Foreign	$000	—	240	252	—	276
U.K.	$000	—	—	—	—	—

Thetix Sales

The market for products similar to Thetix is rising at 5 per cent per annum and will continue to do so for many years. Our share of the market is now steady but will fall unless a new and improved product is introduced at once. Demand will exceed productive capacity in 1969. The factory will be extended immediately and minor improvements made to the product.

A product known as New Thetix will be introduced as soon as possible but it is estimated that it will take four years to complete the market research, the research and development, site preparation and factory construction. Thereafter new types of Thetix will probably have to be introduced every five or six years.

Studies suggest that the cumulative effect on profits compared with Forecast O will be :

		1968	1969	1970	1971	1972
Thetix	$000	—	48	84	120	144
New Thetix	$000	—	—	—	—	72

and capital investment :

		1968	1969	1970	1971	1972
Thetix	$000	120	—	—	—	—
New Thetix	$000	—	—	—	288	—

Note: The following sections indicate the part to be played by each department in the strategies proposed above and show what further measures to improve profits will be taken.

Marketing and Sales Department

By 1970 sales of Hypon may have reached the limits of productive capacity but sales of Thetix may start to decline in spite of the minor improvements made. When this happens the selling effort should be redirected to (a) selling Hypon to competitors and (b) maintaining sales of Thetix.

Efforts should be made, through our Trade Association and that of our customers, to increase the overall market size for products similar to Hypon and Thetix.

Finance Department

Retained profits will be insufficient to meet the expected demand for capital. Loans of approximately $120,000 will be required each year.

The Department will investigate in greater detail what the conditions in Southern Europe are as to capital expenditure, tax, return to U.K. of dividends, etc., and the effects of Britain joining The Common Market on these.

The interest on loans taken up (See Statistical Section) will be (cumulative):

	1968	1969	1970	1971	1972
$000	2.4	16.8	26.4	38.4	48

Production Department
As the Hypon factory will probably cease production by 1980 a substantial reduction in maintenance costs can be made now. In both factories very large savings can be made by a gradual improvement each year in fuel efficiency, transport costs, waste, labour productivity and stock levels by using Work Study, automation, production scheduling, quality control and stock control methods. The cumulative effect on profits compared with Forecast O will be:

	1968	*1969*	*1970*	*1971*	*1972*
$000	31	60	84	108	132

and capital required, mainly for automation:

$000	0	12	12	24	24

Research Department
Several senior scientists will be required to advise on the technical aspects of the Southern European projects and to research any modifications needed to Hypon or the Hypon process to adapt it to conditions there. Research into Thetix will cease at once and all resources directed towards New Thetix. A small team is required to start fundamental studies on the required properties of a Thetix product for the late 1970's.

Buying Departments
Studies and enquiries suggest that substantial reductions in the prices of materials and components can be made by entering into longer term (three or four years) contracts with suppliers. In view of the errors in forecasting demand no contract should involve more than 70 per cent of expected requirements; even so, the savings anticipated are:

	1968	*1969*	*1970*	*1971*	*1972*
$000	4.8	9.6	12	12	12

Staff
A serious weakness of the company is its age structure: a management succession plan should be drawn up to take account of this and the expected changes in the company's business over the next few years. Immediately, the fourteen men over sixty-five should be retired (this is quite in accord with the Constraints) and approximately six men a year will have to

be recruited from 1970 onwards. The cumulative effect on profits of this compared with Forecast O is:

$000	1968	1969	1970	1971	1972
	33.6	33.6	14.4	−2.4	−19.2

Welfare

To meet the Policy of the company new welfare facilities are required at both factories: however no improvement involving capital expenditure will be made at the Hypon factory. At the Thetix factory welfare facilities will be built on to the factory extensions in 1968 and 1972.
Capital required:

$000	1968	1969	1970	1971	1972
	48	—	—	—	72

Offices

Small savings in labour can be made by forming a typing pool based on dictation machines, semi-automatic accounting machines and O and M. The company is too small to warrant the use of its own computer, but further savings could be made by the use of a bureau machine. No new offices will be required for many years.

Organization

Many changes in staff will be required in the next four or five years. Project Managers (not all of whom need be full time on their Project) will be required to supervise, coordinate and report to the Board on:

Hypon development in Southern Europe.
Extension to Thetix factory.
Development and launch of New Thetix.
Profit Improvement plans at Hypon and Thetix factories and in the office.
Sale of Hypon to U.K. competitors.
Organization, Manpower and Staff Changes.

Voluntary Liquidation

The Company will go into voluntary liquidation if and when it becomes clear that no means can be found to provide a return to shareholders of more than 8 per cent d.c.f.

Summary

The Capital required to carry out these plans does not exceed that available from cash flow, grants and loans:

$000	1968	1969	1970	1971	1972
Capital Available (including loans up to 50 per cent of Asset Value)	216	240	264	312	360
Capital Required:					
Hypon – S. Europe	0	240	252	0	276
Thetix Extension	120	0	0	0	0
New Thetix	0	0	0	288	0
Automation, etc.	0	12	12	24	24
Welfare	48	0	0	0	72
TOTAL REQUIRED	168	252	264	312	372

Total cumulative effect on profits will be:

$000	1968	1969	1970	1971	1972
Existing business (Forecast 'O')	192	132	132	67.2	−21.6
Hypon –Europe	—	—	36	84	96
Hypon –U.K.	—	—	—	24	31.2
Thetix	—	48	84	120	144
New Thetix	—	—	—	—	72
Loan Interest	−2.4	−16.8	−26.4	−38.4	−48
Production	31.2	60	84	108	132
Buying	4.8	9.6	12	12	12
Staff	33.6	33.6	14.4	−2.4	−19.2
TOTAL (Forecast 1/67)	259.2	266.4	336	374.4	398.4
Profit Target	268.8	288	309.6	331.2	352.8
Remaining Gaps	−9.6	−21.6	+26.4	+43.2	+5.6

Conclusion

The differences between the target and the profits that the above strategy is expected to yield is not great. However, reference to the Statistical Section[1] indicates that there is a 1 in 10 chance of Forecast O being an over – or under – estimate of the profits to be expected from the existing business. The errors may be:

		1968	1969	1970	1971	1972
$000	±	24	28.8	36	48	60

[1] The Policy Statements would be backed up by a statistical section showing how each major conclusion had been calculated. They would also, of course, indicate what the errors in each forecast were likely to be.

If these proved to be under-estimates then the gaps calculated above may be as much as:

$000	1968	1969	1970	1971	1972
	−33.6	−50.4	−9.6	−4.8	−14.4

The company can tolerate a 1 in 10 chance of missing its targets by up to $12,000 to $14,400 in any of these years but not by as much as $33,600 in 1968 or $50,400 in 1969. (It can tolerate a 1 in 10 chance of achieving only a 5 per cent growth in profits – i.e. in 1968 and 1969 a profit as low as $264,000 and $278,400 respectively.) Accordingly the company will take the exceptional step of postponing maintenance work at both factories until later years. $28,800 will be cut from the 1968 maintenance budget and $40,800 from 1969.

Some Comments on Policy Statements

One interesting feature of the example given above is that special short-term measures had to be taken by Hypothetics to close the gaps in the early years. This is hardly surprising since many of the means by which a company can improve its profits are slow to take effect. It takes time for a ship to alter course. This phenomenon underlines the need for long-term planning, for if it takes two or three years to build a factory then the first sod must be cut two or three years before the output from the factory is needed. It takes a year or two to derive any substantial benefits from introducing Work Study or installing a computer or launching a new product or modifying the design of a product or taking on new staff. The number of actions that can be taken to show an immediate improvement in profits is small – nowadays one cannot use that most effective (but callous) axe – the dismissal of employees with one week's notice. Indeed it must be apparent to most executives today that a company cannot wriggle out of severe short-term dips in their profits and the only hope lies in not allowing severe dips to occur. Furthermore it is an equally obvious corollary that this year's profits may depend far more on the decisions the company took a year or so ago than on any action they can take during the year.

A second interesting feature, related to this one, is that Hypothetics took some care to phase their capital expenditure as evenly as possible over the years. This was done for two reasons: firstly so as not to put too great a strain on the company's resources of manpower (research, development, design, engineering, etc.) as well as not to strain their liquid cash (working capital, etc.) or their capital and loan mechanisms. If it can be arranged to achieve an even growth such as this so much the better – sometimes, of course, it cannot. But an even more important reason for aiming at a steady growth is to provide a steady rise in profit so as to avoid the dips, mentioned above, as far as possible. Once a dip in profits occurs it is hard to continue on the chosen course since the cash flow in that year was intended for re-investment in the following year. If it does not materialize all subsequent profit targets are jeopardized. Indeed one very good reason for introducing a measure of diversification into a company's business is to stabilize a fluctuating profit record. A company whose profits depend largely on having fine weather in August might be well advised to branch out into a product or market that either depends less on this or, better still, that depends on it raining in August! Similarly one that depends on there not being a revolution in South America should search for a source of profit depending on having a revolution there. This desirability of an even growth is particularly important for a highly geared company – i.e. with a large volume of fixed interest loan compared to equity capital.

Notice, incidentally that Hypothetics took several 'combined actions'. One of them killed a good many birds with one stone. This was the idea of the joint venture in Southern Europe with continental competitors and it solved the following problems:

(1) The impending need to build an extension to the Hypon factory to meet U.K. demand.

(2) The longer-term problem of a falling-off in demand for Hypon in the U.K.

(3) Their worries that their high share of the U.K. market might attract the attention of the Monopolies Commission.

(4) Their realization that profits are going to be more difficult to make in the U.K.

At the same time this action took advantage of:

(5) Their enviable reputation in Hypon technology.

(6) The continuing demand for Hypon in Southern Europe.

It is most important that a Policy Statement is not put to a Board containing ideas and suggestions that have not been thoroughly checked for practicability. In the imaginary Statements above, for example, the idea of joint ventures in Europe should have been thoroughly investigated and discussed with several foreign competitors whose reactions were favourable – indeed one must assume that at least one of them had indicated an immediate interest since the first of these ventures was due to start yielding profits in 1970. It would, of course, be grossly irresponsible to put up a strategy based on hope rather than sound study and careful consideration. In the same way one assumes that the corporate planner working for Hypothetics had thoroughly studied the feasibility of erecting an extension to the Thetix factory in 1968 – it seems a very short construction time – and he has presumably obtained this estimate from a competent executive, and, what is more, believes in it himself! One assumes also that he has checked that the company really could afford to give the shareholder a 10 per cent d.c.f. return if the profits rose by 7 per cent per annum: that there were no pitfalls in taxation, dividend cover and so on.

Now it may be asked what would happen if, having completed Stage 4, it becomes apparent that the company does not have the means to achieve its target. The corporate planner will double-check that the target, the forecast and the expected effect of the means are reasonable: this must reveal no obvious error, no undue pessimism; a sense of realism must prevail throughout. Is it quite certain that no means remain to be considered? A merger with a bigger firm, perhaps, or a Government subsidy? Is there really nothing that can be done? If, indeed, there is nothing, then the target may have to be reduced from the level at which it was set, down to the level at which there is a good chance of satisfying the shareholders – *but not below*. It must never be reduced below that level: if even this target cannot be met then the company is duty bound to liquidate while the shareholders' capital is still intact. Survival is not an objective, remember.

On the other hand, if it appears that the target can easily be achieved, then one of two courses is open to the company – assuming, of course, it is confident that no irresponsible optimism exists in the calculations. It can either raise the target, or it can accept the original target and accept the fact that the task of achieving it is likely to be easy. One would certainly be deeply suspicious of a calculation that showed that the task would be easy unless, of course, the company intentionally set itself a target that was not significantly more ambitious than its previous performance. It will be recalled that although Hypothetics set itself a target of 10 per cent d.c.f., knowing that this was significantly better than it had done in the past, it is completely up to each company to decide which race it wishes to enter and where it wants to come in. If it has chosen to race the tortoises although it has the potential to win with the hares, then it can expect an easy life.

The document the corporate planner puts to the Board is an important one, for it is the basis for all the company's actions over the next few years. It is of very great importance that it provides as good a guide to the company's actions as possible. He must have checked and double-checked that the action proposed will not cause some unforseen effect on the company or its environment; this can be done by checking through the Interaction Chart. Thus if it is proposed, for example, to raise the selling price of a product, one can, on checking through the Chart see at once that this will have several effects on the company itself – but what about the effect on certain customers, competitors, the Government, suppliers, importers? Have all these been considered – all too often they are not. What response will Competitor A make? Will any suppliers take the opportunity to put up their prices? Will the Government react? The Interaction Chart will help to remind the corporate planner of these matters, and the effects anticipated must be included in the new forecast. In shaping every plan, in taking every action, the possible effects must be visualized and estimated. (A discussion on sensitivity tests, crawl-out costs and decision theory must be postponed until Chapter XVI, but these are also very appropriate at this stage.)

These Policy Statements represent the end-point of Step 4 in the Corporate Planning process. They are the crux of the process. Everything the corporate planner has done up to this point is done in order to produce them and everything he does from this point on is based upon them. They are the compass-setting for the company. They must be as nearly right as is humanly possible.

Summary of Chapter XII

In Stage F all the corporate planner's analysis, studies, discussions are reviewed, considered, weighed up to produce an overall strategy for the company designed to achieve its profit targets for several years ahead. It requires the utmost care to ensure that the actions proposed are practical and that their effects have been realistically estimated.

(See also Appendix 1.)

CHAPTER XIII

STEP 5   DRAW UP THE PLAN

The distinction between a list and a plan – allocating responsibility – Detailed Specification – Staff Changes.

In Step 4 the corporate planner was concerned mainly with drawing up lists of means by which the company might achieve its target – there was the list of Possible Actions, the Selected Actions and then the final selection from these that were admitted to the Policy Statements. The Policy Statement itself was just another list: now the corporate planner needs to convert this into a plan.

A list differs from a plan. Consider a housewife who, during the week jots down the provisions she requires for the following week. She does this in no particular order but just when each item comes into her mind. The result is a shopping list:

Apples
Sardines
Bananas
Fly-swat

But when she goes shopping she will rearrange these items (mentally if not on paper) according to what aspect she wishes to maximize or minimize. If time is unimportant to her, but cost is, then she may walk right to the other end of the town to get 5 cents off the sardines at Smith's; on the way she calls at Jones' and Brown's:

Apples,   Fly-swat,   Sardines
Bananas,

And if quality is important she might go to Jones' for the apples, but to White's for the bananas:

Apples, Fly-swat, Bananas, Sardines.

And so on. A plan, then, is a list of actions very carefully re-arranged so as to obtain a desired effect. Reverting now to a company's plan one can see that 'build a new factory' is merely one item in a list; 'introduce a new product' is another. These are two examples of actions in a list of actions. In Step 5 the corporate planner does what the housewife had to do – turn the list into a plan. He may also fill in a certain amount of detail: he will almost certainly need to specify for each action who will do what, when and where and why. He need not say how – this is usually the decision of the experts in that field.

Allocating Responsibility

Thus, if the Policy Statement declares that the company will build a new factory, the following details need to be specified:

Who will be in sole charge of the project.
What type and size of factory it will be.
What it will cost.
When it is to be completed.
Where it is to be built.
Why it is to be built – e.g. to yield an extra $500,000 per annum profit.

But he will not say how it is to be done, whether prefabrication methods are to be employed, which contractor to invite to tender, what architect to commission – these are not his concern and require skills and knowledge he does not have.

This Step, then, is quite a short one. It requires only that a specification for action be prepared for each part of the Policy Statements – including the Constraints. If the Policy Statement requires the company to 'treat its employees with respect and consideration' then the corporate planner must see that the company has nominated someone to supervise this, to report to the Board if it is not being observed: a plan must be prepared showing when it is to be done, where, why, what. Again, if the Policy Statement calls for 'a reduction in office costs by 3 per cent per annum' then the corporate planner should ensure that one person has been told that he is solely responsible for achieving this, that he knows why this target has been set, how much capital is available each year should it be necessary, which constraints particularly apply, whether these savings may be sought throughout the offices or whether certain areas are to be excluded.

It is not usually very difficult to add these practical administrative and executive details to any part of a Policy Statement. It may well be difficult for the executive who is given the responsibility to carry out the plan to achieve the results asked of him: this is only to be expected. It is unlikely that a company, having set itself a realistic but challenging profit target, could achieve it by setting its executives anything less than challenging tasks.

It is sometimes stated that corporate planning should consist of a number of types of plan: Financial, Manpower, Product Development, Production Facilities, Research and Development, Marketing, and so on. Up to a point these titles are useful and valid. However, it has been stressed in this book that corporate planning represents an approach to planning the future of a company *as a whole*. It is more in keeping with this philosophy to ignore departmental or inter-subsidiary boundaries when necessary and to prepare overall plans. These, it is true, have often to be split down into specialist sections so that certain parts of the plan can be supervised by departmental staff. Nevertheless many of the imaginary plans discussed so far have been overall ones and can be treated as such, crossing departmental lines even for administrative purposes – the project to launch Hypon in Southern Europe was one for which it would not have made sense to divide responsibility among the departments, it would have been more effective to rely on a single Project Manager for its implementation: his responsibilities would require him to instruct the staff of several different departments and to co-ordinate their efforts in this project. Thus it can sometimes be beneficial to treat some parts of a Strategic Plan as a company, rather than departmental, responsibility. New Production Facilities could well be the responsibility of a Project Manager acting wholly within the Production Department: on the other hand a Manpower Plan – in which the aim is to select and train the right number of employees in the right skills for the company's future needs – is an inter-departmental plan and calls for a Project Manager who is not in any one department (although he could well be someone in the Personnel Department if the company has one).

Detailed Specification

Whichever method is chosen, a clear specification should be drawn up to indicate to the Project Manager precisely what is expected of him. A specification might follow these lines:

PROFIT IMPROVEMENT PLAN

The Policy Statement calls, inter alia, for a reduction in costs of $100,000 per annum by 1970. Of this, $70,000 will be required from improvements in labour productivity especially on assembly work. Mr. Jackson is now solely responsible to the Board for achieving this cost reduction.

He will seek these savings at the Perth and Portsmouth factories only (not at the Plymouth factory). His actions, which must be approved by the respective Works Managers and Unions, may not demand capital expenditure exceeding $10,000 – none of which may be spent in 1968.

He will submit to each April Board a brief report showing (*a*) the savings made to date and (*b*) an outline of the action proposed for the following year showing also what savings are expected from this action. He will report to the Board as soon as he requires their assistance to remove any obstacle to achieving these savings. In the absence of such a request the Board will assume that the target savings will be achieved by the target date.

Specifications of this sort are prepared for each item mentioned in the Policy Statements. Individually they are not difficult to prepare. The difficulty that may exercise the corporate planner's ingenuity is the dovetailing of all these specifications: in practice there could be as many as one hundred individual projects large or small to coordinate. In the case of Hypothetics, for example, the Policy Statements visualized seven major projects:

Hypon in Southern Europe.
Extension to Thetix factory.
New Thetix.
Profit Improvement at two factories.
Profit Improvement in the office.
Sales of Hypon to U.K. competitors.
Organization and staff changes.

But there were also several others as well, for example the note that new types of Thetix would have to be launched at approximately five year intervals, long term buying contracts, dismissal of fourteen employees, co-operation with the Trade Association and so on. Furthermore, some of the seven major projects could conveniently be broken down into separate sections – the extension to the Thetix factory and the New Thetix factory could well be supervised by two different project managers. The dovetailing of these individual projects into a coherent and consistent whole is essential; fortunately it is not too difficult to do since these individual projects all spring from a common source: they are parts of an overall strategy. They are pieces of a puzzle that is known to be complete and whole. It would be quite a different matter if each of these projects were proposed by individual departments and then had to be welded into a coherent and consistent whole. By taking the planning from the top downwards, instead of from the bottom upwards, the task of ensuring cohesion and consistency of action is greatly simplified: indeed, it is almost automatic.

Even so the corporate planner does have to take some care that the breakdown of the puzzle does not go too far – and becomes a too-complex jangle of too-small fragments – or not far enough. If it is not broken down far enough it will consist of too few parts each of which may be unmanageably large for a project manager. Again, care must be taken to phase each part of the plan so as not to overload or under-utilize a part of the company's resources. If it takes two years to produce each product with the existing team of scientists the research department cannot be expected to prepare six new products by 1969.

Staff Changes

As the nature of the company's business changes so its organization structure will change and so also will the skills required of its staff. It is important to plan these changes in staff rather than merely let them happen. Once the company has decided to launch a project in Southern Europe, for example, it should at once ensure that some of the senior men who are going to be concerned with the project learn Italian and Spanish – or whatever. At the same time it should consider in what way the organization structure should be changed – not merely being content to tack on a new Division to the existing structure, but to look afresh at the entire company structure to ensure that this new project did not call for a more radical re-organization from top to bottom. As suggested in the Policy Statement for Hypothetics it would be well worth while nominating one very senior man to take sole responsibility for ensuring that the company's organization structure changed so as to keep in tune with its changing business. Many companies, while appreciating the need for planning the training, promotion, selection, retirement of their staff, have not appreciated the need to plan changes in their organizational *structure*.

This represents the end of the corporate planning process. The company knows what profits it wants to earn over the next five or ten or twenty years; it knows what would happen if it did nothing; it knows what it is in fact going to do and that there is a very good chance of its chosen actions resulting in it achieving its targets; each senior executive has been told exactly what is expected of him and the Board know that the routine and the exception reports they will receive each month will show them the progress the company is making towards its goal.

It is the end of the Five Step Process, but, of course it is only the beginning. Plans have been prepared that will close the profit gaps for the next few years, but only for the next few. What about the years beyond? And what if, as is bound to happen, some event occurs or some new trend emerges that was not forseen and which casts a shadow over the company's future? And what happens if, in spite of all attempts to ensure that the demands made on each project manager and each executive are realistic, they prove unequal to their tasks?

A start has been made. The company has been set upon its course towards its destination, but the compass-setting will only remain valid for a time before it has to be changed. At least the company knows where it is going and knows that it is properly crewed and equipped which is more than could have been said for it before. At least it knows it can meet any storm that is predicted. But what of the storms not predicted, the breakdown of the engines, uncharted wrecks, human frailty among the crew? In the next Chapter the problem of monitoring progress and revision of the plans are considered.

Summary of Chapter XIII
The last Step in the Corporate Planning Process is to draw up individual plans of action designed to put each part of the overall strategy into effect. This is done by instructing one man to take sole responsibility for one part of the plan, giving him a detailed specification of his task and ensuring that he reports progress on a routine basis and whenever he needs assistance.

(See also Appendix 1.)

CHAPTER XIV

MONITORING, REVISING, TIMING

Corporate planning is a continuing task – the need to monitor progress – when to revise the target, the forecast and the plans – the importance of timing decisions – when sorrows come.

No doubt the ink is hardly dry on the corporate planner's notes when a new trend emerges or an event occurs that was not forecast at all or which was forecast to occur but not at the time that it did. All three parts of his work can suffer from this instability: the target, the forecast and the plans. The target was based on assumptions concerning inflation, dividend cover, taxation, yield, Stock Exchange valuation, the profit performance of other companies. If any of these turn out to be significantly different to the assumptions made about them, the target (but not the objective) may need revision. But it will need revision if, and only if, the new trends are thought likely to be *permanently* at variance with the assumptions behind the target figure.

Similarly with the forecast. If it has been assumed that Competitor C would not introduce a new product until 1970 but he does so in 1968, then the forecast will need revision: the corporate planner must check through the Interaction Chart to identify what effects this event will have on the company and on its profits and if the effect is likely to be to alter profits by more than 3 or 4 per cent then he may have to revise his plans to close a new profit gap. Or if, quite unexpectedly, the government applies a substantial Purchase Tax to the company's products, or a hitherto loyal customer deserts them, or their factory in Aden is sequestered or labour costs rise more rapidly or any of a thousand other unexpected events occur, then if these are likely to affect profits by 3 or 4 per cent in any year a revision may have to be made.

Similarly with the plan. If the company hoped to cut labour costs by $20,000 a year but if, in the event, this proves to have been too ambitious a task for the Production Manager to carry out, then some revised plan is called for. Or if their intention to take over a competitor is thwarted, or if the Research Department fails to create that new product, or if the new plant has teething troubles beyond those expected, or if any of a thousand things that can go wrong do so, then a revision may be called for if it jeopardizes the targets by 3 or 4 per cent in any year.

So important is it to keep the planning alive once it is started that most of this Chapter is concerned with how this may be done.

Monitoring

Every important assumption underlying the target, every Factor Affecting Profit and all the expected results of every plan must be monitored continuously. Great trouble has been taken to ensure that the forecast profits will be equal to the target figure each year – i.e. great efforts have been made to ensure that the plans are sufficient to close the gaps – and it is clearly right also to make great efforts to ensure that the Actual result also equals the Target. To ensure that the Forecast equals the Target calls for planning: to ensure the Actual equals the Target calls for control. Control can only be exercised if information as to progress towards the Target is available: this is the meaning of 'monitoring', it is the collection and evaluation of information concerning progress towards the targets.

A list of all these variables is already available to the corporate planner from his notes: the assumptions behind the target (inflation, rate of taxation, etc.); the Factors Affecting Profits (share of market, selling price, fixed costs, behaviour of the Government, competitors, changes in technology, etc.); the expected effect of the plans (profit expected from Management Techniques, new products, extensions to factories, etc.). Against each of these he will record the actual figure as it becomes known. If he expected sales volume to rise to 10,800 units in 1967, then when the actual figure is known he should record it. If it is 9,500, then, if this has affected profits by 3 or 4 per cent he should report this to his Board, together with an explanation of why the out-turn is lower than expected and what action is necessary to counteract its effect on profits. It will be appreciated that the later the information is available – i.e. the greater the time-lag between an event occurring and the knowledge of its occurrence – the less likely it is that corrective action can be taken.

Thus the corporate planner must ensure that he knows, and perhaps also that the Board knows, about these events as soon as and as often as necessary to maintain control. If one of these parameters is subject to frequent variations, any one of which might affect profits by 20 per cent, then clearly it is vital that a close and continuous watch must be kept upon it. If, on the other hand, a parameter is subject to only slow shifts, which are unlikely ever to affect profits by more than a few per cent., then a far less sensitive and sophisticated system of communication is called for. Indeed it would be quite wrong to report these latter changes as frequently as the former.

It is therefore very much part of the corporate planner's job to set up the necessary reporting and communication system such that he, and when necessary the Board, are informed of those changes that they need to know about but not of those that they do not. A company's costing system,[1] the reports from their sales force in the field, the project manager's reports to the Board, their press-cutting system, and other existing or new systems of communication must be designed and redesigned to this end. The company knows what they are aiming to do and how they hope to do it: they must also know if they are actually doing it or look like doing it: and they must know if something is going wrong in time to take action to put it right. After careful study, much consultation and discussion the corporate planner proposed a strategy designed to achieve a worthwhile objective. It was approved by the Board. The executives accepted the challenge. How absurd it would be, if after all this, the company failed to achieve its targets simply because it did not realise in time that it was failing.

Revision

Assuming an adequate monitoring system has been set up so that a careful and continuous watch is kept upon all the most

---

[1] Costing systems usually suffer from two defects in most companies today: (1) they are excessively concerned with historical data, (2) they do not report such non-cost items as the number of customer complaints, for example.

important factors that make up the company's profit, the next problem is to decide when and whether to make a revision to the target, the forecast or a plan.

The target should need revision only very seldom. It makes but little difference to the level of profits to be aimed at even over a period of several years if the target is altered by 1 per cent: there is therefore little point in making this alteration even if it is felt that the target has become inappropriate by that amount. Only if it is thought that the target no longer reflects the intentions of the company by a significant margin need the target be altered. A target of $240,000 profits in five years time is very little different to one of $247,200: indeed no company could expect to control its profits to within such a margin of accuracy. On the other hand a target of $264,000 in five years time may be sufficiently different to one of $240,000 to warrant that it should be officially recognized and recorded as a change.

Much the same is true of the forecast. If the company expected a profit of $240,000 in three years time, but an event occurs that might make this $232,800 then there may be no need to alter the figures or report the alteration to the Board. If the expected change is much greater than this then perhaps there is a need.

And so also with the plans. If these are yielding less than expected by a significant amount, then part of a plan should be revised.

In each of these three cases the gaps will alter. The gaps showed the difference between the Target and the Forecast: it will be recalled that, in the case of Hypothetics, for example, Forecast 1/67 showed that profits were expected to be approximately equal to the Target for each year. But if either their Target *or* the Forecast *or* the expected effect of their plans are changed then the gaps will also change. If these new gaps exceed 3 or 4 per cent of the profit target then, it is suggested, the plans themselves should be reviewed and revised so as to close them up again. Thus the plans will need revision if either the Target or the Forecast or the effect of the plans, or any combination of these, changes so as to open a gap in any year of 3 or 4 per cent. In this way the company maintains close control over its progress towards the targets.

Revisions of the forecast will take place frequently, and of the target less frequently. To guard against confusion in making

these changes, they must be done systematically. It is suggested
that each revision is given a reference number. Thus the first
target adopted by the Board in 1967 could be numbered
Target 1/67 – in the unlikely event of a revision in that year
the revised target would be numbered 2/67. The first forecast
was numbered 'O', and it will be recalled that this was the forecast of profits assuming the company did nothing new and
entered into no new commitments – hence the significance of
the 'O'. But, having laid its plans to yield extra profits, a new
forecast was then made. This was Forecast 1/67, submitted to
the Board in the Statistical Section attached to the Policy
Statements. Now, whenever the figures in this Forecast are
revised, either because of an unexpected trend or event or
because the plans are not yielding the expected profit, then the
corporate planner will notify the Board of the change and
quote a new reference number. Perhaps such a report might
appear as follows:

FORECAST 2/67

In Forecast 1/67 it was expected that unit selling prices would
be:

	1968	1969	1970	1971	1972	1973
$	2.88	2.88	3.00	3.07	2.95	3.26

but recently Competitor B has taken over Competitor C and
because of B's known policy as the industry's price leader it is
now expected that prices will move as follows:

	1968	1969	1970	1971	1972	1973
$	2.88	3.12	3.36	3.48	3.53	3.60

It is proposed to follow Competitor B's prices and, if this has
the approval of the Board, profits will be improved as a result
by 3 per cent per annum to:

	1968	1969	1970	1971	1972	1973
$000	295	310	326	343	360	379

These figures will be known as Forecast 2/67.

A similar report will be made if the plans appear not to be
yielding as expected, although in this case notification of the
fact might come to the Board from a Project Manager rather
than from the corporate planner and it would only be necessary

for him to note briefly what the new reference number was and to draw attention to the new profit forecast and if necessary recommend action.

Revisions of the target and the forecasts are simple – merely a matter of reporting and recording systematically. Revisions to plans are more difficult. If the gaps are expected to become large in any year then new plans to close them have to be proposed. These new plans should be prepared in the same way as the original ones – by studying the opportunities, obstacles, strengths, weaknesses, by intensifying or extending the Profit Improvement Plan, the use of management techniques, in the existing business area or in a new area. Since the need to revise a plan is often caused by an unexpected event, the inspiration for a suitable new plan may come from a study of this event. Thus if a supplier unexpectedly increases the price of his components by such an amount that the company's profits are affected by 3 or 4 per cent, then this event itself might provoke the thought that vertical integration backwards into the manufacture of this component might now be an appropriate plan.

A revision to the existing plans, when required, should be submitted to the Board, perhaps as follows:

'Forecast 3/67 indicated profit gaps as follows:

	1968	1969	1970	1971	1972
$000	9.6	0	9.6	−9.6	16.8

Since then it has become apparent that American competition in Bolawi has intensified against us and since this is tied to their programme of aid for underdeveloped countries, it will not be practical to take action to counter it and the profit gaps could increase to:

	1968	1969	1970	1971	1972
$000	12	7.2	16.8	4.8	23.6

Action to eliminate these gaps is required. It is proposed to cease exporting to Bolawi from 1968 and instead transfer our agents to Urana where the potential for export is evidently rather greater than previously estimated. It is expected that at least 5,000 more units can be sold there at £40 each and the profit gaps would become: (Forecast 4/67)

	1968	1969	1970	1971	1972
$000	12	2.4	9.6	−4.8	19.2

Approval is sought for this change.'

Assuming approval is obtained, it would be necessary to revise the specification of the plan given earlier to the manager in charge of exports and ensure that he and everyone concerned knew that he was solely responsible for carrying out the change.

It has been emphasized several times that corporate planning is a continuing activity. To take Steps 1 to 5 for the first time is a long and difficult task, but to reach the end of Step 5, the detailed specification of the plans, is not the end of the task by any means. It is only the beginning. There follows three continuous cycles of revision: the targets may have to be revised every few years; the forecast almost continuously as new trends and events appear that are thought likely to affect profits by 3 or 4 per cent; the plans whenever they appear likely to have been miscalculated so that the actual results might differ from those previously expected so as to affect profits by 3 or 4 per cent. Whenever the profit gap for any year alters by 3 or 4 per cent of the target, a revision of the plans is called for, whether the gap alters because the target alters, or the forecast is changed or a plan goes astray or a combination of any of these.

The revision process is not represented by the diagram:

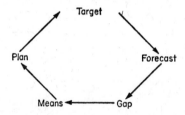

It is not that sort of cycle at all. Each part of the planning process is revised at different times, for different reasons and as a result of different stimuli. In summary:

Revise the Target when assumptions as to tax, cover, yield, etc., appear to be permanently and significantly invalidated by new trends or events.

Revise the Forecast when new trends or events are considered to be likely to alter the profit forecast by 3 or 4 per cent.

Revise the Plans when it is realised that, contrary to expectations, the existing plans will fail to close the gaps by 3 or 4 per cent. or when, for whatever reason or combination of reasons, the gaps alter by 3 or 4 per cent of the target profit for any year.

Timing

One important duty the corporate planner has to perform is to ensure that the volume and timing of reports to the Board are conveniently phased. The point has already been made that reports should only be made when the matter to be reported seems likely to affect profits by 3 or 4 per cent – this level of significance is not chosen arbitrarily, it is chosen because to lower this level of significance could result in an indigestible flood of reports, while to raise it may result in the Board being left in ignorance of trends and events that may seriously affect the company's future. This prescreening is important, therefore.

But of equal importance is the need to ensure that decisions to take action are appropriately timed. It will readily be appreciated that to take action too late might be disastrous for the company. To give the order to build a factory in September of 1967 when it is required to be in operation that year is obviously a situation to be avoided. One reason that decisions are taken too late is that the calculation, discussion, examination necessary to determine what action to take is often a protracted exercise. A decision, after all, is the act of choosing between alternative actions and in order to make this choice it is desirable to consider the effect of many possible actions on the future of the company. The time it takes to make this evaluation is often underestimated and the corporate planner has a useful part to play in initiating the study of a possible project sufficiently early to ensure that it is done thoroughly.

On the other hand, just as it is important not to take a decision too late, it is important not to take it too early. It is important for two reasons. The first is obvious; if action is taken too early the company's resources can be committed unnecessarily soon and this is wasteful. Secondly, and less obviously, decisions are based on their expected effects: to determine these effects a forecast has to be made. But the greater the time-span of a forecast the more likely it is to be inaccurate. Thus the longer one can delay a final decision, the longer one can postpone an irrevocable act, the more likely it is that later and therefore more reliable information will be available. *When* to take a decision is often as important as *what* is decided.

A useful and very simple means of ordering the timing of decisions is the Decision Diary. Imagine a company whose existing plans are expected to close the gaps in 1968, 1969 and 1970, but in 1971 a small gap is expected and a much greater one in 1972. How can the company decide when to start taking action to close these and, equally important, how can they decide when to start considering what this action should be? It is necessary to determine the 'lead time' for the proposed action or study. The 'lead time' is simply the time it takes for the action to have the desired effect or the time it takes to make the study. If it has been decided that the best way to close the gap in 1971 is to build a new factory, then, if it takes a year to build it, the order to the contractor must go out in 1970. If it takes a further year to design the factory then this must start in 1969. If it has not been decided yet what to do about closing the 1971 gap, and if it might take a year to decide this, then, bearing in mind that one means may be to build a factory which takes two years, the process of deciding what to do must begin in 1968.

In the case quoted above one might place a reference number against the 1971 gap as follows:

	1968	1969	1970	1971	1972
Gap $	0	0	0	12,000	28,800

4/68

This reference number, 4/68, refers to the month and year in which action must be taken to get this project under way so that the factory is ready when it is needed. At the same time as the corporate planner makes this entry he also makes a note in an ordinary five-year diary under April 1968 to remind him that action is required to initiate this project or its study. And when April 1968 comes, he will notify the Board that this study is about to begin and will thereafter keep them informed as to its progress. Whenever a change in the profit target or the forecast causes a new gap to emerge in any year, however, he may have to revise this decision diary.

Although all this is very simple there is one important principle involved. It is that this recognizes that there are many occasions when one does not yet *need* to decide what action one is going to take. There may be no need to know, in 1967, what action is going to be taken to close a gap in 1975: one may not need to know, in 1967, what sort of factory one is going to build in 1970 nor what size nor its location. Too much planning is nearly as bad as too little.

The decision diary should contain notes concerning decisions required in all the areas of a company. If, for example, it had been decided, in adopting the Policy Statement, to maintain the company's share of the market at 30 per cent, and if it is forecast that it may fall below this after 1972, then a note might well be made in the diary for 1970 reminding the company that it should consider what action should be taken to counteract this trend. Again, if the Policy Statements call for maintaining the company's lead in product quality, then, if no plans exist to upgrade the product quality after 1970, a note might be made in the diary for 1968 to initiate the necessary research. Or a reminder in 1969 to start the process of raising a $24 million Debenture for 1971. Or a reminder that a lease, a contract, a patent or a licence expires in 1975 or the replacement of a retiring director in 1980. And so on – including the Constraints, of course: if the Policy Statements called for the gradual transfer of wage-earners to staff status, then a note might appear in the diary for 1970 to remind the company to consider whether new measures are needed to accelerate progress. In this way the company will ensure that its policies are being put into action systematically, and that sufficient time is allowed for careful consideration to be given to each project before a final decision has to be made. Panic, last-minute guesses can be avoided in this way, but care has to be taken not to allow any final decision to be made or commitment entered into until the last possible moment. For the earlier a final decision is made the more likely it is that there may be large errors in the forecast data on which it is based. As far as possible commitments should be postponed to allow the latest information to be included in the decision-making process; only when a further delay is unlikely to reveal better data or when it is likely to jeopardize the essential completion date of the project should the final decision be made and the company's resources committed.

A note in the Decision Diary should also be made to remind the company to carry out a 'post-mortem' examination of each major project after, say, five years of operation. Much can be learnt from these. But they can only be carried out if the company's accountants have been able to set up a costing system designed to monitor the results and this is best done when the project itself is approved – indeed they should perhaps certify that they are satisfied that sufficient information is likely to be available to enable them to do this for each project.

One other note should be made in the Decision Diary. In Step 2 certain factors that might affect profits by more than 3 or 4 per cent were considered to be so unlikely to occur that no cognizance was taken of them in the subsequent steps. These were classified as 'Less likely trends and events'. However, some of these possible trends or events could, if they did occur, cause a crisis – they could affect profits disastrously. It is always extremely difficult to know whether to take some action – actions cost money – to insure against the effects of a very improbable event. The weighing up of the cost of the action, which is known with fair accuracy probably, with the effect of the event if it did occur is never easy. No doubt some 'contingency' plans will be necessary, i.e. plans, however embryonic, designed to be put into action if one of these improbable but momentous events occurred.

It is recommended that any such plans be prepared after the main strategy has been approved. In this way the contingency plans are more likely to be made so as to dovetail – or at least not run counter to – the strategy. So that these are not lost sight of it might be sensible to make a note in the Diary that outline plans are needed to meet these contingencies and these can be discussed when there is a lull in the corporate planner's activities.

When Sorrows Come

'When sorrows come they come not single spies but in battalions.' However careful the planning and energetic the execution, something is certain to go wrong. Sometimes there is the time (and the resources) available to put it right, but by no means always. One single event might occur, against which the company has taken no precautions or for which there is no precaution it can take, that cuts its profits by 10 per cent or 20 per cent or 100 per cent. Or, much more probably, it is not one momentous event but a series of minor troubles, which taken together cut its profits by such amounts. The whole of its future growth is jeopardized because the cash flow available for reinvestment just does not materialize. Naturally one tries not to commit money that is not yet safely in the bank (another good reason for postponing action until as late as possible) but it is not always possible to avoid this.

When this uncontrollable drop in profits occurs one has but two courses of action; either to cut back the intended rate of growth for the time being, hoping to catch up later, or to borrow the amount needed to maintain the target. This latter course is preferable in most situations but it assumes that the company has some remaining capacity for debt: it could certainly be good practice to ensure that it had.

One might think that if such setbacks can occur to a company even though it has embraced corporate planning, then it does not say much for the efficiency of corporate planning. There is no denying that corporate planning cannot possibly insure a company against all setbacks: nothing can. The point of this approach is that by looking forward into the future one can foresee *some* of the rocks and sunken wrecks that lie ahead. One cannot see them all and even if one could no company has the resources to defend itself against them all. The choice is between sailing the ship with no look-out, no navigator, and having a look-out posted even though he may not see everything and having a navigator even though he cannot avoid every rock nor always steer into favourable currents.

This vulnerability to unforeseen setbacks must not be underestimated: the number and variety of events, large and small, that can strike a company in the course of a single year is astonishing. Equally astonishing is the proportion of these that depress profits compared with those that enhance them. In one year there can be an economic depression, a *coup d'état* in one's main export market, a rail strike, one's new plant can be months behind schedule, one's suppliers raise their prices by 20 per cent, import duties removed, bank rate soars, Managing Director dies. . . . It would indeed be a wise and farsighted corporate planner who could set up a system by which the company could steer a course through the sea of troubles that a business is sometimes heir to.

Summary of Chapter XIV

The corporate planner's task is by no means over even when the strategic plans have been approved. An efficient communication system must be designed to enable a close watch to be kept on all the really important trends and events so that action can be taken in time. If any new trend emerges or an unexpected event occurs such that a new profit gap equal to more than 3 or 4 per cent of the profit target appears, then a revision to the forecast or the existing plans may be required.

A simple system, such as the Decision Diary, helps the corporate planner to ensure that decisions are made neither too early nor too late and that sufficient time is allowed for careful study of each decision before it is made. It enables him to plan his planning.

(See also Appendix 1.)

CHAPTER XV

HOW FAR AHEAD SHOULD ONE FORECAST?

Why plans and forecasts are needed – the next immediate action – sensitivity tests and crawl-out costs – when not to forecast – how far ahead – Long Range and Short – the purpose of planning.

It will have been noticed that the examples of the forecasts and plans for the imaginary companies with which this book is illustrated are shown for periods varying from three to twenty years. So far no attempt has been made to indicate the logic that should lie behind the decision as to how far ahead a forecast or a plan should be made – indeed in the examples so far given, the choice of the period shown has been determined mainly by the number of figures that can conveniently be shown on a page! This difficult question must now be tackled: it is difficult because to answer it correctly takes one deep into the very nature of planning.

Why Plans and Forecasts are needed
Consider first the distinction between a plan of action and an action itself. A plan is a list of actions that one intends to take and which one arranges in the best way to achieve a given objective. The important word in this context is 'intends': a plan is a declaration of intent only, nothing is actually altered by it, no one signs a contract, speaks into a telephone, presses a button. Nothing is done by anyone to commit the company to anything. An action is quite different. Here someone does sign something, does pull a lever, does alter the company or its environment in one way or another. Many actions, once taken, cannot be reversed, they leave their imprint on the world forever; others have an effect that can be reversed by some

counteraction taken later. An action, then, affects the future. All actions affect the future, some for a short period of it only, others for all time. Indeed the whole purpose of any action *is* to alter the future to bring about some circumstance that might not otherwise have occurred and which is thought to be beneficial to the company in some way. Now, in order to alter the future to one's greater advantage one must know enough about it firstly to know that it *requires* an alteration and secondly to know whether one's action will have the desired effect.

A forecast, then, is made to identify whether action is needed to alter the future, and if so, when such action should be taken, what it should be, how it should be taken and by whom in order to change the future of the company or its environment to improve the company's chances of achieving its targets. A forecast is necessary to determine which actions are to be taken now, immediately, today and which can be postponed until later. Today's actions to commit the company and tomorrow's actions that do not yet commit it are determined by the forecast, because the timing depends upon when the action is required to take effect and its 'lead time'.

In normal parlance the word 'forecast' refers to the attempt to predict trends and events outside one's control: action by the government, competitors, suppliers, the emergence of new technologies, social trends, and so on. But to forecast these things only does not represent a complete description of the future as one sees it: there is one element missing, namely those trends and events over which the company *has* a measure of control. The future course of these depends mainly on the company's own actions – so one needs a forecast of one's own actions as well as a forecast of other people's. A forecast of one's own actions is a plan: a plan is a forecast of one's own actions. The forecast and the plan together form as complete a picture of the company's future as it is possible to achieve.

The next immediate action

The next point to be made in this discussion is that there is no merit in knowing now what action the company intends taking later except insofar as the later action may affect the action to be taken now. The point being made is very elementary and yet so often neglected. It is this: A forecast and a plan are made, not to illuminate future decisions, but to illuminate *today's* decisions. It is one of those popular misconceptions that planning is done merely to decide what actions one proposes to take in the distant future. The whole purpose of planning is thus missed. One has to decide now what actions to take in the future because, *and only because*, these may affect an action to be taken today.

If it is true that plans and forecasts are made to illuminate today's decision then the question 'how far ahead to forecast and to plan?' can be answered. One should forecast and plan as far ahead as is necessary to take today's decision. If the decision involves the commitment of the company's resources for four months (or forty years), then the forecast and the plan should be for four months (or forty years) – or so one would have thought. In fact there are three reasons why this answer is too naïve. The first is that there may be an event *beyond* the period of the commitment which could cast its shadow forward into the period. Thus, before signing a five-year contract for materials with a supplier a company might try to forecast prices for five years ahead: it would ask 'What events in the next five years might affect the price?' But it is possible that, had they looked into the sixth year, they could have foreseen that an event could take place of such importance that it would affect prices in the fifth or fourth or even third year of the contract. One such event might be the exploitation of a new source of the material and another might be an action by the company itself (such as to integrate backwards or to cease using this material). Thus the forecasts and the plans need to be made *beyond* the period of the commitment.

The second reason is that the period of commitment may not be accurately known. A decision to shut down a factory in a year's time may later have to be reversed thus extending the period in which the company's resources are committed. The third reason is that a company is a complex entity and a decision to alter one part of it may affect every other part: a decision to commit the resources of the sales department for six months might inevitably commit some of the resources of the production department for a year. For these three reasons it is not possible to lay down a simple rule such as 'If your next immediate action commits some of the company's resources for two years then forecast two years ahead.'

Sensitivity Tests and Crawl-out Costs

In fact simple rules of this sort are probably founded upon a misconception as to the nature of decisions. A decision is the act of choosing between alternative courses any of which might have the desired effect but one of them, it is assumed, is more likely to achieve it than the others. In the context of this discussion a decision means the choice between alternative ways of attaining the profit targets of the company, and the best approach to such a decision is to try to calculate the effect on profits of each possible course of action.[1] This is the same approach as was used in Chapter XI when the corporate planner listed all possible actions and then selected the one which, it was felt, was most likely to succeed. In making this choice one has to bear in mind the likely future course of events in the company and in its environment – in other words one needs a forecast and a plan. Given both of these it is then possible to imagine the effect on the company's profits of any action taken today and hence to choose the best action. In making these appraisals it is not only necessary to evaluate each action against a set of assumptions about the future but also to test the effect of one or more of these assumptions being wrong: it must never be forgotten that forecasts are nearly always wrong and, since a plan is a forecast, that may be wrong too. Just as a wrong forecast can invalidate an action so a changed plan can too.

Thus a series of sensitivity tests should be made for each possible action: action A may be better than B so long as event E really does take place in 1971 as predicted – but what if it did not? Might action B then be preferable? And suppose action C depends crucially upon event F occurring, but, as so often happens, one simply cannot say if F will occur or not? And suppose event G would wreck the beneficial effects of action D, what would be the cost of crawling out ('the crawl-out[2] costs') if G does occur? These questions demand an answer, but one must know a good deal about the future before one can answer them. All too often one cannot answer them and each decision of this sort becomes a leap in the dark: but this is part of the fabric of business, risk-taking is part of an executive's

[1] Using the contribution method, of course.
[2] The Author apologizes for this lapse into jargon – but this particular example is so eminently expressive!

job. All that one can do is to take one's decisions today in the light of the best information about the future that is available today.

When not to forecast

It must be added that some decisions do not require a knowledge of the future except in a very trivial sense and others require no knowledge at all. Any action that has an effect that can easily be reversed needs no forecast as a background – to take on an office boy who requires only one week's notice of dismissal is a commitment to the company which may last for weeks or months or years – but this is irrelevant since what really matters is that this commitment can be ended in a matter of days. Virtually no forecasting and no planning are needed. Similarly, but for quite different reasons, some decisions require no forecast because the action would be taken come what may. Constraints are of this type; a company may decide to treat its employees with consideration regardless of what the future may bring, regardless of how other companies treat their staff, or how the staff treat the company, or whether profits rise or fall.

It costs money to obtain information of any sort and it is a waste of that money if the information is filed away rather than put to use. It is a waste of money to obtain information about the future that does not improve the quality of one's next immediate action. One need not therefore attempt to forecast events that do not have a bearing on one's next immediate action – this simple rule is so often broken by planners who feel it necessary to try to dot every i and cross every t whenever they make a forecast or a plan. There are many things about the future that one simply does not need to know and one should forecast and plan for as far into the future and in as much detail as the information so obtained has a significant bearing on one's next immediate action.

In Appendix 3 an attempt has been made to illustrate by a concrete example some of the points made in this chapter so far. The example is a mathematical one showing how a hypothetical company decided what size of factory to build on the basis of a sales forecast and the steps through which it went to arrive at its decision were basically as follows:

1. The Sales Director made a forecast of sales volume which suggested that new production capacity was needed in two years

time. (This illustrates the point that a forecast can act as a warning that something in the company or its environment needs to be changed.)

2. Since it will take two years to get the factory operating satisfactorily action is needed now. It cannot be postponed. (Here the forecast also indicates *when* action has to be taken.)

3. The company now has to decide what size the factory should be. They calculate the probable effect on profits of several different factory sizes. (This illustrates the meaning of the word 'decision' as 'choosing between alternatives'.)

4. One particular size turns out to be the most promising one, but it is not the size that common sense might have suggested from the Sales Director's forecasts because the calculations take account of the likely errors in his forecast. (Forecasts are nearly always wrong – a point never to be ignored in planning and decision-making.)

5. Before taking action on this result they decide to test it against the possibility of the forecast being even more inaccurate than it is believed to be. (This illustrates the need for sensitivity tests. In this example in Appendix 3 it was found that the indicated size for the factory was highly sensitive to errors in the sales forecast. It was even possible to calculate, in this example, what the effect on profits might be if it was possible to obtain more accurate information.)

6. Finally, one wonders what the result of the calculation might have been if the forecast was made for a greater or lesser timespan. (The point illustrated here is that one only needs information that really does affect a decision to be made today: unless the decision is sensitive to data referring to twenty or thirty years ahead then there is no merit in forecasting that far ahead. On the other hand, of course, it could be worth spending a great deal of time, effort and money to obtain a better forecast if the decision *is* sensitive to this extra data.)

The work involved in making calculations of the sort illustrated in Appendix 3 is considerable and could not be justified for every minute decision that a company has to make. It could certainly be justified for some of the more important ones, however, and one would go further and recommend that the calculations in this Appendix should be considered the minimum required for major decisions because the sensitivity tests were applied to only one of the factors involved – sales volume – and ignored the errors in such forecasts as for selling price, construction costs, and so on. These should also be tested. Risk-analysis calculations involving two or more variables can nowadays be done using a computer. By this means the 'risk profile' for a very large number of complex alternative decisions can be calculated. However, the emphasis of this chapter is intended to be on the basic principles that underlie the need for a forecast and for a plan, rather than on the need to make certain calculations. Even if these calculations are not made the principles can be applied to all decisions of any sort.

All decisions should be made on these lines even if it is not possible to make any calculations at all. Thus: if a sales forecast suggests that the company will need to buy 1,000 units of Component A next year, how many should they buy – 1,000? Not often will this answer be right. The chances are that the sales forecast is wrong – they may not know how wrong, and so cannot make any calculations but it is still possible to use this Decision Theory approach. For if the penalty for buying too many of these components is likely to be greater than buying too few that is all they need to know: they would buy less than 1,000 in that case. How much less they would have to judge by experience. What is important is that they should ask themselves the question 'If sales are higher than forecast and we have to go out and buy more of Component A towards the end of the year, will this be more or less costly than buying more now?' To answer this they need to judge (or better, of course, to calculate) the probable change in price, the cost of holding Component A in stock, the cost of running out of stock, etc., etc. Clear thinking is needed but not to make this type of decision-theory approach is tantamount to failing to do the job properly. This is the key to decision-taking whether in planning or in the executive field of action.

How far ahead?

The basic points being made are that one needs a forecast to decide whether any action has to be taken and if so whether it need be taken now, immediately. One then needs to know as much about the future as necessary to enable one to choose the best action to take, and the future consists essentially of trends and events that are beyond one's control (revealed by forecasting) and those that are within one's control (revealed by planning). Broadly speaking the more one knows about the future the more likely is one to choose correctly, but this is true only insofar as the data obtained has a significant bearing upon one's next immediate action.

General rules cannot be laid down as to how far ahead any company should forecast and plan. If a company has no commitments of more than three months then it probably need not forecast or plan much more than four or five months ahead – but there are bound to be exceptions. If a company has a commitment of ten years then it should forecast and plan for those items that might affect this commitment at least ten years ahead – probably for fifteen. Companies who have to build factories or offices or plant forests may need to know whether the goods or services that they propose to sell will be valid in fifteen or fifty or one hundred years time: if they cannot forecast to such distant horizons, at least they should estimate the risks they are taking in not being able to. At the other end of the scale, companies engaged in one of the fashion industries may never need to look beyond one year for they may long ago have given up trying to forecast what their next line would be: instead they simply organize their business so it can cope with change, that is to say they make as few long term commitments as possible.

Long Range or Short
One popular misconception is that long range planning[1] is somehow different to short range planning: it is different in degree only, not in kind. A policeman on traffic duty may have the same objective as the Road Planning Department of the Council he works for – to improve the flow of traffic through the town. However, the policeman can treat the buildings as fixed parts of his environment and need worry only about the volume of traffic that he can see now and that he can forecast as likely to appear in the next few minutes. Thus he has few variables

---

[1] Long Range Planning is incidentally not synonymous with corporate planning. Corporate planning often calls for long range planning but long range planning is not corporate. The essential difference is that corporate planning is concerned with the analysis and determination of objectives as well as plans. A long range planner is only concerned with a plan – the objective having presumably been set by someone else. Corporate planning is sometimes concerned with the short range as well as long.

and little forecasting – in a word, he has little uncertainty to cope with. The Road Planning Department can consider buildings and roads as variables and they have to rely on a forecast of traffic through the town in several years time – this forecast could be very inaccurate. In other words the Road Planning Department have to make decisions under conditions of greater uncertainty and greater complexity than does the policeman. However, both are subject to the same set of rules, namely that their next immediate decision is determined by a forecast of what might happen if they do not take action immediately and the action they choose to take is conditioned by their forecast of other people's possible actions and a plan of their own possible actions. Both estimates may be inaccurate – other people may not do as they expect them to and they themselves may later change their plans – but the action they take now is taken in the light of the best information available to them at the time when the action can no longer be postponed. There is a difference of degree in the number of variables and the accuracy of the forecast, but no differences in kind. There would be a difference in kind only if one of them need not forecast at all. If the policeman decided to control the traffic only on the information that was *certain* – i.e. to take account only of the cars he could actually see to be in line, and to disregard any that he could only forecast where approaching him – then his activity would be different in kind to the Road Planning Department.

The purpose of planning
This simple analogy brings us to the point of planning. If a policeman controls the traffic only on the basis of what he *knows* is happening rather than on what he *expects* to happen the traffic will flow less smoothly. He will not, for example, have taken action at 4:55 to clear New Road ready for the employees who will be streaming out of Jones & Co. at 5. This is the fundamental difference between planning and not planning; one decides now on a course of action believing that if this is not done now the objective will be less easily attainable: one can only come to such a belief if one has forecast what the future would be like if the action was taken now compared with if it was taken at some other time or in some other way; not to plan implies that action is taken without heed to the

future at all. To the extent that one can forecast the future, planning is more likely to lead to achievement of an objective than not planning. There are occasions when the errors in forecasting are so great, or when so little is known about the future, that planned actions lead to grave failures – failures as great as might have occurred if no heed had been paid to the future at all.

It seems likely, however, that such disasters may be due to a breach of one of the rules of planning which is: never take action to commit resources further ahead than the factors that significantly affect the decision can be forecast unless the crawl-out costs are acceptable. In other words, if one is signing a lease for fifty years and can only see a valid use for the property for twenty years ahead, then one should estimate the cost of negotiating one's way out of the last thirty years of the commitment. If, in spite of this, this course is likely to cost less than any other alternative, then sign, otherwise consider the next best alternative course of action.

The purpose of planning, then, is to enable the decision-maker to make his next choice with the necessary knowledge of the future. To forecast other people's actions is not enough, one must forecast one's own as well. Now there are three ways in which it is possible to learn more of the future – and the more that one knows of the future of the factors affecting a decision, the better that decision may be. One is to forecast more accurately by the use of advanced techniques (exponential smoothing, etc. – see Appendix 2) or by deeper studies or wider enquiries: one of the best ways of improving the accuracy is to postpone the decision as long as possible so it is based on the latest data. A second is to plan more of one's future actions so that, when the time comes to make a decision, many of the future actions that might affect this decision are known in some detail. The third way to better decisions is to take control over more of one's environment. It has been suggested that a forecast is one's expectation of how those trends and events that are *beyond* one's control will behave in the future. Forecasts are nearly always inaccurate. Plans, on the other hand, are actions one intends to take to alter factors that are *within* one's control. Plans are not always adhered to but at least the decision to carry them out or not is also within one's control.

Now, since the quality of a decision depends upon one's knowledge of the future, and since a plan is likely to be a more reliable estimate of the future than is a forecast, it follows that the more the future is within one's control the better will be one's next decision. This is to say nothing new; it is, however, still worth saying. The fact that a forecast of one's own actions is more reliable than a forecast of someone else's actions lies behind the perpetual drive to extend man's domination over Nature; it lies behind the trend towards even larger companies who, because of their size, can control a larger proportion of their environment; it lies behind the urge of all governments to control national economies, social and political movements, and, unfortunately, the liberty of the individual itself. Mercifully, most organizations apply Constraints to the lengths they will go to in attempting to extend control over us.

Summary of Chapter XV

Forecasts and plans are made to illuminate the next immediate action, for the more that is known about the future the more likely is it that the action decided upon will achieve the objective. A forecast is an estimate of the future behaviour of those factors that are beyond one's control. A plan is a forecast of one's own actions. Plans are usually a more reliable estimate of the future than are forecasts. The higher the proportion of the future that can be planned, by bringing it under one's control, the more likely is it that one's next immediate action will be successful in achieving the objective.

A forecast and a plan should be made as far ahead as the next immediate action requires. This action should only be taken after choosing it from among several (perhaps thousands) of other possible actions and this choice (or decision) depends upon an estimate of the power of each action to achieve the target. To make this estimate it is necessary to determine how each action will affect and be affected by the future. It is necessary therefore to forecast or to plan those future trends and events that have a bearing on these actions – it is not necessary to forecast or plan any that do not. For this reason some long range plans and forecasts need not be in great detail.

Forecasts and plans may turn out to have been wrong: this fact is usually crucial to decisions, although there are some decisions that can be made without much forethought (those that do not commit significant resources for a significant period of time) and some that can be made without any heed for the future at all (many moral decisions including some Constraints). Any actions that do commit the company significantly must be taken in the light of their sensitivity to the errors in forecasting and planning. If this cannot be calculated satisfactorily, due to the uncertainty of the future, then the decision should be made in the light of the crawl-out costs.

CHAPTER XVI

ORGANIZING FOR PLANNING

What the corporate planner does – his qualifications – his department – how long will it take? – the effect on existing employees – two warnings.

INEVITABLY when the spotlight is turned on to one actor, the other actors appear to stand in the shadows. The impression may have been given that the corporate planner prepares the plans that shape the company's future single-handed: he sits in an ivory tower while the rest of the senior executives pace up and down outside waiting for his triumphant emergence bearing, in trembling hands, the tablets of stone on which are written the Policy Statements. Nothing is further from the truth. In this chapter it is proposed to consider what the corporate planner does do, the qualifications he needs to do it, how long it takes and, of course, what part the other executives must play if the corporate planning approach is to succeed.

What the Corporate Planner does
A corporate planner need do only two things: firstly get the corporate planning system going and secondly see that it keeps going. He is, after all, a specialist in a particular field, not the Managing Director: he is there to show a company how to do something they are not doing, not to run the company as an executive. In theory he need do nothing but ask questions in a certain order without himself supplying any of the answers – indeed he could not possibly know the answers if they were of a technical nature in a field that was foreign to him.

Consider what the corporate planning process is. In essence it is a *systematic* way of running a company: it is not a new way of making a take-over bid, or a better way of carrying out research – it *is* a way of relating take-over bids or research to the totality of the company's affairs. It is a way of bringing method into the process of making decisions about bids or research, etc. The corporate planner's task is to introduce a decision-making system, not to take the decisions. To illustrate this distinction let us repeat the 5 Steps outlined in earlier chapters – not to review what has already been said, but to note what part the corporate planner plays and what part the other executives play at each step.

In Step 1 he does not tell the company what its objective is, he asks his colleagues what they think it is. He does challenge their answers if he is not satisfied with them, just as any senior employee would do. Nor does he tell them what their profit target should be, although, having studied their past performance and having examined the records for the relevant competitors and industries, looked up averages and indices, discussed it with the Finance Director and financial advisers and experts, he might suggest a suitable target. His colleagues might challenge it, it might be modified, but eventually, when a figure was chosen it would be one agreed by all as being appropriate.

In Step 2, it is true, he would have to do most of the research into the past records of the company himself. However, he would not list the Factors Affecting Profits without extensive discussion with his colleagues to ensure that only those that might affect profits by 3 or 4 per cent were included – and that none were excluded. He would make the Projections himself, mainly to assist him to learn about the company's possible future just as his probing into the records taught him about the past. But he would not make any of the forecasts without prolonged discussion with the executives most knowledgeable in the relevant factors – again, he would feel entitled to challenge any forecast that appeared to conflict with other facts and forecasts: it will be remembered how important it was to cross-check the forecasts thoroughly.

He would take Step 3 himself as far as merely calculating the gap, but, to estimate the errors, he would certainly call upon his colleagues' experience in forecasting in their own fields.

His part in Step 4 would be limited to asking questions and noting the replies: it is not for him to lay down the company's moral code; nor could he possibly know enough about the company's affairs to put forward a full list of possible means. His contribution at this stage would be to elicit these from his colleagues although the framework within which the thinking and discussion would take place would be provided by him – this framework was the six stages of Step 4 and, by examining each of the seven categories of means in a systematic way, it is certain that more ideas would be produced than otherwise.[1] Again, the overall strategy would not be his but the result of much discussion and thought within the top echelons of the company.

In Step 5 his part would be mainly to ensure that detailed plans were being drawn up in accordance with the strategy.

His part in maintaining the system is likely to be extensive. He has to ensure that communications are such that the company's progress towards its targets can be monitored, he will be responsible for warning the company when progress is not satisfactory and for calling for revised plans. He will be responsible, by using the Decision Diary, for warning the Board when new plans are needed and when it is time to start the long deliberations that must precede a major project. He must ensure that everyone who needs to know does know what the company's task is, how it is to be done and what their part in it is.

The job described above is unlike any other in industry today. If it has a parallel at all it is closer to that of the Navigator in a ship or aircraft. When he steps aboard the company the corporate planner's first question to the Captain and the Officers is, 'What is our destination?' As has been stated many times before, the curious fact is that few companies know the answer to this simple, fundamental question and, if he does nothing else, to extract a clear definition of the objective is almost a sufficient justification for the corporate planner in itself. Having obtained a satisfactory answer he then pores over the charts, the weather forecasts, learns the capacity of the ship as to speed, stability in various types of weather, its ballast and so on. This done, he reports to the Captain, 'we will fail to reach our destination on time unless we (a) sail at 12 knots, which is beyond the present power of the engines, (b) take on more fresh vegetables to prevent scurvy and (c) modify the engine-room telegraph system'. It will be noticed that some of these recommendations are beyond the competence of a real Navigating Officer and the analogy has broken down – this was inevitable since the corporate planner

[1] The Brainstorming technique is sometimes useful here – see Appendix 2.

is concerned with every aspect of the company while every other officer in every other organization is concerned with only one aspect of the organization – with the sole exception of the Captain or Managing Director or Chief Executive who alone is responsible for all aspects. And yet the corporate planner is in no sense a Chief Executive or his Deputy or Vice. He is not an executive at all. To return to the analogy, however: the ship, suitably modified, sets out and for a time is seen to be on course. Then, an engine breakdown, or unexpected gale, sickness among the crew, or something of the sort is reported: the navigator considers the implications and reports to the Captain with a suggested change of course – not necessarily his suggestion, but one which all agree is appropriate to the situation.

This analogy is not a good one but it may be the best there is. The increasing trend towards division of labour and specialization has brought with it a disintegration in the management of organizations. Each executive attends to his own department: only one man, the Managing Director, is left to attend to the Company – and he usually has no supporting staff whatever to help him. Only the Managing Director has the task of plotting the future course of the entire company – as opposed to the future of each part of it – and he seldom has the time to do this. The corporate planner's task is not to do this for him but to enable him to do it by pre-digesting all the data, eliminating that which is unimportant or worthless, passing on that which matters and is worthy of action.

The corporate planner is not a new type of Managing Director nor is he a clerk. He lies somewhere in between – perhaps anywhere in between. That is to say, it might be practical for a corporate planner to be effective if he was little more than a clerk; his job could be restricted to reminding the Board that it was time for them to consider x or to submitting calculations to them showing the expected outcome of action y. He would leave it to the Board to take all the actions, ask all the questions, set up the system. Such an arrangement would be possible but to succeed it would require the whole Board to be thoroughly familiar with and committed to corporate planning: it would further require that they should be able, of their own accord, to concentrate on the future rather than the present, and it would also require that they should be thoroughly objective in their outlook, capable of identifying their own strengths and weaknesses. It might be practical but, on the whole, it is suggested that a corporate planner should be introduced at Board level where he can discuss the company's future directly with and on an equal footing to those who are responsible for it.

His qualifications

It is unlikely that a corporate planning system as rigorous as the 5 Step Process could be introduced into a company by anyone with less than a university education. This alone might rule out a corporate planner whose status was that of a clerk or a little above.

Corporate planning is wedded to the use of modern techniques of analysis: mathematical methods of forecasting, analysis of risk, the measurement of error, discounted cash flow, critical path analysis, costing systems, decision theory, computer languages, simulation models and so on. Clearly a knowledge of these is essential but the level of education and intelligence required for their proper understanding and use is high.

However this is not the prime requirement of the corporate planner: these techniques are merely the tools of his trade. What is vital is that he should be endowed with a spirit of enquiry coupled with a scepticism born of practical experience. The last thing any company needs is a corporate planner who is content to sit in his ivory tower doing complex calculations and making his recommendations on the results of these alone. He must have had a sufficiently rough industrial upbringing to know what is possible and what is not; what people can do if they are challenged and what they cannot; how customers react to marketing ploys, how the government reacts to monopolies, what sort of people the shop stewards are, what scientists can and cannot do. A young Operations Research worker[1] would be ideal as a wielder of the tools of corporate planning but quite useless as a corporate planner. Without doubt, a man who has had less than ten years practical experience in the field would not have the healthy scepticism for the results of purely mathematical calculations that is so necessary.

On the other hand a man whose long experience in one specialist field has taught him only what cannot be done is

[1] Or accountant, economist or scientist.

equally unsuitable. There are times when a corporate planner needs to challenge the opinion of specialists who declare that something is impossible. Nor must he be insensitive to the rate of change of the modern world, to the sound of the iron cataract of scientific thought, to the new trends in morality and in society: he must be attuned to the present and to the future – this sense of alignment is not often found in men who have spent twenty years in one specialist field. Furthermore he must be attuned to so many fields of activity in the present and the future. He must know something of economics, politics, science, accounting, company law, personnel and union matters, marketing and promotion, sales techniques, production, social and moral trends. He need not know much about any of these – only a paragon could – but he should have a feeling for them. As stated many times corporate planning concerns the whole company within the whole environment. He must know whether the results of any calculation, a report in a newspaper, an opinion of a colleague, really fits in with all the relevant facts, or whether it should be challenged. 'Plastics won't affect our business.' 'Well, there'll always be daily newspapers won't there?' 'But there is a tariff on it – always will be.' These are the remarks that any of us can overhear or make ourselves: the corporate planner needs to know enough about the world to know whether they should be challenged or not.

Although many of the ideas and suggestions put forward to improve the company's profits will come from the executives themselves, the corporate planner should not merely passively accept or reject these. He should be capable of throwing out his share of creative thought. He should have the imagination to visualize the effect of change as well as to calculate it.

Finally, his colleagues must respect him enough to tell him all they know, to share their ideas, to discuss the future of the company – and hence their own future – with him.

Three qualifications, then, are essential:

(1) He should have a university degree with some knowledge of mathematics, statistics or management techniques.

(2) He should be old enough to know what is practical politics and what is mere fancy: he is unlikely to have learnt this in less than ten years, preferably in more than one department of more than one company in more than one industry. The

minimum age might therefore be as low as thirty. But he should not be so old that he has lost a sense of the times he lives in, nor should he have spent long in one specialist field. The maximum age is more difficult to state since some men have been left behind by the pace of change while only in their forties: one would guess, however that sixty is too old to start as a corporate planner. Perhaps for most people the early fifties is quite late enough.

(3) He should be acceptable to his colleagues. If he is to be on the Board he should be of director material; if just below then of the same calibre as the men at this level in the company. If a company has a man answering this description in its employment then he could well be suitable. If not, or if the Board could do with 'new blood' then he should be brought in – an outsider's views are often fresh and untainted by traditional attitudes.

His Department

For any company employing less than a thousand people the corporate planner needs no permanent staff at all. It would help him to have a temporary assistant seconded to him for a few weeks at a time at various stages – notably when he is examining the company's past records and making the projections in Step 2 and again when considering the possible means in Step 4. In general it is better for him to do as much of the work himself since, as has been stated before, the important thing is for him to understand how the profits are affected by any trend and event rather than to produce figures accurate to several places of decimals. It is the quality of his understanding of the mechanism that is important, and to some extent this depends upon him being able to make all the calculations himself: to that extent, then, he may lose some of the 'feel' if he relies too much on an assistant or a computer to make these for him.

However, in a very large and complex company he may have to have assistance if his work is not to be intolerably delayed. As a rough rule, then: no permanent assistant if the company employs less than say, 1,000 people; a temporary assistant seconded to him part-time if it employs say 1,000 and full time if it employs, say 3,000; more than 3,000 employees suggest a need for a full-time assistant; two or more if it employs more than, say, 5,000. The number of employees is not the best guide to the volume of his work but the true criterion is so complex a mix of the number of products, assets overseas, extent of diversification, need for urgent action, that it is hardly possible to set out a meaningful rule.

It is suggested that he, or his department, should fit into the company's organization in one of two ways shown below: in each case he would report direct to the Managing Director – this is quite essential from the nature of his job: to report to any other executive would be meaningless.

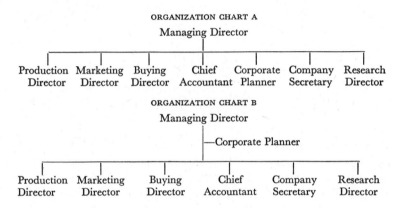

than, say, 5,000. The number of employees is not the best guide to the volume of his work but the true criterion is so complex a mix of the number of products, assets overseas, extent of diversification, need for urgent action, that it is hardly possible to set out a meaningful rule.

ORGANIZATION CHART A
Managing Director

Production Director | Marketing Director | Buying Director | Chief Accountant | Corporate Planner | Company Secretary | Research Director

ORGANIZATION CHART B
Managing Director

—Corporate Planner

Production Director | Marketing Director | Buying Director | Chief Accountant | Company Secretary | Research Director

Of course in neither of these Charts is any significance to be attached to the order in which the various titles appear when read from left to right. The only merit of the layout in Chart B is that the corporate planner's status is not revealed – this may hide the intention that he should be very much senior or very much junior to the other Board-level employees while still reporting to the Managing Director. It would, one might suggest, be better to have his status clearly defined (preferably as an equal to the other directors as in Chart A), but if it is thought desirable to conceal this then it can be done as in Chart B.

How long will it take?
Assuming the corporate planner obtains assistance on the scale suggested above and assuming also he obtained the willing co-operation of his colleagues and that fairly adequate past records are available, the 5 Step process should be completed

within one year. Very approximately the various stages could be completed as follows:

Step 1 Get everyone's agreement that the company's fundamental purpose is to make a profit – one day. Identify the
owners – a few hours. Select a target in terms of d.c.f. to
owners – one week.

Step 2 Examine past records, identify trends and project them –
one month. Identify Factors Affecting Profits – one month.
Prepare the forecasts – one month. Total three months.

Step 3 Calculate the Gap and spell out the task – one week.

Step 4 Examine all possible means – six months. Decide overall
strategy – two months. Determine constraints – one week.
Total eight months.

Step 5 Specify plans – a few weeks.

The timetable suggested above is only a rough guide, of course. Concurrently with the latter stages the corporate planner should begin designing the information system to monitor progress towards the targets and to ensure that the constraints were being observed. One would expect that no improvement in profits would appear for a year or more after the overall strategy had been initiated right at the end of the process. This is true in the main since many of the proposed actions could well be large-scale projects or represent fundamental changes that would take time to bear fruit. However, about half-way through the first year – sometimes earlier – several fairly fundamental facts would have come to light and it might be possible to take action to improve profits then rather than wait until all the details of the overall strategy had been worked out. For example it might become quite clear from the forecasts that Product A made in the Aberdeen works would be a useful line for many years ahead – one would not hesitate therefore to bring in a Work Study man to improve the efficiency of this factory since it is evident that it will not be closed down for years. Suppose on the other hand it was evident that product B made in the Bedford works would be a liability in five years time it might not be sensible to cut back on maintenance at once – at least not until it was certain that the Strategy yet to be devised would not call for the continuance of some form of production at the Bedford factory, or its sale as a going concern, or any other action that might be precluded by poor maintenance.

A trickle of results affecting profits might appear within one year of the corporate planner starting work: there should be a useful flow after two years.

The effect on existing employees

Without doubt the main effect of the introduction of corporate planning is felt by the Board. It will become geared to the future. It will be fed with information that carries a threat or a promise of a change in profit of 3 or 4 per cent or more but will not be required to consider any trend or event that is not likely to have such an effect.[1] It will be informed of the progress of each project to close each year's gap from the time the first discussions take place to the time the gap is actually closed (or not). The importance of each event, each piece of information, each project will be graded according to its potential effect on profits. They will know by heart the several dozen Factors Affecting Profits. They will know which executive is responsible for each project and what help he needs from them. They will know the importance of each decision they make, when it has to be made, what are the major factors affecting its success or failure. They will know, because they decided it, exactly what the company is trying to do, how it is proposed to do it, what is not to be done, and what progress they are making. They will know what to demand of each department and each executive.

As a result each department and each executive will know what is expected of him. The Sales Director will know how much he must sell and what the effect on profits will be if he fails. The Research Director will know that he must prepare this new product by 1970 or that new process by 1969 or find a new use for Product P by 1971. The Works Engineer knows he must keep Machine M in full production for the next four years but can allow Plant P to deteriorate since it will be scrapped in two years time. The Work Study Officer knows he must cut labour costs by 5 per cent per annum for the next twenty years and the Engineer knows that by then the plant must be so automated that it can be run by ten men. Mr. Jones knows that in addition to being Sales Manager for Scotland he is also solely responsible for launching a Subsidiary Company in Eire by 1969. Mr Smith is in sole charge of devising ways of reducing

---

[1] Other than matters referring to legal, moral or personal matters which most Boards would wish to continue to control closely.

the labour relations problems at the Portsmouth factory. Mr Thomson knows he alone is responsible for selecting and training the staff the company will need in 1970–1972.

Each man has his own target – these are each fragments of the company's target but, and this is important, these individual targets are broken down from the company's overall target. Not, as so often is the case, a set of individual targets, arbitrarily set, which when added together form the company's overall performance – done in this way two risks are run: firstly the sum of these targets may be inadequate. Secondly many of the targets may call for a substantial improvement – possibly at the cost of some capital expenditure – in some part of the company that it is later decided should be closed down. It must be more appropriate to set targets from the top downwards rather than from the bottom upwards. In this way a hierarchy of objectives is set for the hierarchy of executives. The objective of a junior manager being one of the means by which his senior expects to achieve his objective.

Thus the Board will delegate to each appropriate executive the authority to deal as he thinks best with any event or trend that is likely to affect profits by less than 3 or 4 per cent – or whatever figure is decided upon. It will be the appointed executive's responsibility to take appropriate action or, if he considers that profits could be affected by more than this figure he should inform the Board. There is little difficulty in identifying such trends and events: in a company earning profits of $2.4 million a year the 3 or 4 per cent deadline is approximately $84,000. For example: a salesman suspects his best customer may go to a competitor – what effect would this have on profits? The answer is readily calculated for if the contribution is $24 per unit and this customer takes 1,000 units a year then the effect is likely to be about $24,000 – no need to alert the Board, although no doubt the Sales Director should be told: and if he learns of several such customer defections and believes they form a pattern – then the 3 or 4 per cent level is reached. In this way a hierarchy of reporting can be built up. The Board to be told if 3 or 4 per cent is involved, Directors if 1 per cent, Section Heads if 0.2 per cent and so on.

The Board will not only delegate routine and continued responsibilities in this way but will also delegate *ad hoc* duties: each project will have a manager, of course, but also each executive is given a target as described above. A Company Target is expressed in terms of profit and as far as possible all other targets should also be in these terms. The lower down the line the less appropriate does this measure become, however, and certainly at shop floor level it should be stated in physical units rather than in money: the boiler operator's target could be given in terms of CO_2 content of the flue gas for example. Care has to be taken, though, that, in an attempt to hit their target the employees do not become careless of all else, a salesman can easily reduce the company's profit by selling in an uneconomic area in order to boost his sales volume, but this particular problem can be overcome by setting the target for salesmen in terms of contribution – i.e. volume multiplied by margin. No doubt it will eventually come to be realized that, ideally, salaries should be related to the effect that each man has (or can have) on the company's profits.

It will have been noted that the corporate planner is concerned with short term plans as well as long term – for any trend or event that either occurs or is thought likely to occur should pass into his system if it affects profits in any year, including the current one, by more than 3 or 4 per cent. For if such an event does occur it may mean the alteration of an existing plan – and since this could affect some future plan it is right that he should know of it and have some say in what is to be done. It might be thought that this is an unnecessary complication to the decision-making process of a company: perhaps it is, but of all the functions that a Board or a Director should perform in a company, the most important is to shoulder responsibility for those decisions that significantly affect the company's profits – a decision that affects profits by as much as 3 per cent of the total annual profit is surely in that category. If this view is challenged then by all means alter the critical level to a higher figure, 5 per cent perhaps, or 7 per cent, or even 10 per cent: or the view might be quite the opposite – that 1 per cent is the appropriate level.

The sequence of events, in which the Board, the corporate planner and the company's executives all play their parts is as follows. A note in the Decision Diary for the current month reminds the corporate planner that it is time to consider a particular circumstance, for example, that there is a gap of $24,000 between the target for 1970 and the latest forecast for

1970. He will advise the Board that it is time to consider how this gap should be closed. At the same time he reminds them of the circumstances surrounding this gap: the sales forecast, the drop in profits due to materials prices, the expiry of a contract, the introduction of a new product planned for that year, and so on. (Note that action may soon have to be taken and before taking action that commits the company's resources, as much as possible should be known about the relevant future, therefore forecasts of other people's actions and plans of one's own are needed.)

If there is no obvious action to take the Board might set up a small committee to propose a suitable means of closing the gap. Together with the corporate planner they examine the seven Categories of Means, just as for the Strategy exercise described in Chapters XI and XII. It soon becomes evident that one action above all others is most likely to overcome the obstacles predicted for that year, or take advantage of an opportunity or whatever. This is put to the Board who may approve it, appoint the Project Manager and state how frequently they wish to be kept informed of progress. (Or, alternatively, because the proposed action will bear fruit within a few months, action is delayed until it *has* to be taken and an entry made in the Decision Diary for that date.)

Whether a committee has to be set up or whether the corporate planner and just one executive can prepare the plan depends upon the circumstances. It may be very obvious that all that needs to be done to close the gap can be done by the Buying Director or the Chief Engineer in which case no committee is needed. Again, there may be no need to appoint a special Project Manager since all the actions that are to be taken can be taken within one department under one executive – he is automatically the Project Manager *ex officio*. It is rare, however, for a project to require action only by one department[1] and almost certainly other executives will be drawn in to play their part: when action is spread fairly equally over several departments a special Project Manager may be needed.

Meanwhile the executives continue to supervise the day-to-day affairs of their departments. They are opportunists in this role, reacting as they think best to their environment, referring

---

[1] Remember that we are discussing *corporate* planning – i.e. planning the company as a whole, not operational planning or departmental planning.

to the Board only when an event or a proposed action might affect profits by 3 or 4 per cent.

At the same time the corporate planner is responsible for ensuring that each department knows if their plans are likely to be affected by the plans of another department. He must ensure that the Personnel Department, which is probably responsible for Manpower Planning, knows how the company will change over the next few years and how, therefore, its manpower needs will change. The Production Department must know about the Product Development Plans. The Finance Department about capital expenditure proposals – and so on.

Two Warnings

One word of warning to those who wish to set up a corporate planning department is necessary. The role of the corporate planner is to see that corporate planning is done, not to do the company's planning for it. He is there to see that a system is installed, that the obvious pitfalls (a forecast without an indication of its errors, for example) are avoided, that the full advantages of treating the company as a corporate whole and looking far enough ahead are reaped. He is not there to run the company nor to do its planning – only to see that it is done. If the corporate planner does start doing the planning he will need more staff; gradually he will take over long range planning, first perhaps the financial planning, then manpower, and so on. With these disastrous results: his department will grow; he will take over those parts of planning that interest him to the neglect of other parts; the other executives will become hostile in an attempt to preserve their jobs which they feel he is threatening; and worst of all it will be difficult to define at what point his 'long range planning' should end and when the project should be handed over to an executive. If the corporate planner has taken over Product Planning, for example, is this limited to new products only? Or to modifications of existing products? Does his planning include research and promotion? – and so on. Severe pitfalls open up once the corporate planner starts doing the planning instead of merely seeing that it is done. Not only is the definition of the boundaries between the plans that he prepares and those that the executive departments prepare difficult to delineate, but his knowledge of the company and its affairs is bound to be less than adequate. There is another reason why he should only help, guide and control the planning. The men who plan should also be the men who are in touch with reality and who are going to have to play an executive part in carrying out the plans – the advantages of this arrangement are obvious. The disadvantages are, as stated before, (1) they cannot usually take an overall company view, (2) they have not the time or the knowledge of planning techniques to do the job thoroughly, (3) they do not know the company's objective and therefore cannot tailor their plans to achieve it. Now it is these three disadvantages that the corporate planner is employed to eliminate. He ensures that they *do* know the company's objective, that a company view *is* taken, that they *do* know how to plan and do find time to do it – if they have not the time or knowledge he is there to assist if necessary.

In order to do these things, in order to supervise the whole process of planning, he should as far as possible stand back from the day-to-day affairs of the company to preserve an objective bird's-eye-view of it. He should not be so far away as not to hear the sound of battle (or not to help in it when necessary) but nor should he be so near as to be unable to see the surrounding countryside as well: he should be able to see the enemy troop-movements.

It is strongly recommended therefore that his task is limited to warning the Board when a plan is required to close a gap, helping them to identify what the most appropriate plan might be, assisting others to draw it up and generally ensuring that the forecasts, the analysis of problems, the use of the seven categories of means, the sensitivity tests, the monitoring system, etc., etc., were of the high standard that the system demands. He may well have to do some of the calculations himself if no one else can do them, and should lose no opportunity to make useful suggestions as to the appropriate use of management techniques, possible ways of overcoming weaknesses, and so on, but as a rule, he should see that the planning is done well, not do it himself.

Another word of warning is necessary. It will be clear that in corporate planning the emphasis is as much on 'corporate' as on 'planning'. That is to say, although it is a planning system its main pillar is in its treatment of a company as a whole rather than as a collection of departments. One would not therefore expect to find a corporate planner in a Subsidiary Company of a Group of companies any more than one would expect to find one in an individual department of a company. A Group of companies who decide to initiate corporate planning would appoint their corporate planner so as to report to the Managing Director of the Main Board, not to one of the subsidiaries. He, and the Main Board, would then decide the target for the Group and, in searching for means of achieving the target, would look upon each subsidiary as a potential vehicle for extra profit just as the Board of a single company looks upon each of its products or services as a potential vehicle. The corporate planner would discuss the future with the Managing Director of each subsidiary just as, in the case of a single company, he would have discussed it with the heads of the departments. And in the same way as in a single company the Main Board of a Group would agree with the Managing Directors of each subsidiary what contribution to profits was expected of him and his company over the following years and broadly how these were to be earned – each Managing Director would thus be, in effect, a project manager. If it is objected that this leads to the centralization of control, one cannot deny it. Where else should the exercise of control lie? Nor need this trend stifle initiative: on the contrary, if the company's executives chose to do so they can set themselves and their junior colleagues a really worth-while, challenging, task.

The trend towards greater centralization of control is likely to continue in all organizations, for corporate planning is not the only force behind this movement. Another is the computer which brings with it the rapid collection, transfer and digestion of the data by which companies can be controlled. Another is such management techniques as Linear Programming with its capacity to show the best actions to take in complex situations and especially in its ability to optimize the costs and revenues from many different departments at once. Many trends are thus blurring the traditional departmental boundaries and the result must be for new organization structures to emerge. Increasingly, also, companies are coming to look upon their products (and Groups are coming to look upon their subsidiaries), as portfolios; the choice of product lines, diversification, bids, mergers are becoming increasingly likened to the selection of a portfolio to achieve a given return or a given stability of returns. All these trends, especially corporate planning, can, given good management, result in a company benefiting from centralization by reason of a greater coherence and cohesion; a drawing together of all parts of the company to give each of them a fuller meaning.

Summary of Chapter XVI

The role of the corporate planner is to introduce and maintain a corporate planning system: his task is to ensure that the company's planning is done in this highly methodical way – it is not to do the planning himself. This continues to be the task of the existing executives.

To carry out this job he should be a university graduate, needs to be skilled in the techniques of planning, experienced in industry, attuned to the future, and acceptable to his colleagues. Ideally he should be appointed as a director since it is with top policy that he will be mainly concerned. He will need an assistant only if the company is large and complex.

Results should start to affect profits within one year to a small extent – but, by the second year these effects should be more extensive. The really important effects on the company will be that the Board know very clearly what the company is trying to do (because they have decided it), what factors are important to the achievement of this task and what part each of the senior executives should be asked to play. Each executive will know what his part is and will know when he must report to the Board and when he need not.

It is important to ensure that the corporate planner is not asked to do the company's planning for it since he will have neither the staff nor the specialist knowledge to do it properly. He should concentrate upon seeing that the planning was done – not do it himself.

CHAPTER XVII

THE ESSENCE OF
CORPORATE PLANNING

Corporate planning can be used in all types of organization –
the essential ingredients of the system – the essential nature
of the corporate planner's job – the essential nature of
corporate planning.

IT is hardly possible to overstate the importance of organizations to mankind – wherever a need arises, however trivial and fanciful, someone will form an organization to meet it. This proclivity seems to be almost universal (one is considered to be somewhat eccentric if one is a member of no organization), we form organizations at the drop of a hat. Business organizations – Companies – are just one particular type, although they nowadays stand out as being perhaps the most successful class of organization since The Church, the Greek City States, the great Armies of Imperialism.

Every organization provides a benefit to someone, i.e. it satisfies a need or a desire. If an organization failed, or was thought to have failed, to provide sufficient benefit to the beneficiaries it would soon cease to exist. Conversely if it was thought to be providing an adequate benefit to a sufficient number of beneficiaries it would continue and perhaps grow. Unfortunately many organizations have not defined for themselves what their objective really is: they have not determined precisely what benefit they are meant to be providing nor who shall be the beneficiaries. Very few have gone one stage further and set themselves a target for the amount of benefit to be provided to the beneficiaries. Unless they know what they are trying to do it is difficult to see how they can *possibly* decide how to do it. What, one might ask, is the true objective of The Church, a prison, a parish council, the Boy Scouts, the United Nations, the Coal Board, the State, a school, a learned society, a family, the Automobile Association? If one did ask, would one receive one precise answer or half a dozen approximations? Certainly in some of these examples one would receive a clear and distinct definition of the benefit and the beneficiaries and possibly even some sort of target figure relating to it. But not with all of them – for them no clear objective, nor, one would expect, was a clear course of action to achieve it possible.

Determining the objective is often difficult because it is essentially a moral question but it must be done if the organization is to be efficient, if its actions and the uses to which it puts it resources are not to be wasteful. Some organizations do not need to be efficient, perhaps, and others are run by people who do not or cannot make them efficient; for these people the most effective way of hiding this inefficiency is to ensure that the objective *is* blurred and ill-defined. Then no one can tell whether the organization is making good progress towards its goal for no one knows what its goal is. This may be the most powerful reason for the pre-eminence of companies among the organizations: it can so readily be seen, merely by referring to the published record of profits, whether the organization is successful or not. Those who run companies know this.

The Essential Ingredients of the Corporate Planning System

This book has been mainly concerned with the detailed methodology of the Five Step Process. Now it is time to stand back from the detail and consider the essential ingredients of the corporate planning approach to the management of companies and other organizations.

Basically corporate planning is concerned with today, not with tomorrow. Basically it is concerned with actions not with plans. It is founded on two propositions: that one cannot decide what action to take unless one knows what one wants to achieve; and that action taken today can best be directed towards the achievement of the objective if one knows as much as possible about the future. In short, Action Today depends on The Objective and The Future.

That any action depends upon what it is intended to achieve must be self-evident. It appears to be universally true and no exceptions exist. It is probably also true that the more precisely an organization knows what its objective is the more precisely can it tailor its actions to achieve it: in other words, the more efficient the action. And yet it seems also to be true that many companies have not determined even approximately what their objective is, many more have not determined precisely what it is. Some have several objectives. Some, who have determined one single objective are aiming at a mirage such as survival or to maximize profits, others are aiming to increase their share of the market or their Return on Capital Employed which, though related to profits, are not closely related. Some are aiming at an objective that is more appropriate to a department than to a whole company. It follows that if 'the more precise the objective the more efficient the action' is true then there must be a great deal of inefficient activity in many companies. Corporate planning recognizes the essential need to determine the objective for organizations. Nothing else is worth doing until this is done properly. It cannot be done properly unless the objective is the one that the company *as a whole* is aiming to achieve.

That action also depends upon the Future also seems to be incontrovertible. An action is taken to change the environment in some way so as to make the objective more attainable. And yet, if one knows nothing about the future how can one know that it requires to be changed? And how can one know what effect one's action will have? Corporate planning recognizes that the more one knows about the future the more likely is one's actions to have the desired effect: great efforts are therefore made in Step 2 to forecast the future as nature and as other people would have it and in Step 4 to forecast the company's own plans to alter it. Both these aspects must be known as accurately as possible if today's actions are to be effective – and the limits to this accuracy is itself a vital factor in deciding between alternative possible actions.

There are, however, two types of action that can be taken without the need to forecast. One is the action that alters the future in such a way that it can be altered back again at no cost and at a moment's notice. Another type is what we have called the Constraints, those actions having a moral basis and, since the basis is a moral one, they can often be taken without regard to the consequences. A forecast of their effects on the environment is therefore not always necessary: Corporate planning recognizes, therefore, that there are occasions when actions can be taken without making a forecast or a plan:

there are occasions when one simply does not need to know about the future.

Corporate planning also recognizes that due to the great length of time that it takes a company's actions to bear fruit and because of the duration of some of its commitments, a longer term forecast and plan must be made than is the usual practice in industry today. The further into the future one attempts to look – whether one is predicting other people's actions or one's own – the more liable to error will one's estimates be. As the range increases therefore the need to subject one's next immediate action to sensitivity tests becomes more crucial: one needs to know how robust or delicate it is to possible errors. One even needs to test it against a total ignorance of the distant future by estimating the crawl-out costs.

These studies of the company-environment system are at times bewildering in their complexity. A thoroughly systematic, methodical, approach is necessary often calling for advanced mathematical techniques,[1] although an understanding of the profit-making mechanisms of the company within its environment is recognized as being more important than the useless pursuit of accuracy.

To put the essence of the corporate planning approach in a nutshell:

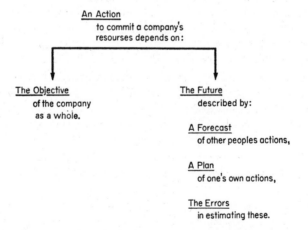

An Action
to commit a company's
resourses depends on:

The Objective
of the company
as a whole.

The Future
described by:

A Forecast
of other peoples actions,

A Plan
of one's own actions,

The Errors
in estimating these.

[1] Some of these have had no mention in this book since they are still in their infancy. They include the concepts of cybernetics, games theory, evolutionary operation, marketing models, portfolio selection, cost benefit analysis, etc., etc.

The Essential Nature of the Corporate Planner's Job

It is strongly recommended that the corporate planner does not do any planning, he should only see that it is done. Of course the company cannot use the corporate planning approach until the system has been created and this is certainly part of the corporate planner's job. In essence corporate planning is a detailed, systematic study of a company's aims and means and the corporate planner's job is to ensure that the company *can* make this study and that it *does*. He cannot do either unless the Managing Director and the Board want him to – indeed they must be fully behind him in all his work.

They must be behind him when he sets up the communication network to monitor the target, the forecast, the plans and the company's progress towards its targets. They must be behind him when he is setting the target, when he is seeking past data, when he is listing the Factors Affecting Profits, when he is collecting creative ideas and imaginative suggestions for improving profits. They must be behind him when he is analysing strengths and weaknesses. He is not a threat to their own position in the firm: corporate planning is not Financial Planning which may be the preserve of the Finance Director, or Product Planning which the Marketing Director may feel is his concern, or Manpower Planning or Research Planning or Production Planning. It is *Company* Planning. It shows how each of these Departmental planning endeavours could best be geared to the achievement of the profit targets.

Executives are so preoccupied with present means that they frequently lose sight of the future and the objective. The corporate planner's job is to redress the balance. He can provide a system by which the objective is kept constantly in mind and the future is constantly reviewed so that the next immediate action is best suited to the company. This action is not chosen by him alone but by the executives whose knowledge of the business is an essential ingredient of any decision.

The Essential Nature of Corporate Planning

Companies, indeed any organization, need three constituents in their make-up. An objective to aim at, the means of achieving this and the executive action necessary to give effect to these means. A company blest with an objective, the means and a vigorous executive will almost certainly be successful. If any of these three are absent it may fail. Even the most powerful executive action will not lead to the objective if the means are lacking. Nor will executive action succeed in achieving the objective if no one knows what it is. Nor can an objective be achieved, even if the means are at hand, if the executive action is lacking in strength. Corporate planning is concerned with two of these fundamental constituents – the objective and the means. It is not concerned with the vigour of the executive. Or, to be more precise, it is concerned with it, but it is not designed to strengthen the energy with which executive action is taken. It is intended and designed to guide the direction that executive action should take. It is intended to point the company in the right direction but whether the company gets there or not depends on the executives. Corporate planning cannot add to the qualities of leadership displayed by the company's senior men. It can give the ship a rudder and can plot the course, it cannot provide a good Captain.

There are many companies with good Captains: some of these have also clearly defined their destination and know how to reach it. *They do not need corporate planning.* They are doing it already, by instinct, without giving it a special name. Many companies who also have good Captains have not decided what sort of company they wish to become, nor how to achieve this, nor whether their company will be able to sit profitably in the environment of the future. They do need corporate planning.

Consider a few of the changes that may take place within the span of most executives' lives and within the span of many companies' normal commitments of resources – say twenty years or so. What changes there will be! The increasing variety of surface transport including hovercraft, jet propulsion, linear motors, monorails; new tunnels and bridges, roads and ports. The advances in medicine: new drugs, new diseases, spare parts, auxiliary parts to boost the natural strength of minds and bodies. Materials of new strength, resistance to temperature, weight, pliability, rigidity, disposibility, longevity and resistance to corrosion. Electronics, with its filaments of wire invading data transmission, automation, miniaturisation. New synthetic foods, desalination of water. New sources of power, mobile and fixed. New methods of construction and new shapes for buildings. Powerful trends in the social mores, in education, in leisure. Political kaleidoscopes in Africa and Asia; the emergence of a more unified Europe. Freer trade across national boundaries, reduction of resale price maintenance. No company can remain unaffected by these changes. But what will be their effects? When will they first be felt? Will this company benefit from them, and will that company fail because of them? What can be done, now, to meet them?

These are momentous questions. A company that sits comfortably in its environment today may not do so tomorrow unless it alters its posture. What its new posture should be can only be determined by a careful and detailed analysis of possible problems leading to creative and imaginative solutions. Of equal moment are the Constraints, those actions that a company will or will not take on moral grounds even if they render the objective difficult to attain – or *even if they make it unattainable.*

Above all is the need for a company to identify its objective – its permanent, unalterable, reason for continuing in existence at all. What it is *really* for? And once having decided this then they also need to know *how much* profit it should aim to make – which race does it want to enter and where does it want to come? Not all companies have to beat the field, some are fully entitled to jog along at their leisure if that will satisfy the owners. Others do have to try to win against all-comers.

Introduced into a company led by dynamic men, corporate planning can add a new dimension. Its emphasis on clarifying the Objective for the company as a whole, the systematic study of its future, the methodical analysis of possible Means and Constraints blended with the entrepreneurial flair and wisdom of its senior executives can result in a combination of great power.

APPENDIX I

OUTLINE OF THE FIVE STEP PROCESS

STEP 1

Determine the Objective
Determine who the owners are
Set the Target

STEP 2

Stage 1   Analyse revenue, volume, costs
Stage 2   The Projections
Stage 3   The Factors Affecting Profit
Stage 4   The Forecasts
Determine errors

STEP 3

Calculate the Gap
Decide the Task

STEP 4

Determine the Constraints
Decide the Means:
Stage A Review the seven possible means
Stage B Review the three possible business areas
Stage C Test the means in the existing business area
Stage D Test the means in new business areas
Stage E Consider liquidation
Stage F Draw up the Policy Statements

STEP 5

Draw up detailed plans

Monitor and Revise continuously

LIST OF MANAGEMENT TECHNIQUES[1]

MANAGEMENT techniques, a few dozen of which are described briefly below, are tools – as with any tool some care and skill is required in their use. And, as with any tool, some are more useful than others. Again, each technique can be used to help solve only one type of problem. What this list of techniques is intended to do is to identify some of the important problems that can occur in each Department of a Company and to indicate which techniques can be used to tackle each problem. For that purpose the list is divided firstly into Departments – Sales, Production, and so on – then into Problems of the type encountered in each Department, and thirdly into the techniques that can be used to tackle each of these problems.

The list is classified in another sense. Those techniques that usually lead to good results compared with the effort required to learn and use them are given a *** rating, those that produce goods results but need rather more effort have ** and those that call for considerable effort only get *. Those that are still being developed are given † and will become even more valuable in the future than they are now if their present rate of development is maintained. The rating system is described in greater detail below.

Four things ought to be said about these techniques:—

1 They are highly specific: one cannot use Linear Programming to improve human relations or T.W.I to create a new idea for a product or Critical Path to improve quality.

2. A problem that is of profound importance to one company may be of only slight significance to another. Therefore no two companies have the same need for any technique or set of

---

[1] This appendix is based on two articles that appeared in *Management Today* in April and August 1966. The author is grateful to his co-author, Crispin Rope, and to the Editor of *Management Today* for permission to re-publish the substance of these articles here.

techniques. Some problems are, however, so general that most companies could profitably use some of these techniques.

3. Some problems are so severe in some companies that it could be sensible to use not only the *** but possibly even the *.

4. Most of these techniques can be used to improve the efficiency of any organization, not only profit-making companies. After all, they are in essence nothing more than thoroughly *systematic and detailed procedures* for studying and improving the way things are done.

The ratings used are as follows:

*** Essential aid to good management. No organization can afford to be without one man trained in its use to ensure that it is used whenever necessary. Most of these are relatively simple to learn.

** Useful technique. Can be used by most companies to advantage but some of them require considerable training for their proper use.

* Some of these require highly specialised knowledge or equipment for their correct use. Probably only a few dozen people in the country fully understand them.

† When these become fully developed their impact on industry will be profound. Some are already used widely and will become increasingly essential to good management in all companies. Some are as yet barely understood by more than a few experts. Progress in these should be carefully watched.

ADMINISTRATIVE DEPARTMENT
How to Decide Overall Company Strategy

*† *Corporate Planning*
This approach to top-level management problems emphasizes (*a*) the need for the company to decide exactly what its objectives are; (*b*) the need for long-range planning in every part of the company to achieve these objectives. Highly systematic versions of this approach are beginning to appear.

Decision Theory
Technique for helping to make decisions under conditions of uncertainty and risk. All decisions are based on a forecast; all forecasts are likely to be wrong. Given the criteria selected

by the decision-maker, Decision Theory points to the best possible course, whether or not forecasts are accurate; for example, how large a plant to build when sales demand is uncertain.

* Decision Trees

Managers are very often faced with not one decision, but a whole network extending into the future. Displaying these as a branching tree diagram in which the probabilities of the outcomes of each decision are shown can help to evaluate the best immediate choice.

* Games Theory

A mathematical theory has been developed for the description and analysis of competitive situations. While not sufficiently developed to deal with most real-life problems, its use can sometimes assist in determining which strategies are best (for example, in bidding for contracts).

* Company Models on Computer

Using such techniques as simulation (q.v.) and mathematical programming (q.v.), it is possible to build a model of the entire operation of a company, from which the complex effects of any decision or alternative decisions can be studied. Building the model is often a huge task, not made any easier by lack of marketing information (for example, the effect on sales volume of a promotion campaign is seldom known).

How to Evaluate Capital Expenditure Proposals

*** Discounted Cash Flow

A method of evaluating capital expenditure projects taking into account taxation, etc., and the fact that the earlier a return is obtained, the more valuable it is – the cash can be reinvested to earn further interest. (More properly known as Internal Rate of Return; see also Net Present Value.)

*** Net Present Value

A rate of return is applied to cash flows in order to determine whether their discounted value is greater than the cost of the investment. This method and Discounted Cash Flow (above) give a more accurate assessment of investment proposals than simpler techniques such as pay-back period and average return. Neither, however, allows for the risk element.

** *Replacement Theory*
This is a body of mathematical and statistical techniques to help decide the optimum life for an item of plant such as a fork-lift truck. It takes account of second-hand values, increasing repair bills and breakdowns as the plant gets older, tax implications, etc.

* *Decision Theory and Decision Trees* (above)

* *Markovitz Portfolio Selection*
Takes into account the risks associated with an investment and the risks associated with any investment related to it; for example, if a project to make umbrellas may be risky, so is one to make sun-shades – but together the risks are lessened. The difficulty is to determine the risks.

How to Improve the Flow of Information Needed to Control an Organization

*** *Costing Systems*
It is important to know whether costs are rising or falling so that someone can take action to control them. Some immensely elaborate and detailed systems exist allowing managers to know what each activity is costing almost as it happens. Very useful to have a 'standard' or 'budget' cost against which the managers can compare actual costs – but only if the 'standard' has been correctly set.

*** *Reporting by Responsibility*
Some costing systems fail because all costs are reported to everyone; managers are swamped by figures. It is sensible to report only those costs that a manager is responsible for and has control over. Same principle applies to all reports calling for action.

*** *Management by Exception*
Another way of preventing a manager being swamped by figures. A report is made to him if, and only if, something

exceptional has happened. Too often he has to wade through figures which all indicate that everything is going according to plan. He really only wants those figures which show that something is going wrong.

** *Organization and Methods*
The study of the best form of organization and the clerical (in the broadest sense) methods to be used in a business. Much wider than 'work study in the office', for it is concerned with such questions as who should receive what information. Also concerned with: office equipment, printing, copying and duplicating, typing services, office layout, etc. By appropriate study of methods and laying down standards of performance (sometimes allied to incentives) for clerical work, it is often possible to make substantial savings.

** *Systems Analysis*
Before putting any information system on to a computer it is essential to find out exactly who wants the information, when it is required, why, and in what form. Only when this has been thoroughly studied can a computer programme be written for the job. Often major economies are made, whether or not the work is in the end computerized.

**† *Computers for Data Processing*
Apart from a saving of clerical staff, a computer can so speed up the calculations associated with costing systems (above) that managers are better able to control their costs.

* *Computers for Information Retrieval*
It is becoming increasingly difficult for managers and especially research workers to find information among the mounting mass of published works. The computer can assist by storing and retrieving such data very rapidly. Before the potential benefits can be obtained much detailed work on indexing and classification must be done.

* *Random Observation*
Rather than record everything a man or a machine does throughout the day, it is possible to build up an adequate picture by making observations at random intervals of time.

Information Theory
The mathematical theory describing the coding and transmission of information. Used in telecommunications, it may eventually have a place in studying communication problems in an organization.

* *Cybernetics*
The science of control, especially of complex equipment, man-machine relations and organizations. It can often give a useful insight into such problems, but is not yet sufficiently developed to give precise answers.

How to Launch a New Project

*** *Critical Path Method*
A technique for planning complex projects. The approach involves:

(a) Breaking down the project into a set of individual jobs.
(b) Arranging these jobs into a logical network according to the sequence in which they must be performed.
(c) Estimating the duration of each job.
(d) Examining the network to find out which jobs determine the time to complete the project (the critical path). These are the ones that really matter and to which the project manager should give much of his attention. Uses include: planning construction projects, marketing a new product, and production planning of batch processes.

* *PERT*
One variant of Critical Path Method. How long each job is going to take is given an optimistic and a pessimistic time as well as an expected time. Statistical methods are used to find the most probable completion time for the project.

* *PERT/Cost*
Costs are also estimated for each task so that the cost of altering the required completion date can be calculated.

* *Branching Network*
Sometimes there will be several ways of completing a project. But until it has progressed to a certain point, it cannot be

decided which way it should be completed. Branching networks can be used in these cases.

* Resource Allocation
The available resources (men, machines, money, etc.) are so allocated to the various tasks in the project as to minimize the time and/or resources required to complete it.

* Use of a Computer
It is sensible to use a computer on all types of Critical Path Methods when there are more than about 100 separate tasks in any project; it is essential to use a computer in Resource Allocation.

MARKETING AND SALES

How to Forecast Demand

*** Exponential Smoothing
Future levels of demand can often be forecast from recent levels. The more recent the data, the more relevant to the future it may be. This technique gives progressively greater weight to the more recent data.

** Moving Averages
This is a simpler calculation to make than Exponential Smoothing. But it may be less accurate, since the same weight is given to recent as to older data.

** Market Research
By examining published statistics a good idea of the potential demand for a product can be obtained. An even more accurate estimate can be made from a special enquiry in the field designed to provide the answers to specific questions.

* Time Series Analysis
Allows the best method of forecasting to be developed by the analysis of past data. Besides the simple approach, it is often necessary to incorporate provision for analysing trends and seasonal patterns.

* Regression Analysis
Where immediate past data alone are insufficient to give a good forecast of future levels of activity, this can sometimes

be related to the level of some other activity which can be forecast more easily (for example, sales of cars are related to the
standard of living). Regression Analysis is a way of establishing
such a relationship.

* Box Jenkins

Is a technique that takes into account the difference in error
of the two previous forecasts. It is likely to be particularly useful
when errors in sales forecasts, for example, are complementary;
for example, a month of low demand followed by a high one
and vice versa.

* Leontieff Input-Output Tables

Describe relationship between inputs (for example, raw
materials) and outputs (for example, consumer durables) in an
economy or part of it. Can be used to predict consumption of one
product when production and consumption of some related ones
are known.

† Use of Computer with Forecasting Techniques

A computer is not always necessary when doing simple moving
averages, exponential smoothing and so on. It is necessary when
a lot of data is to be handled, or when Box Jenkins, Regression
Analysis and Times Series Analysis are used.

How to Generate New Product Ideas

** Market Research

Enquiries in the field amongst potential customers may reveal
an unfulfilled need for a new or revised product.

** Brainstorming

A group of people, not necessarily all from the marketing
department, get together to answer a question such as 'In how
many ways can we improve our product (or packaging, or our
service, etc.)'. If suggestions, however wild, are vigorously
encouraged and all criticism of them is banned – this is vital –
a large number of ideas, some of them entirely new, are often
created.

* *Value Analysis*
By carefully analysing what each component of a product is for, why it is that shape, why made of that material, etc., it is often possible to simplify the product, reduce its cost, improve its appearance. Often combined with brainstorming (above).

How to Launch a New Product

** *See Critical Path Method*

How to Determine the Profitability of a Product or Product Line

** *Marginal Costing*
A manager often needs to know what it would cost to produce and sell one more unit (or one less) than the level currently planned. It is no good taking the 'unit cost' as a guide because this carries its share of the company's overheads. To produce one more or ten more (or less) units probably will not affect these overheads at all. So only those costs that are actually altered by the altered level of sales are relevant.

** *Contribution Analysis*
Is designed to show by how much profits (as opposed to costs) will be affected by altering sales volume or mix. Only the revenue and the costs that are actually altered should be used to calculate the contribution to overheads and profits that the proposed alteration will make.

** *Profit Volume Ratio*
It is possible to draw a graph showing profits from any sales volume.

** *Breakeven Charts*
It is possible to draw a graph showing at what level of sales the contribution (i.e. revenue less directly variable costs) equals the company's fixed costs.

** *Linear Programming*
This technique (q.v.) can determine what is the best mix of products in order to make the most profitable use of the company's manufacturing facilities.

How to Improve Product Design

** *Market Research*
Asking actual or potential customers questions about the product – for example how they use it, when, what difficulties they have with it – can provide a useful guide as to what is wrong with its design.

* *Value Analysis* (q.v.)

* *Ergonomics*
This is the study of the physical relationship between man and machine and is used to decide the best shape for a typist's chair, the least fatiguing position for a steering wheel, best height for accurate reading of a temperature gauge, etc.

PRODUCTION

How to Remove Factory Bottlenecks

***† *Production Control by Computer*
Production control is the biggest problem of all in some industries. Very often the complexity and number of processes or products makes practical solution too difficult without employing the high speed of a computer to make use of mathematical programming, simulation, critical path methods, and so on.

*** *Critical Path Methods* (q.v.)
Can be very valuable for batch processes, as in building and construction, aircraft production, plant maintenance and overhauls. Of much less value in continuous processes such as chemicals, food canning, etc.

**† *Simulation*
One of the most versatile of all Operational Research tools. A mathematical model of the factory is made to represent the random breakdowns of a machine, regular shift changes, stock levels, arrival of customers, and so on. It is then possible, using a computer, to imitate several weeks' or months' operation in a few minutes to show under what circumstances bottlenecks appear, queues form, stocks run out, etc. Effect of changes (for example, of installing an extra machine or altering working hours) can be studied.

* *Monte Carlo Method*
One particular method of Simulation.

* *Queuing Theory*
A mathematical description of what happens when queues form. Most practical problems of this sort are better solved by Simulation.

How to Improve Product Quality and Reliability

*** *Statistical Quality Control*
A number of statistical methods have been developed to aid in checking and controlling the quality of manufactured goods. The general aim of these techniques is to balance the cost of inspection against the penalties of allowing faulty materials to escape detection. Thus total cost is minimized.

*† *Process Control by Computer*
The control of manufacturing processes can be improved by the online use of a computer to control the plant: useful only for certain types of process at present.

* *Evolutionary Operation*
A technique by which plant performance can be improved by experimentation on the plant with minimal upsetting of normal operating conditions.

* *Adaptive Control*
Techniques for making adjustments to operating conditions as external factors vary.

How to Cope with Complex Mixes

*† *Mathematical Programming*
If a company has only one factory, it supplies all the customers – there is no choice. But if the company has two, each with different capacity and production costs, there is a choice between which customer to supply from which factory to achieve minimum cost of production and transport. And if there are many factories delivering through dozens of warehouses (each with a different storage capacity and handling cost) it is beyond human ability to calculate the production and distribution

pattern that gives lowest cost. A similar 'complex mix' problem occurs when several products (each of different profitability) made from many components (each of different cost) are made on several machines (each of different capacity) – which mix of products made from what selection of components on which machines would give maximum profits?

These problems can be solved using a computer by Mathematical Programming techniques. They are all based on an organized trial and error procedure which progressively selects better solutions until the best is found (i.e. lowest cost or highest profit). Mathematical Programming techniques include:

Linear Programming
The most useful. It can solve all such problems except when the following have to be used:

Quadratic Programming
When some relationships are quadratic – e.g. if cost of production goes up as the square of output.

Separable Programming
When the relationships are variable – e.g. if cost of production goes up as the square of output for the first 100 units then goes up in direct proportion to output.

Integer Programming
Linear Programming gives the answers to several decimal places; e.g. 'make 3·37 units at factory A'. This is not good enough if the 'units' happen to be battleships. Is the right number three or four? Integer Programming gives the most profitable answer in whole numbers.

How to Cut Labour Costs

*** *Method Study*
Part of 'Work Study'. By systematically studying any job, it is possible to eliminate any part of it that does not contribute usefully, or improve the way it is done, or reduce the labour to do it. Can be applied to almost any type of work from tying a piece of string to building a skyscraper. Usually includes Time Study – measuring the amount of work needed to complete a job.

* Incentive Schemes
Modern version of 'piecework' or payment by results. In its
best form some part of a man's pay will depend on the work he
puts into his job as measured by Time Study techniques.

* Ergonomics (above)
A man will usually be more productive if the machine he is
operating has been designed on good ergonomic principles.

*† Productivity Bargaining
Attempt to obtain a *quid pro quo* for any rise in wage rates.
The employer grants a rise in pay only on condition that its
total cost is recouped by improvements brought about by a
productivity-rise, due, for example, to abandonment of excessive overtime, reduction in overmanning, elimination of a
restrictive practice.

How to Improve Labour Relations

** T.W.I. Job Relations Programme
A very simple but extremely effective course, run by the
Ministry of Labour, designed to help supervisors and foremen
prevent human relations problems occurring at the shop-floor
level.

PERSONNEL
How to Improve Training Methods

** Programmed Learning
A new method of writing textbooks. At the end of each page
of the textbook a question is asked and the student chooses one
of several answers against each of which a page number appears.
If he chooses wrongly, the page explains his error; if he is right
the next stage in the subject is reached. The same method can be
employed with a Teaching Machine, in which the pages are
shown on a screen like a TV, and the pages are selected by
pressing buttons opposite the suggested answers. Gives added
incentive to learn.

* Business Games
Several groups of students form imaginary companies operating
in a carefully defined competitive market. Umpires (or a

computer) evaluate each company's decisions (for example, to spend more on research, less on advertising). At the end of the game one company is seen to have done better than others. The game itself and analysis of results teach appreciation of company problems.

*How to Bring Order and Equity into
Wages and Salary Schemes*

**** Job Description*
This is a carefully thought-out written description of a job, showing what it involves, how it is to be done, responsibilities, duties etc. Only when it is known exactly what a job is can one decide (*a*) how much payment the job is worth; (*b*) what qualities are needed to do it.

Job Evaluation
A systematic way of weighing up how much a job is worth in wages or salary compared with some other job – i.e. establishing a differential between jobs. Must be preceded by a Job Description.

*** Merit Rating*
A systematic way of weighing up how much a man is worth compared with some other man. Factors such as standard of work, time keeping, loyalty, are included.

*** Salary Progression Curves*
As a man get older his salary usually rises until middle age, then levels off. Plotting the rate of rise against age and comparing one man's graph with another provides a check on whether men of similar abilities are similarly paid.

** Time Span of Discretion*
In some jobs a man's supervisor checks on his work every few hours, in other jobs a check is made only every few weeks or months. It is possible to relate salary levels to this time span.

How to Recruit the Right Number of the Right Type of People
*** Manpower Planning*
In addition to normal replacement due to resignations and retirements, knowledge of how a company will develop over the

next few years (see Corporate Planning) should show approximately what new types of vacancy in what numbers will occur and what present jobs will be redundant. Some idea of the qualifications required for these jobs can be estimated and recruitment planned accordingly.

* Intelligence, Personality and Aptitude Tests
Very variable results: intelligence tests are a good guide to some sorts of intelligence but must be supplemented by an interviewer's personal assessment. Personality tests are still very suspect, although they may uncover otherwise unsuspected traits. Aptitude tests are a useful guide in some cases.

PURCHASING
How to Check Quality and Reliability of Raw Materials
*** Statistical Quality Control
General term for statistically designed methods of checking that goods that are received are up to the specification on which they were bought.

** Quality Protection
Several types of scheme can be designed: to protect the company against one particular batch of goods being below standard, for example, or against average quality being below standard.

** Statistical Sampling Methods
A very large amount of data is generated in any large organization. It is worth collecting some of this in full detail on a routine basis. In other cases a sample of the data may be sufficient to give any information that is required. Statistical Sampling allows the correct method and frequency of sampling to be determined.

* Sequential Analysis
Allows one to determine whether sufficient accuracy has been achieved from the samples already taken, or whether a further sample should be taken.

How to Cut Down the Cost of Purchasing and of Holding Stocks
*** Statistical Stock Control
Stocks of material are normally held so as to allow demand to be met without having to re-order material from the supplier

(or factory) on each occasion it is needed. Stock Control is concerned with the relationship between:

(*a*) The cost of placing an order.

(*b*) The discounts obtainable by taking delivery in large quantities.

(*c*) The cost of holding stock (interest on capital tied up, physical deterioration, obsolescence, cost of warehouse space, etc.).

(*d*) The cost (or loss of profit) in being unable to meet demand through shortage of materials.

(*e*) The amount and variability of demand.

A large number of models have been developed for different combinations of the conditions. (Simulation can often be usefully employed.)

A number of computer manufacturers supply standard programmes for the analysis of stock levels. While useful in many cases, these should be treated with caution – they do not apply to all circumstances.

** *Methods of Forecasting Demand*
(see under Marketing)

** *Economic Batch Re-ordering Quantities*
The larger the batch of materials that can be ordered, the lower the cost of placing the order and the better the quantity discount is likely to be. On the other hand, the higher will be the cost of storage and working capital. One can calculate the batch size that minimizes all these costs.

**† *Simulation by Computer*
Stock control and Economic Batch Size calculations are often complex. It may be preferable to build a mathematical model of the stock problem and use simulation on a computer.

RESEARCH
How to Reduce the Time Taken to Complete Research
*** *Method Study* (q.v.)
Can be used with great effect to improve methods of carrying out routine research experiments.

*** *Critical Path Methods* (q.v.)

** *Statistical Design of Experiments*
Proper design can ensure that an experiment will be as sensitive as possible to the factors under investigation, that it will not be subject to systematic bias and that the results will be capable of statistical analysis. Factorial Design, Latin Squares, etc., can minimize the experimental work required for a given accuracy in the results.

**† *Scientific Calculations on a Computer*
Many scientific calculations (for example, stresses in a structure) can be rapidly and cheaply made either on general-purpose computers or small scientific machines costing no more than $50,000 or so. For this type of work the availability of standard computer programmes and programming languages (for example, FORTRAN and ALGOL) is particularly important. Now becoming possible to do engineering design work and engineering drawings on a computer.

* *Simulation by Computer*
Provided a mathematical model can be built which reproduces the scientific problem under study, it is possible to conduct 'experiments' in the computer rather than with physical objects. Particularly useful in studying changes in methods of operation of chemical plants, etc.

AN APPLICATION OF DECISION THEORY[1]

FOR thousands of years man has searched for a key to the future. At first we thought that it was revealed to us in dreams and visions, then we appealed to the oracles or examined the entrails of animals and then we tried crossing the gypsy's palm with silver. Now at last, after many centuries of disappointment, we have come to realise that the key to the future lies where we had least expected to find it – in the past. Why did it take so long to find? Perhaps because it was only comparatively recently in our history that adequate records of the past were kept, perhaps the necessary mathematics were unknown; perhaps we had to wait for the computer; whatever the reason, forecasting, based on the principle of induction, can now take its place among the sciences.

There is, of course, a snag. As our records of the past become more detailed and as our mathematics become more sophisticated, our forecasts will become more and more accurate – but they can never become dead accurate. It is astonishing that such an obvious statement needs to be made: it can certainly be argued, however, that in the excitement of devising better methods of forecasting we all seem to have lost sight of this stark fact. All over the world managers and mathematicians are working to improve the accuracy of their forecasts apparently quite oblivious to the fact that nature has imposed a strict limitation upon it. We may have found the key to the future, we may have cleaned it and oiled it but, alas, it is imperfect.

What is needed now is to recognise that forecasts are the basis of plans, that forecasts are bound to be more or less wrong and, therefore, that plans must always have to be made

---

[1] This appendix was first published as an article in *Scientific Business* by the author and Tony Brooks. The author is grateful to Tony Brooks and to the Editor of *Scientific Business* for permission to reprint this article here.

taking this into account. It is not the making of forecasts but the using of them that now needs all our attention. The question has had some attention; mathematicians have developed decision theory; there are volumes of equations describing the optimum course of action when decisions have to be taken under conditions of uncertainty. So far as can be ascertained, however, not one real life practical decision has ever been taken by an industrial manager using the equations of decision theory. Perhaps the reason is that managers simply do not understand these equations, and quite rightly dare not make a multi-million-dollar decision on the basis of a calculation they do not understand. And yet so crucial to good planning and correct decision making is it to recognize that forecasts are usually inaccurate that it must be right to attempt to develop a decision-making procedure that both takes this into account and that can be understood and used by an industrial manager.

The sort of problem that is being discussed is found in every field of human activity: for how many patients should a hospital be built, for what flow of traffic should a highway be designed, for how many diners should a restaurant chef prepare? All these problems are characterized by someone having to make a decision on the basis of a forecast that is known to be inaccurate and at the same time it is known that there are penalties to be paid whether the forecast turns out to be either too high or too low. What action should be taken which minimizes the penalties or at least which avoids the worst penalty? In this paper the authors wish to illustrate a method of decision-making designed to take account of the inaccuracy of a forecast but which contains no advanced mathematics and which is broken down into such simple steps that it can be used by an industrial manager. This method was developed for use in a situation very similar to the one described:

In 1965 Hypothetics Ltd. made and sold 600 tons of Hypon. Their sales director, in his routine annual report, forecasts that the sales of Hypon for the following seven years would be:

	1966	1967	1968	1969	1970	1971	1972
Tons	800	1,000	1,200	1,300	1,300	1,300	1,300

The production director at once points out that their present plant could be stretched to produce 1,000 tons and no more and suggests that, since it takes two years to put down a new plant, they should order a 300 ton plant immediately. Now – would this be the right decision?

By looking back in the records it was seen that the sales director had made similar seven-year forecasts every year for the past fifteen years and, of course, the actual out-turn can easily be compared with his forecasts for many of these years. A junior statistician then drew up a table of confidence limits at the 90 per cent level showing what error could be expected from a forecast relating to one year ahead, two years ahead and so on as follows:

For a one-year-ahead forecast the error was at least five per cent on one occasion in ten.

For a two-year-ahead forecast the error was at least eight per cent on one occasion in ten.

For a three-year-ahead forecast the error was at least ten per cent on one occasion in ten.

For a four-, five-, six-, and seven-year-ahead forecast the error was also at least ten per cent on one occasion in ten.

(The decision-making procedure being described can make use of confidence limits that widen out; it just happens that, in this case, based on real life, they did not apparently widen beyond the three-year forecast). Now this means that, when Hypothetic's sales director published his latest forecast, what he really meant to say was:

'There is a 1 in 10 chance of selling less than 1,080 tons in 1968 and 1,170 tons in 1969 and beyond; and there is a 1 in 10 chance of selling more than 1,320 tons in 1968 and 1,430 tons in 1969 and beyond: I cannot be expected to do better than a ten per cent error either way when making a three-year-ahead forecast'.

This puts a wholly different complexion on the problem for it implies that if Hypothetics put down a 300 ton plant in 1968, there is a 1 in 10 chance of it being hopelessly inadequate after one year or alternatively of it running at little more than half capacity.

The next step is to take the forecast tonnage and the tonnage at the 90 per cent confidence level for each of the years relevant to the decision (in this case, since the new plant cannot come on stream for two years it is only 1968 onwards that is relevant) and add two figures midway between the forecast and the confidence limits:

	1968	*1969* *onwards*
Lower confidence limit	1,080	1,170
Mid point	1,140	1,235
Forecast	1,200	1,300
Mid point	1,260	1,365
Upper confidence limit	1,320	1,430

The reason for inserting these two figures is to give more points on the graphs that are to be drawn later and to aid the next step: we know that there is a 1 in 10 chance of *exceeding* 1,320 tons in 1968 but we now want to know what is the chance of *attaining* 1,320 tons, or any other tonnage figure in any of these years. It turns out that there is a 12 per cent chance of attaining 1,320 tons in 1963. Of course no-one in Hypothetics need know how this is done[1] – all they need to do is to establish what their past forecasting errors have been, obtain the confidence limits and put in the mid-points to which they can simply ascribe the standard probabilities listed below:

Probability of attaining lower limit	0.12
Probability of attaining lower mid-point	0.24
Probability of attaining forecast figure	0.28
Probability of attaining upper mid-point	0.24
Probability of attaining upper limit	0.12

We can now solve the problem for, knowing the probable demand in any year, one can calculate the probable revenue and hence determine what sized plant is best. In Hypothetic's case they know that if they put up a plant that is too small they can buy in some Hypon from the Continent and re-sell it at a contribution to overheads and profits of $24 per ton, while, for any sales they can meet from their own plants their contribution will be $264. They also know that whereas they would incur no extra fixed costs from merely factoring Hypon, they would incur an extra $12,000 in fixed costs if they built a new plant. They can, for example, calculate that the probable contribution from a 300 tons per annum plant would be

[1] It is done, as statisticians will recognize, by taking a band ¾ σ-wide and deriving these probabilities from the normal distribution tables.

$47,448 in 1968, because for every ton over and above the capacity of their old plant (1,000 tons per annum) they will make $240 from the new plant compared with factoring. In 1968 there is a 0.12 probability of selling 80 tons and making a contribution of $19,200 from the new plant – a probable contribution of $2,304. And for all five levels of demand the contribution is as follows:

Probability of selling 80 tons at $240 per ton contribution is 0.12 = $2,304.

Probability of selling 140 tons at $240 per ton contribution is 0.24 = $8,064.

Probability of selling 200 tons at $240 per ton contribution is 0.28 = $13,440.

Probability of selling 260 tons at $240 per ton contribution is 0.24 = $15,000.

Probability of selling 300 tons at $240 per ton contribution is 0.12 = $8,640.

Total probable contribution = $47,448.

The reader will notice one interesting point: the maximum likely demand in 1968 was 1,320 tons of which 320 tons would have been required from the new plant: but the capacity of this is only 300 tons so they can only claim 300 × $240 of contribution: fortunately there is only a 12 per cent chance of this happening but if it does happen it means having to import 20 tons of Hypon. But in 1969 matters get worse.

Probability	Demand	Actual Output	Contribution $	Probable Contribution $
0.12	170	170	40,800	4,896
0.24	235	235	56,160	13,560
0.28	300	300	72,000	20,160
0.24	365	300 (buy in)	72,000	17,280
0.12	430	300 (buy in)	72,000	8,640
		Total Probable Contribution		$64,536

There is now 0.36 chance (0.24 plus 0.12) of the company having to buy in and this will also apply to the years beyond 1969. It looks as though Hypothetics are going to have to buy in fairly large quantities at a contribution to fixed costs and overheads that is very much lower than the contribution they could achieve if they made this material on their own plant. It looks as though a 300 ton plant might be too small for maximum profitability and that they should do the same calculation to see what would happen if they had a 400 ton plant. In fact we are going to try four different sizes of plant to get four points on a graph. The probable contribution from each of these plants for each year calculated as above is shown below:

Plant size	200 t.p.a.	300 t.p.a.	400 t.p.a.	500 t.p.a.
1968	$41,088	$47,400	$48,240	$48,240
1969 onwards	$71,136	$64,536	$71,136	$72,000

We must now subtract the $12,000 per annum fixed costs and overheads which are virtually the same for each size of plant over this range. And then we must discount the cash flows. Since Hypothetics have several projects competing with this one for capital and some of these other projects could yield 15 per cent d.c.f. this is the appropriate discounting rate to use. But we must remember that the cash flow derived above is cash before corporation tax and without investment allowances so a rather complex calculation now has to be made and it is wise to call in the company's finance department to do it. All they need are the figures above for revenue each year for each plant and the capital cost of each plant which are as follows:

Plant Size	200 t.p.a.	300 t.p.a.	400 t.p.a.	500 t.p.a.
Capital Cost	$103,200	$120,000	$132,000	$141,600

When the finance department has adjusted the revenue for corporation tax and allowances and has discounted the cash flow at 15 per cent and added up these net profits for the five years for each plant it is necessary then to subtract the capital cost of each plant to get the present value of the net revenue from each of these plant sizes.

Plant Size	200 t.p.a.	300 t.p.a.	400 t.p.a.	500 t.p.a.
Total profit over five years	$100,800	$141,600	$165,600	$168,000
Capital Cost	$103,200	$120,000	$132,000	$141,600
Net Present Value	−$2,400	$21,600	$33,600	$26,400

Now these figures should be plotted on a graph:

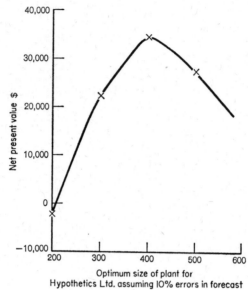

Optimum size of plant for
Hypothetics Ltd. assuming 10% errors in forecast

FIG. 1.

The net present value is at a maximum when a plant of 400 t.p.a. is built and this is the size that Hypothetics should decide upon.

It is interesting to notice the difference in net present value between a 300 and a 400 t.p.a. plant. The graph shows that this amounts to $12,000 after tax: thus the difference between the Production Director's original suggestion to put down a 300 ton plant and our suggested 400 ton plant is equivalent to simply giving away $20,160 gross in 1967 – a fairly large sum for a firm the size of Hypothetics, a sum that represents a substantial blunder. (Incidentally it will be noticed that the net present value of building a 200 ton plant is – $2,400 and this indicates that it would be preferable to risk buying in raw materials rather than build this size plant – this observation happens to be irrelevant in the present circumstances since it is not intended to build this size of plant.) At this point we must warn that to build a plant that is 'too big' is not always correct nor is it always correct to sign a long term contract that is for 'too small' a quantity although this often turns out to be the case. A careful examination is always needed to determine where the balance of penalties lies.

We have for brevity taken only a five year period for our calculations and this is far too short a period for most industrial
decisions involving the building of new plant. It is possible to
draw another graph showing the relation between the best size
for a plant and the number of years over which the calculations
should be made. In the particular case discussed above the
graph would look like this:

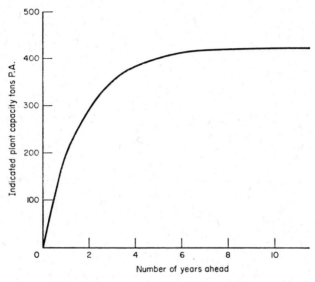

FIG. 2. Effect of increasing the Forecast Period

Thus if Hypothetics Limited decided to look only two years
ahead they would have obtained the answer that the optimum
size plant would be 300 tons – an incorrect decision as we have
seen. On the other hand to look much further ahead than five
years would only increase the optimum plant indicated by a
few tons capacity. A graph of this sort should always be drawn
to ensure that a sufficiently long period ahead had been looked
at: this is indicated when the inclusion of one more year in the
calculation results in a change in the plant size that is too small
for the plant designer to take account of in his calculations, or
that makes no significant difference to the costs of the plant.

To keep the calculations simple we have assumed above that
the demand for Hypon would level off after a few years and

this is a perfectly respectable assumption. In practice of course the method outlined can accommodate any forecast pattern of sales whether variable, rising or falling.

Another point which is of great importance: we postulated that Hypothetic's sales forecasts were more than ten per cent wrong on one occasion in ten, but suppose this had been five per cent or 20 per cent wrong? A third type of graph should be drawn showing how the inaccuracy of a forecast affects the size of the plant indicated; the graph for Hypothetics would look like this:

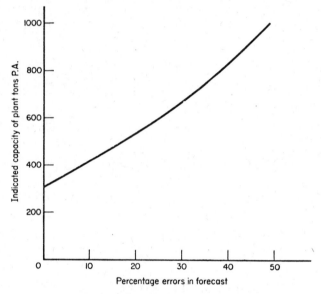

FIG. 3 Effect of Errors in Forecasts

From this it can be seen that if only Hypothetics could make a slightly more accurate forecast they could cut the size and therefore the cost of their plant considerably. By spending, say, $1,000 on market research or perhaps by using exponential smoothing on a computer they could save themselves several thousand dollars in capital expenditure on the plant. Instead of asking what size plant should be built based on a forecast of given inaccuracy it might perhaps be more pertinent to ask how accurate it is necessary to make a forecast in order to take a reasonable decision.

The system described yields the solution giving the maximum probable net present value; but one should always be on the look-out for a solution that, while giving this, may also contain an enormous penalty. For example, looking back at the probable contribution calculation earlier on all the contributions were positive – but it is possible to have a situation such as the following:

0.12 chance of $28.8 million loss
0.24 chance of $2.4 million loss
0.28 chance of $9.6 million profit
0.24 chance of $2.4 million profit
0.12 chance of $28.8 million profit
Total probable profit $9.6 million

The total looks harmless enough but there is a slight danger of incurring a very large loss indeed and this may be a risk that the company dare not expose itself to: the table of probable contributions should always be searched for such results. If there are a large number of losses or if the probability of a loss is high then there may be a case for using utility theory: this would be beyond the capabilities of the management of Hypothetics to calculate – and that is making the generous assumption that utility can be calculated at all in the present state of the art.

The way that forecasts can be made more accurately than ever before is impressive but the way forecasts are used, even today, to make far-reaching decisions is highly questionable; we hope we have demonstrated the striking differences between the common-sense use of forecasts and our own. That this type of approach should be used in all decisions involving the long term commitment of extensive resources, whether in industry, in town planning, in civil or social engineering we have no doubt. We are sure that our method or something like it is sufficiently simple for there to be little excuse for not using it.

GLOSSARY OF TERMS AS USED

Action   An action taken by an executive alters or commits the company's resources for a period of time.

Constraint   Any action that, for moral, religious, aesthetic, political or personal reasons, the officers of the organization have decided to take or not to take *whether or not* it may help to achieve the objective. (cf. Means).

Contribution   The contribution made to a company's fixed costs and profit from the sale of one or more unit of product.

Crawl-Out Costs   The cost of correcting a decision after action has been taken to commit the company's resources and when it is seen that the decision has been proved wrong by events.

Decision   The act of choosing between two or more possible courses of action. Decisions do not commit the company's resources (cf. action).

Decision Diary   A simple diary in which the corporate planner can note when decisions have to be made to enable adequate consideration of alternatives to be made before action has to be taken.

Environment   Everything in the world except the company.

Factor Affecting Profits   Any trend or event that might occur and which might affect profits by a significant percentage either way.

Forecast   The qualitative or quantitative estimate of events or trends that one believes may occur in the future.

Gap The differences between a target and a forecast. (The gap shows the extent to which one must take action to achieve the target.)

Interaction Chart A chart showing what impact each Factor Affecting Profits might have on each other Factor.

Management Technique A systematic, methodical analysis of management problems. Some of these techniques take years to achieve results.

Means Any action that might help the organization to achieve its objective (cf. Constraints).

Objective The permanent unalterable *raison d'être* of an organization: this can only be fully described if it specifies both the benefit that the organization is intended to bring and who the intended beneficiaries are. In the case of companies the objective is to provide a satisfactory return on the shareholder's capital.

Obstacles & Opportunities Trends or events that are likely to occur in the company's environment that suggest a possible decline or improvement respectively in the company's ability to achieve its objective (cf. Strengths).

Plan A plan is a list of actions arranged in whatever sequence is thought likely to achieve an objective.

Plan, Contingency A plan prepared to take advantage of or to minimize the effect of an event which is considered to be unlikely to occur but, if it did, to have a considerable impact on the organisation's ability to achieve the objective.

Plan, Short Range Long Range No theoretical difference marks the distinction between short and long range planning. In practice short range is usually considered to be less than three years ahead and long range more than two years. The degree of uncertainty to be taken into account normally increases as the range increases, as do the number of variables.

Planning The act of drawing up a plan (cf. Corporate Planning).

Planning, Corporate	A systematic and disciplined study designed to help identify the objective of any organization or corporate body, determine an appropriate target, decide upon suitable constraints and devise a practical plan by which the objective may be achieved (cf. Planning).
Planning, Operational	Short term planning in response to day-to-day events. Usually consists not of planning so much as revision of plans.
Profit, the four Components of	Selling Price, Volume, Variable costs and Fixed Costs.
Profit Improvement Plan	A deliberate, systematic campaign to improve revenue and reduce costs often carried on for many years.
Projection	The simple extrapolation of a past trend into the future on the assumption that the future will be the same as the past.

Return on Capital

(1) Return on Capital Employed: the ratio of Gross Trading Profits to the Capital Employed in the company.

(2) Return on Capital Invested: the ratio of gross profit earned by a project to the capital invested in the project.

(3) Return on Shareholder's Capital: the total amount of cash (after tax) received by a shareholder compared with amount of cash he invests in the company. Best expressed in d.c.f. terms.

(4) D.c.f. Return on Capital Invested: the rate of interest earned by capital spent on a project – all figures in after-tax terms.

Sensitivity Tests	Calculations made to determine whether a given course of action would still be taken even if certain of the data relating to the decision was wrong.
Strategy	A long term plan, usually in broad outline, indicating the main lines of action by which the objective may be achieved.
Strengths and Weaknesses	Advantages and disadvantages respectively present in the company itself (cf. Obstacles).

Target   The quantitative, numerical expression of an objective.

Top-down   When the Board decides how profitable a com-
Bottom up   pany is going to be and then asks the employees to work towards this it is known as 'top-down' management. When the Board asks the employees what they are going to do and then decides if this is sufficient to result in an acceptable profit, it is known as 'bottom-up' management.

INDEX

Numbers Italicised refer to pages on which a definition will be found.

Absurdities, 88, 102, 103, 112
Accountants, 21, 218
Accuracy, 62, 76, 79, 110, 256
Actions, 183, 191, 202-205, 233, *266*
Appropriateness of Target, 63, 68, 124, 192
Assumptions, 75-76, 104, 137, 189-190

Benefit, 231
Board, effect on, 223-226, 235
Bottom-up planning, 22, 224, *269*
Brainstorming, 216, 246
Budgets, 21-22, 25

Capital gains, 47, 60
Capital investment, 137-138, 145-148, 162, 178
Capital, return on—*see* Return
Centralization, 229
Combined actions, 166-169, 179
Communications, 191, 235
Computers, 65, 148, 208, 222, 241, 246
Confidence, 113, 116, 258
Constraints, 32, 127-135, *266*
Contingency Plans, 107, 199, *267*
Contribution, 86, 108, 205, 247, 259, *266*
Control, 190, 211
Convertible Loan, 63
Co-operatives, 39-41
Corporate Planner's qualifications, 218-220
Corporate planning, definitions of, 13, *267*
  department, 220-221
  need for, 14, 20, 236
Costing system, 191, 242
Costs, *see* Fixed and Variable
Crawl-out costs, 181, 205, *266*
Creative thought, 219, 235, 237
Cross-checks, 88-89, 112

Decisions, 196-199, 204, 207, 215, 256-265, *266*
Decision Diary, 196-199, 216, 225-226, *266*
Decision Theory, 122, 181, 208, 240, 256-265
Departmental Plans, 23-25
Direct Costs—*see* Variable
Discounted Cash Flow, 49, 52, 61, 149, 241, 261
Diversification, 137, 144, 161-165
Divestment, 154, 170
Dividend cover, 57, 64, 67
  growth of, 47, 67
  yield, 47, 67

Environment, 13, 209, 211, *266*
Errors, 63, 110-118
Executives, 12, 224-225
Existing business, 137, 144, 151-161
Experience, corporate planner's, 112, 218

Factors Affecting Profits, 90-106, 140, 152, 215, 235, *266*
Family business, 39
Five Step Process, 16-18
Fixed Costs, 76-78, 259
Forecasts, 21, 70-109, 245-246, *266*
  cross checking, 88-89, 112
  and errors, 110-118
  need for, 202, 206
  and plans, 203
  See also Revisions, Zero
Forecasting techniques, 70-109, 245-246

Gaps, 73, 119, 145, *267*
Growth, 47, 59, 121, 179
  and return on capital, 65

Inaccuracies, inevitable, 111, 256
Inflation, 57-60, 75, 83
Integration, 137, 144, 161-165
Interaction Chart, 98, 100, 181, 267
Ivory tower, 214, 218

Liquidation, 138, 145, 164, 176
Lists and Plans, 183
Loan capital, 63, 67, 139, 146
Long range, 209, 267

Management, fragmentation of 25, 217
Management by objectives, 142, 157
Management techniques, 137, 143, 158,
    164, 239-255, 267
Marketing, 142, 174
Market research, 246, 248, 264
Maximize, 44
Means, 32, 136-165, 166, 267
    and constraints, 130
Models, mathematical, 65, 241
Monitoring, 189-191, 216
Moral codes, 36, 127-129, 215

Nationalization, 39-41

Objectives, 28-35, 267
    and constraints, 127-130
    hierarchy of, 224
    ill-defined, 28-34, 44-47, 232
Obstacles and Opportunities, 137, 139,
    151-155, 162-163, 267
Organization, structure, 187-188, 221
    and organisms, 34
Overheads—see Fixed Costs,
Owners, 37-42

Partnerships, 39-40
Patterns of cash flow, 49-52, 55
Penalty, 257-265
Plan, 267
    detailed specification for, 184, 195
    and forecasts, 203, 211
    inadequate, 23
    and lists, 183, 202
    need for, 202, 210-212
responsibility for, 184, 230
    see also Contingency, Corporate,
    Departmental, Long range, Oper
    ational, Revisions, Short range

Policy Statements, 133, 166-182, 198,
    214
Post Mortem, 198
Product, life cycle, 80, 101-103
    function of, 160
Professional standards, 15-16
Project Managers, 185, 193, 226
Projections, 86-91, 215, 267
    and forecasts, 92-105, 111
Profit, components of, 87, 268
    gap, 73, 119, 145, 267
    maximise, 44
    morality of, 36, 127-128
    and survival, 34
Profit Improvement Plan, 137, 142,
    157, 164, 267

Research, 141, 175
Responsibility for planning, 184, 230
Return on Capital Employed, 45-46,
    64-65, 89
    and growth, 65
Return on capital, satisfactory, 38-42,
    180
    Shareholders', 46-47, 67
    Types of, 64, 149-150, 267
Revenue, Analysis of, 78
Revisions, 17, 66, 107, 124, 191-195, 216
Risk, 120-124, 208

Sales Volume, 76-88
Satisfactory Return, 38-42, 180
S-Curve, 101-103
Sensitivity Tests, 181, 205, 207, 268
Shareholder's capital, 47
Shareholders, types of, 38-42
Short range, 209, 267
State owned firms, 39-41
Statistical techniques, 112, 245
Strategy and Tactics, 136, 170, 216, 268
Strengths, 137, 140 ,155,163, 268
Subsidiary Companies, 229
Survival, 33, 180

Tactics, 136
Take-over bids, 141
Targets, 21, 67, 268
    appropriate, 63, 68, 124, 192
    choice of, 42, 53-57, 62, 192
    ill-defined, 21, 44-47
    revision of, 66, 68, 124, 195

Taxation, 60-61, 67, 146
Test Questions, 28-33, 38, 128
Timing, 189, 196-199
Top down, 22, 224, *269*

Uncertainty, 210, 257
Utility Theory, 122, 265

Variable Costs, 76-88
Volume, Sales, 76-88

Weaknesses, 137, 140, 156, 163, *268*

Zero, forecast, 105, 151, 193